Historical Dynamics

Why States Rise and Fall

PRINCETON STUDIES IN COMPLEXITY

SERIES EDITORS

Philip W. Anderson (Princeton University); Joshua M. Epstein (The Brookings Institution); Duncan K. Foley (Barnard College); Simon A. Levin (Princeton University); Martin A. Nowak (Harvard University)

Lars-Erik Cederman, *Emergent Actors in World Politics: How States and Nations Develop and Dissolve*

Robert Axelrod, *The Complexity of Cooperation: Agent-Based Models of Competition and Collaboration*

Peter S. Albin, *Barriers and Bounds to Rationality: Essays on Economic Complexity and Dynamics in Interactive Systems*. Edited and with an introduction by Duncan K. Foley

Duncan J. Watts, *Small Worlds: The Dynamics of Networks between Order and Randomness*

Scott Camazine, Jean-Louis Deneubourg, Nigel R. Franks, James Sneyd, Guy Theraulaz, Eric Bonabeau, *Self-Organization in Biological Systems*

Peter Turchin, *Historical Dynamics: Why States Rise and Fall*

Historical Dynamics

Why States Rise and Fall

Peter Turchin

PRINCETON UNIVERSITY PRESS

PRINCETON AND OXFORD

Copyright © 2003 by Princeton University Press
Published by Princeton University Press,
41 William Street, Princeton, New Jersey 08540
In the United Kingdom: Princeton University Press,
3 Market Place, Woodstock, Oxfordshire OX20 1SY

Library of Congress Control Number 2003110656
ISBN: 0-691-11669-5
British Library Cataloging-in-Publication Data is available

The publisher would like to acknowledge Peter Turchin for providing
the camera-ready copy from which this book was printed

Printed on acid-free paper.

www.pupress.princeton.edu

Printed in the United States of America

10 9 8 7 6 5 4 3 2 1

Contents

List of Figures

List of Tables

Preface

Many historical processes are dynamic: growth and decline of populations, territorial expansion and contraction of empires, trends in political centralization/decentralization, and the spread of world religions, to name just a few examples. A general approach to studying dynamical systems is to advance rival hypotheses based on specific mechanisms, translate the hypotheses into mathematical models, and contrast model predictions with empirical patterns. Mathematical modeling is a key ingredient in this research program because quantitative dynamical phenomena, often affected by complex feedbacks, cannot be fully understood at a purely verbal level. Another important ingredient is the full use of statistical techniques (such as time-series analysis) for quantitative and rigorous comparison between model-predicted and observed patterns. This general approach has proved to be extremely successful in natural sciences. Can it be instrumental in increasing our understanding of historical processes?

Historical Dynamics is an attempt to answer this question. The specific problem chosen for analysis is the territorial dynamics of agrarian states. In other words, can we understand why some polities at certain times expand, while at other times they contract? The advantage of focusing on territorial expansion/contraction is that we have reasonably accurate empirical data on this aspect of historical dynamics (historical atlases). The focus on agrarian polities is motivated by the extent of empirical material (roughly, from the third millennium B.C.E. to 1800 C.E.) and the greater simplicity of these societies compared to modern ones, potentially making them easier to understand and model.

Although the main focus of the book is on territorial dynamics, it is clear that the ability (or inability) of states to expand depends very much on their internal characteristics. Thus, in order to understand how and why states expand and contract, we need to study military, economic, demographic, ethnological, and ideological aspects of social dynamics. I consider four sociological theories potentially explaining territorial dynamics. The first is the geopolitical model of Randall Collins. This theory has been very clearly formulated and requires minimal work to translate into a mathematical model. The second one, by contrast, is an original development. Starting from ideas of the fourteenth century Arabic thinker Ibn Khaldun and recent developments in sociobiology, I advance a theory attempting to explain why the capacity for collective action may vary among different societies. The third theory addresses the issue of ethnic assimilation/religious conversion dynamics. Finally, the fourth theory focuses on the interaction between population dynamics and sociopolitical stability. The connection between population growth and state breakdown is based on the demographic-structural model of Jack Goldstone (another well-formulated theory that is easily translated into a dynamical model). To this model, I add the feedback mechanism, postulating how state breakdown and resulting sociopolitical instability negatively affect population numbers. The four theories address somewhat different aspects of historical dynamics, and thus logically are not mutually exclusive. However, alternative hypotheses about particular empirical patterns can be derived from them and tested with data. I present several such empirical tests.

ACKNOWLEDGMENTS

Many people provided extensive comments on previous book drafts or draft chapters. I am particularly indebted to Tom Hall, Jack Goldstone, Sergey Nefedov, and the anonymous reviewer who read the whole draft and provided numerous and truly excellent comments and criticisms. I also wish to express my deep gratitude to Marc Artzrouni, Robert Boyd, Christopher Chase-Dunn, Randall Collins, Lev Ginzburg, Robert Hanneman, John Komlos, and Nikolai Rozov for their comments on various parts of previous drafts. Many thanks to Svetlana Borinskaya, Andrey Korotayev, and other members of the Social Evolution group in Moscow for constructive critique and general encouragement. I am grateful to Marc Artzrouni for providing the graphical output of his simulation model for Figure 2.4. Finally, I wish to thank Jennifer Slater for excellent copyediting, Kathy Tebo for help with typing and proofreading, and Mirko Janc for his "TeXpert" typesetting.

Historical Dynamics

Why States Rise and Fall

Chapter One

Statement of the Problem

1.1 WHY DO WE NEED A MATHEMATICAL THEORY IN HISTORY?

Why do some polities—chiefdoms and states of various kinds—embark on a successful program of territorial expansion and become empires? Why do empires sooner or later collapse? Historians and sociologists offer a great variety of answers to these and related questions. These answers range from very specific explanations focusing on unique characteristics of one particular polity to quite general theories of social dynamics. There has always been much interest in understanding history, but recently the theoretical activity in this area has intensified (Rozov 1997). Historical sociology is attempting to become a theoretical, mature science.

But why do historical sociologists use such a limited set of theoretical tools? *Theory* in social sciences usually means careful thinking about concepts and definitions. It is verbal, conceptual, and discursive. The theoretical propositions that are derived are *qualitative* in nature. Nobody denies the immense value of such theoretical activity, but it is not enough. There are also formal, mathematical approaches to building theory that have been applied with such spectacular success in physics and biology. Yet formalized theory employing mathematical models is rarely encountered in historical sociology (we will be reviewing some of the exceptions in later chapters).

The history of science is emphatic: a discipline usually matures only after it has developed mathematical theory. The requirement for mathematical theory is particularly important if the discipline deals with dynamic quantities (see the next section). Everybody is familiar with the paradigmatic example of classical mechanics. But two more recent examples from biology are the synthetic theory of evolution that emerged during the second quarter of the twentieth century (Ruse 1999), and the ongoing synthesis in population ecology (for example, Turchin 2003). In all these cases, the impetus for synthesis was provided by the development of mathematical theory.

Can something similar be done in historical sociology? Several attempts have been made in the past (e.g., Bagehot 1895; Rashevsky 1968), but they clearly failed to make an impact on how history is studied today. I think there are two major reasons explaining this failure. First, these attempts were inspired directly by successes in physical sciences. Yet physicists traditionally choose to deal with systems and phenomena that are very different from those in history. Physicists tend to choose very simple systems with few interacting components (such as the solar system, the hydrogen atom, etc.) or systems consisting of a huge number of identical components (as in thermodynamics). As a result, very precise quantitative predictions can be made and empirically tested. But even in physical applications such systems are rare, and in social sciences only very trivial questions can be reduced to such simplicity. Real societies always consist of many qualitatively and quantitatively different agents interacting in very complex ways. Furthermore, societies are not closed systems: they are strongly affected by exogenous forces, such as other human societies, and by the physical world. Thus, it is not surprising that traditional physical approaches honed on simple systems should fail in historical applications.

The second reason is that the quantitative approaches typically employed by physicists require huge amounts of precisely measured data. For example, a physicist studying nonlinear laser dynamics would without further ado construct a highly controlled lab apparatus and proceed to collect hundreds of thousands of extremely accurate measurements. These data would then be analyzed using sophisticated methods on a high-powered computer. Nothing could be further from the reality encountered by a historical sociologist, who typically lacks data about many aspects of the historical system under study, while possessing fragmentary and approximate information about others. For example, one of the most important aspects of any society is just how many members it has. But even this kind of information usually must be reconstructed by historians on the basis of much guesswork.

If these two problems are the real reason why previous attempts failed, then some recent developments in natural sciences provide a basis for hope. First, during the last 20–30 years, physicists and biologists have mounted a concerted attack on complex systems. A number of approaches can be cited here: nonlinear dynamics, synergetics, complexity, and so on. The use of powerful computers has been a key element in making these approaches work. Second, biologists, and ecologists in particular, have learned how to deal with short and noisy data sets. Again, plentiful computing power was a key enabler, allowing such computer-intensive approaches as nonlinear model fitting, bootstrapping, and cross-validation.

There is another hopeful development, this time in social sciences. I am referring to the rise of quantitative approaches in history, or *cliometrics* (Williamson 1991). Currently, there are many investigators who collect quantitative data on various aspects of historical processes, and large amounts of data are already available in electronic form.

These observations suggest that another attempt at building and testing quantitative theories in historical sociology may be timely. If we achieve even partial success, the potential payoff is so high that it warrants making the attempt. And there are several recent developments in which application of modeling and quantitative approaches to history have already yielded interesting insights.

1.2 HISTORICAL DYNAMICS AS A RESEARCH PROGRAM

Many historical processes are *dynamic*. Generally speaking, *dynamics* is the scientific study of any entities that change with time. One aspect of dynamics deals with a phenomenological description of temporal behaviors—trajectories (this is sometimes known as kinematics). But the heart of dynamics is the study of mechanisms that bring about temporal change and explain the observed trajectories. A very common approach, which has proved its worth in innumerable applications, consists of taking a holistic phenomenon and mentally splitting it up into separate parts that are assumed to interact with each other. This is the dynamical systems approach, because the whole phenomenon is represented as a *system* consisting of several interacting *elements* (or *subsystems*, since each element can also be represented as a lower-level system).

As an example, consider the issue raised at the very beginning of the book. An empire is a dynamic entity because various aspects of it (the most obvious ones being the extent of the controlled territory and the number of subjects) change with time: empires grow and decline. Various explanations for imperial dynamics address different aspects of empires. For example, we may be concerned with the interacting processes of surplus product extraction and warfare (e.g., Tilly 1990). Then we might represent an empire as a system consisting of such subsystems as the peasants, the ruling elite, the army, and perhaps the merchants. Additionally, the empire controls a certain territory and has certain neighboring polities (that is, there is a higher-level system—or *metasystem*—that includes the empire we study as a subsystem). In the dynamical system's approach, we must describe mathematically how different subsystems interact with each other (and, perhaps, how other systems in the metasystem affect our system). This mathematical description is the model of the system, and we can use a variety of methods to study the dynamics predicted by the model, as well as attempt to test the model by comparing its predictions with the observed dynamics.

The conceptual representation of any holistic phenomenon as interacting subsystems is always to some degree artifical. This artificiality, by itself, cannot be an argument against any particular model of the system. All models simplify the reality. The value of any model should be judged only against alternatives, taking into account how well each model predicts data, how parsimonious the model is, and how much violence its assumptions do to reality. It is important to remember that there are many examples of very useful models in natural sciences whose assumptions are known to be wrong. In fact, all models are by definition wrong, and this should not be held against them.

Mathematical models are particularly important in the study of dynamics, because dynamic phenomena are typically characterized by nonlinear feedbacks, often acting with various time lags. Informal verbal models are adequate for generating predictions in cases where assumed mechanisms act in a linear and additive fashion (as in trend extrapolation), but they can be very misleading when we deal with a system characterized by nonlinearities and lags. In general, nonlinear dynamical systems have a much wider spectrum of behaviors than could be imagined by informal reasoning (for example, see Hanneman et al. 1995). Thus, a formal mathematical apparatus is indispensable when we wish to rigorously connect the set of assumptions about the system to predictions about its dynamic behavior.

1.2.1 Delimiting the Set of Questions

History offers many puzzles and somehow we must select which of the questions we are going to address in this research program. I chose to focus on territorial dynamics of polities, for the following reasons. Much of recorded history is concerned with territorial expansion of one polity at the expense of others, typically accomplished by war. Why some polities expand and others fail to do so is a big, important question in history, judging, for example, by the number of books written about the rise and fall of empires. Furthermore, the spatiotemporal record of territorial state dynamics is perhaps one of the best quantitative data sets available to the researcher. For example, the computer-based atlas CENTENNIA (Reed 1996) provides a continuous record of territorial changes during 1000–2000 C.E. in Europe, Middle East, and Northern Africa. Having such data is invaluable to the research program described in this book, because it can provide a *primary data set* with which predictions of various models can be compared.

The *dynamic* aspect of state territories is also an important factor. As I argued in the previous section, dynamic phenomena are particularly difficult to study without a formal mathematical apparatus. Thus, if we wish to develop a mathematical theory for history, we should choose those phenomena where mathematical models have the greatest potential for nontrivial insights.

Territorial dynamics is not the whole of history, but it is one of the central aspects of it, in two senses. First, we need to invoke a variety of social mechanisms to explain territorial dynamics, including military, political, economic, and ideological processes. Thus, by focusing on territorial change we are by no means going to be exclusively concerned with military and political history. Second, characteristics of the state, such as its internal stability and wealth of ruling elites, are themselves important variables explaining many other aspects of history, for example, the development of arts, philosophy, and science.

1.2.2 A Focus on Agrarian Polities

There are many kinds of polities, ranging from bands of hunter-gatherers to the modern postindustrial states. A focus on particular socioeconomic formation is necessary if we are to make progress. The disadvantages of industrial and postindustrial polities are that the pace of change has become quite rapid and the societies have become very complex (measured, for example, by the number of different professions). Additionally, we are too close to these societies, making it harder for us to study them objectively. The main disadvantage of studying hunter-gatherer societies, on the other hand, is that we have to rely primarily on archaeological data. Agrarian societies appear to suffer the least from these two disadvantages: throughout most of their history they changed at a reasonably slow pace, and we have good historical records for many of them. In fact, more than 95% of recorded history is the history of agrarian societies. As an additional narrowing of the focus for this book, I will say little about nomadic pastoralist societies and leave out of consideration thalassocratic city-states (however, both kinds of polities are very important, and will be dealt with elsewhere).

This leaves us still with a huge portion of human history, roughly extending from −4000 to 1800 or 1900 C.E.,[1] depending on the region. One region to which I will pay much attention is Europe during the period 500–1900 C.E., with occasional excursions to China. But the theory is meant to apply to all agrarian polities, and the aim is to test it eventually in other regions of the world.

1.2.3 The Hierarchical Modeling Approach

There is a heuristic "rule of thumb" in modeling dynamical systems: do not attempt to encompass in your model more than two hierarchical levels. A model that violates this rule is the one that attempts to model the dynamics of both interacting subsystems within the system *and* interactions of subsubsystems within each subsystem. Using an individual-based simulation to model interstate dynamics also violates this rule (unless, perhaps, we model simple chiefdoms). From the practical point of view, even powerful computers take a long time to simulate systems with millions of agents. More importantly, from the conceptual point of view it is very difficult to interpret the results of such a multilevel simulation. Practice shows that questions involving multilevel systems should be approached by separating the issues relevant to each level, or rather pair of levels (the lower level provides mechanisms, one level up is where we observe patterns).

Accordingly, in the research program described in this book I consider three classes of models. In the first class, individuals (or, perhaps, individual households) interact together to determine group dynamics. The goal of these models is to understand how patterns at the group level arise from individual based mechanisms. In the second class, we build on group-level mechanisms to understand the patterns arising at the polity level. Finally, the third class of models addresses how polities interact at the interstate level. The greatest emphasis will be on the second class of models (groups–polity). I realize that this sounds rather abstract at this point; in particular, what do I mean by "groups"? The discussion of this important issue is deferred until chapter 3. Also, I do not wish to be too dogmatic about following the rule of two levels. When we find it too restrictive, we should break it; the main point is not to do it unless really necessary.

1.2.4 Mathematical Framework

The hard part of theory building is choosing the mechanisms that will be modeled, making assumptions about how different subsystems interact, choosing functional forms, and estimating parameters. Once all that work is done, obtaining model predictions is conceptually straightforward, although technical, laborious,

---

[1] Negative sign refers to years B.C.E.

and time consuming. For simpler models, we may have analytical solutions available (to solve a model analytically means to derive a formula that gives a precise solution for all parameter values). However, once the model reaches even a medium level of complexity we typically must use a second method: solving it numerically on the computer. A third approach is to use agent-based simulations (Kohler and Gumerman 2000). These ways of obtaining model predictions should not be considered as strict alternatives. On the contrary, a mature theory employs all three approaches synergistically.

Agent-based simulation (ABS), for example, is a very powerful tool for investigating emerging properties of a society consisting of individuals who are assumed to behave in a certain way (by redefining agents to mean groups of individuals or whole polities, we can also use this approach to address higher-level issues). Agent-based models are easily expandable, we can add various stochastic factors, and in general model any conceivable mechanisms. In principle, it is possible to build a theory by using only agent-based simulations. In practice, however, a sole emphasis on these kinds of models is a poor approach. One practical limitation is that currently available computing power, while impressive, is not infinite, putting a limit on how much complexity we can handle in an agent-based simulation. More importantly, ABSs have conceptual drawbacks. Currently, there is no unified language for describing ABSs, making each particular model opaque to everybody except those who are steeped in the particular computer language the model is implemented in. Small details of implementation may result in big differences in the predicted dynamics, and only in very rare cases do practitioners working with different languages bother to cross-translate their ABS (for a rare exception, see Axelrod 1997). And, finally, the power of ABSs is at the same time their curse: it is too easy to keep adding components to these models, and very soon they become too complex to understand.

The more traditional language for modeling dynamical systems, based on differential (or difference) equations, has several advantages. First, it has been greatly standardized, so that a model written as a system of differential equations is much easier to grasp than the computer code describing the same assumptions. This, of course, assumes that the person viewing the model has had much experience with such equations, which unfortunately is not the case with most social scientists, or even biologists, for that matter. Still, one may hope that the level of numeracy in nonphysical sciences will increase with time, and perhaps this book will be of some help here. Second, analytical results are available for most simple or medium-complexity models. Even if we do not have an explicit analytical solution (which is the case for most nonlinear models), we can obtain analytical insights about qualitative aspects of long-term dynamics predicted by these models. Third, numerical methods for solving differential models have been highly standardized. Thus, other researchers can rather easily check on the numerical results of the authors. To sum up, differential (difference) equations provide an extremely useful common language for theory building in dynamical applications.

Note that I am not arguing against the use of ABSs. In fact, I find the recently proposed agenda for doing social science from the bottom up by growing artifical societies (Epstein and Axtell 1996) extremely exciting (for an excellent volume illustrating the strength of this approach when applied to real problems in the social sciences, see Kohler and Gumerman 2000). Rather, I suggest that the ABS should always be supplemented by other approaches, which may lack the power of ABSs, but are better at extracting, and communicating, the important insights from the chaos of reality. The best approach to building theory is the one that utilizes all the available tools: from pencil-and-paper analysis of models to numerical solutions to agent-based simulations.

1.3 SUMMARY

To summarize the discussion in this introductory chapter, here is my proposal for a research program for theory building in historical dynamics.

- Define the problem to be addressed: the territorial dynamics of agrarian polities. The main questions are, why do some polities at certain times expand? And why do they, at other times, contract, or even completely disappear? More luridly, what are the causal mechanisms underlying the rise and demise of empires?
- Identify the primary data set: the spatiotemporal record of territorial dynamics within a certain part of the world and a certain period of time. The data set serves as the testing bed for various mechanistic theories. The success of each theory is measured by how well its predictions match quantitative patterns in the primary data.
- Identify a set of hypotheses, each proposing a specific mechanism, or a combination of mechanisms, to explain territorial expansion/contraction of polities. Many of these hypotheses have already been proposed, others may need to be constructed de novo. The list of hypotheses does not have to be exhaustive, but it should include several that appear most likely, given the present state of knowledge. Hypotheses also do not need to be mutually exclusive.
- Translate all hypotheses in the list into mathematical models. Typically, a single hypothesis will be translated into a spectrum of models, using alternative assumptions about functional forms and parameter values.
- Identify secondary data. These are the data that we need for each specific hypothesis and its associated spectrum of models. For example, if a hypothesis postulates a connection between population growth and state collapse, then we need data on population dynamics. Secondary data provide the basis for auxiliary tests of hypotheses (in addition to tests based on the primary data). Thus, predictions from a hypothesis based on population dynamics should match the observed patterns in the population data. On the other hand, a hypothesis based on legitimacy dynamics does not need to predict population data also; instead, its predictions should match temporal fluctuations of legitimacy.

- Solve the models using appropriate technology (that is, analytical, numerical, and simulation methods). Select those features of the models' output where there is a disagreement among hypotheses/models, and use the primary data set to determine which hypothesis predicts this aspect better than others. Take into account the ability of each hypothesis to predict the appropriate secondary data, how parsimonious is the model into which the hypothesis is translated, and any degree of circularity involved (for example, when the same data are used for both parameter estimation and model testing). Make a tentative selection in favor of the model (or models) that predicts various features of the data best with the least number of free parameters.
- Repeat the process, by involving other hypotheses and by locating more data that can be used to test various models.

Clearly this is a highly idealized course of action, which sounds almost naive in its positivistic outlook. In practice, it is unlikely that it will work just as described above. Nevertheless, there is a value in setting the goal high. The rest of the book presents a deliberate attempt to follow this research program. As we shall see, reality will intrude in a number of sobering ways. Yet I also think that the results, while failing to achieve the lofty goals set out above, prove to be instructive. But this is for the readers to judge.

Chapter Two

Geopolitics

Geopolitics, in the narrow sense that I use in this book, concerns itself with the spatial aspects of historical dynamics. There are two major kinds of mechanisms invoked in geopolitical models: the ability to project power at distance, and the effect of spatial position. Thus, geopolitics is a natural place to start in my review of theories for territorial dynamics of states. Additionally, it is one of the best-theorized areas in historical sociology (for example, Collins 1978, 1986, 1995), and perhaps enjoys the greatest number of already existing formal models (see below). However, my argument in this chapter indicates that geopolitical models (in the narrow sense) are insufficient for the explanation of empirical patterns; in particular, they fail to account for a sustained decline of formerly powerful and territorially extensive polities.

2.1 A PRIMER OF DYNAMICS

Rather than starting immediately with geopolitical models, I first review some basic facts about general kinds of behaviors that can be exhibited by dynamical systems. Although these facts are fairly elementary, they are worth discussing, because (1) they may not be well known to people lacking extensive experience with dynamic models, and (2) it gives me a chance to introduce a simple classification scheme, to which I can then refer throughout the book. An excellent introduction to dynamical social systems can be found in Fararo (1989).

2.1.1 Boundless Growth

The simplest possible dynamics is linear growth, obeying the differential equation

$$\dot{X} = c \tag{2.1}$$

Here X is the variable that is changing, $\dot{X}$ is the rate of change of X (often written as dX/dt), and c is a constant. A familiar application of this model is Newton's first law, in which X is the position of a body and c a constant velocity. (The first law states that, in the absence of any forces acting on the body, it will move with constant velocity.) The solution of this equation is $X(t) = X_0 + ct$, where t is time and X_0 is the initial position of the body, $X(0) = X_0$. The solution says that X will change linearly with time (Figure 2.1a), and that the rate of change is c. Thus, I refer to this kind of dynamics as *linear growth* (or decline, if c is negative).

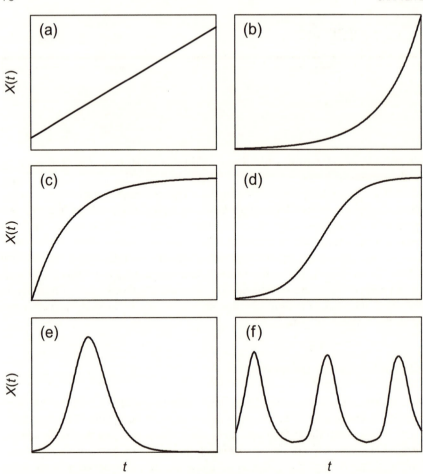

Figure 2.1 Qualitative types of dynamics: (a) linear, (b) exponential, (c) asymptotic, (d) logistic, (e) boom and bust, and (f) sustained oscillations.

Another simple model of growth obeys the following differential equation:

$$\dot{X} = rX \tag{2.2}$$

This is the *exponential growth* model. The parameter r is another constant, called the *relative rate of change* (because the total rate of change is the product of the relative rate r and X). Because the rate of change of X is assumed to be proportional to X itself, this type of growth is sometimes called *autocatalytic*: the more X there is, the faster it grows. The exponential equation provides the simplest model for the growth of biological populations and can be thought of as the first law of population dynamics (Turchin 2003). The autocatalytic part arises because the more animals there are in the population, the faster the population grows (since each animal can reproduce). The solution of the exponential model is a curve bending up (Figure 2.1b).

The linear and exponential models are examples of *boundless growth*. Such models often provide good starting points for modeling dynamical systems, because they make minimal assumptions about the system. In other words, they are *null models*, and that is why the first laws of mechanics and population dynamics belong to this class. But boundless growth models, by themselves, are not good models for the overwhelming majority of dynamic phenomena, because few real-life systems exhibit limitless growth. We need to add other mechanisms to the right-hand side of equations.

2.1.2 Equilibrial Dynamics

Few real-life processes grow without bound. Usually, there are some mechanisms—generally called *negative feedbacks*—that act to impose upper and lower limits on growth. One of the most important characteristics of a negative feedback mechanism is the lag time with which it operates. Some feedback mechanisms operate on a time scale that is much faster than the time scale at which the modeled variable X changes. In such cases we usually neglect the lag and assume that the feedback is instantaneous. A simple model that adds an instantaneous negative feedback to the linear growth is

$$\dot{X} = c - dX \qquad (2.3)$$

Here two processes affect the dynamics of X. One force increases X at a constant rate c, but there is also a counteracting force, whose strength increases proportionately to X. At some point (specifically, when X reaches $X^* = c/d$), the strengths of the positive push and negative pull balance each other, and X stops growing. The point X^* where the rate of change of X is zero is called an *equilibrium*. Equilibria can be stable or unstable. For this model, the equilibrium X^* is stable, because when X is below the equilibrium, the positive push overwhelms the negative pull; and vice versa, if X somehow gets above X^*, then the negative pull will overwhelm the positive push, and return X back to the equilibrium. A typical trajectory for X predicted by equation (2.3) is initially linear (at low X) and then slows asymptotically as X approaches equilibrium (Figure 2.1c). I will refer to such dynamics as linear-asymptotic or *asymptotic growth*, for short.

Adding a negative feedback to the model of exponential growth is also simple. In this case, let us assume that the relative growth rate r is a linear function of X: $r(X) = r_0 - gX$. This leads to the *logistic* equation

$$\dot{X} = r(X)X = (r_0 - gX)X \qquad (2.4)$$

Logistic growth is illustrated in Figure 2.1d.

Both asymptotic and logistic dynamics belong to the class of single-dimensional or first-order differential models. The general form of first-order models is $\dot{X} = f(X)$, where $f(X)$ is some arbitrary function of X. For example, in the logistic model, $f(X) = (r_0 - gX)X$ is a quadratic function of X. These models are called first order (or one dimensional) because there is only one structural variable, X. (In mathematical applications structural variables are called *state* variables, because they describe the state of the system. The use of this standard terminology in dynamical systems, however, would create unnecessary confusion because the main subject of this book is states in the meaning of polities.)

In addition to the kinds of dynamics illustrated by the asymptotic and logistic models, in which the system is always attracted to a unique stable equilibrium, single-dimensional models can also have a more complex behavior, called *metastable* dynamics. For example, if $f(X)$ is a cubic polynomial, so that the model is

$$\dot{X} = a(X - b)(c - X)X \tag{2.5}$$

(a, b, and c are positive constants), then there are three equilibria: two stable ones (a low and a high equilibrium), and one unstable in the middle. If X is initially below the unstable equilibrium, the trajectory will be attracted to the low equilibrium. Alternatively, if X starts above the unstable point, the trajectory is attracted to the high equilibrium. One social science application of such an equation is in modeling "tipping" behaviors (see Chapter 6).

One very important fact that we need to know for later is that first-order differential models are incapable of oscillatory dynamics. They cannot even exhibit a single (rise-and-fall) oscillation. *Fast negative feedbacks, operating without an appreciable lag, cannot cause a dynamical system to oscillate.* They can only cause it to return asymptotically to an equilibrium, if a stable equilibrium exists (if it does not, then the system will run away to $\pm\infty$). In order for oscillations to arise, a negative feedback must operate with a delay. We model such slow feedbacks either explicitly, by adding other structural variables to the differential equation model, or implicitly by using discrete-time (difference) models.

2.1.3 Boom/Bust Dynamics and Sustained Oscillations

In order to model rise/fall dynamics of X with differential equations, we need to identify another structural variable, call it Y, which is affected by X and, in turn, itself affects X. Thus, X is affected by a negative feedback loop that is mediated by Y. Consider the following simple biological model of a population of consumers living on a nonrenewable resource:

$$\dot{X} = caXY - dX$$
$$\dot{Y} = -aXY \tag{2.6}$$

where X is the number of consumers at time t and Y is the current amount of resources. Looking first at the Y equation, we see the term $-aXY$ representing the rate of consumption (the minus sign indicates that consumption reduces the amount of resources present). Consumption is assumed to be proportional to the product of X and Y, for the following reasons. First, more consumers deplete resources faster. Second, when resources are plentiful, each individual consumer depletes resources faster than when resources are scarce. Turning to the X equation, I assumed that consumers increase in proportion to the amount of resource consumed, with c being the constant of proportionality (this is the term $caXY$).

Additionally, consumers die off at a rate proportional to X (the proportionality constant d is known as the relative or per capita death rate).

The dynamics of this model are illustrated in Figure 2.1e. Assuming plentiful initial resources, consumers will first increase because their "birth rate" ($caXY$) will exceed the "death rate" (dX). Meanwhile, resources are depleted, and at an increasingly faster rate, because consumers are becoming more and more numerous. Eventually, resources fall beyond the point where consumer birth rate exceeds death rate, and the consumers start declining. Since consumers are still depleting resources, even during the decline phase, there is no end to the collapse: X will keep decreasing to 0. The boom is inevitably followed by the bust.

It is very easy to modify Model (2.6) to cause it to go through repeated boom/bust cycles. For example, we can add the assumption that the resource is renewable, and grows exponentially in the absence of consumers. Adding the exponential growth term bY to the second equation, we have

$$\dot{X} = caXY - dX$$
$$\dot{Y} = -aXY + bY \tag{2.7}$$

This is the famous Lotka-Volterra model of predator-prey cycles (a typical trajectory of X is shown in Figure 2.1f).

Second- and higher-order differential models (models with two or more structural variables) are capable of very diverse kinds of dynamic behaviors. They can have a stable equilibrium, approached either monotonically (as in one-dimensional models) or in an oscillatory fashion. They can exhibit stable cycles, characterized by a certain period and amplitude. Models with three or more structural variables can oscillate chaotically (predicting irregular-looking dynamics) or quasiperiodically (two or more cycle periods superimposed on each other). There are many kinds of fascinating mathematical phenomena, but we do not need to be concerned with them in the investigation of social dynamics, at least not for a long time yet. The important general class of dynamics for our purposes is second-order oscillations. Whether they are limit cycles, quasiperiodicity, or chaos is not critical at the current state of the art. The important feature, which distinguishes them from first-order dynamics, is sustained periods of increase followed by sustained periods of decline.

One further important result from nonlinear dynamic theory is that there is a close relationship between the time scales at which negative feedback loops operate (how fast they are) and the time scale of the dynamics (for example, the average period of oscillations). In differential equation models such as (2.7), the speed with which negative feedback acts is explicitly related to parameter values of the model, typically those whose units are [time] or [time]$^{-1}$. In the Lotka-Volterra model, there are two parameters whose units are [time]$^{-1}$: d and b. The parameter d measures how fast the numbers of consumers would (exponentially) decline in the absence of resource; b, analogously, measures how fast resources would (exponentially) increase in the absence of consumers. These two parameters determine the periodicity with which the consumer-resource system oscillates. In fact, the period is inversely related to the geometric mean of b and

d (for the mathematically inquisitive: the period of oscillations near the neutrally stable equilibrium is $2\pi/\sqrt{bd}$). Thus, the faster consumer and resource populations change in time, the shorter is the oscillation period. In models more complex than the Lotka-Volterra model the formula for the period is more complicated, but the qualitative insight carries over: faster feedbacks cause faster oscillations (and if feedbacks are too fast, then we cannot even obtain oscillations, because dynamics tend to be stabilized by very fast feedback mechanisms).

2.1.4 Implications for Historical Dynamics

Our discussion of dynamics, so far, has focused exclusively on *endogenous* factors—variables that participate in dynamic feedbacks. In a purely endogenous system any fluctuations are solely a result of the interaction of endogenous variables; such systems are "closed" with respect to influences from outside. Historical social systems, by contrast, should always be affected by outside forces: climate fluctuations causing crop failure, sudden appearance of new epidemics, hostile invasions, spread of new religions, and so on. Factors that influence a dynamical system, but are not themselves influenced by its variables, are called *exogenous*. The distinction between endogenous and exogenous factors is not sharp, and usually depends on the questions we choose. For example, if we are focused on the internal dynamics of a single polity, then we will model invasion by other polities as an exogenous factor. But if we decide to expand the model to cover the dynamics of the whole system of interacting states, or the *world-system* (Wallerstein 1974; Chase-Dunn and Hall 1997), then invasion occurrence is endogenized.

The open property of historical social systems presents no problem to the dynamical systems approach. The most natural way to model such influences is to add an exogenous structural variable to the system of equations. For example, if we already have endogenous variables X and Y, and add an exogenous variable Z, then the equations look something like

$$\dot{X} = f(X, Y, Z)$$
$$\dot{Y} = g(X, Y, Z)$$
$$\dot{Z} = h(t)$$

where f, g, and h, are some functions. That is, the rate of change of X and Y depends on all three variables in the system, while the rate of change of Z is given by some time-dependent function. There are two general ways to model Z: (1) as a stochastic variable or (2) as a deterministic trend. Which approach we choose depends on the nature of the exogenous variable, and the questions we wish to ask.

In Sections 2.1.1–2.1.3 I identified three fundamental types of dynamics characterizing purely endogenous systems. The simplest type encompasses systems that are not affected by negative feedbacks. I will call such dynamics *zero order*. Next, there are systems that are affected only by feedbacks acting very rapidly, which I will call *first-order* dynamics. Finally, there are systems that incorporate multiple endogenous variables, leading to negative feedback loops acting with a time delay. These are *second-order* systems.

Allowing exogenous variables leads to a natural generalization of this order typology as follows. Zero-order systems are characterized by this general model:

$$\dot{X} = f(Z(t)) \tag{2.8}$$

In effect, X itself is the exogenous variable. Examples of such systems are various kinds of random walks (biased or otherwise), stochastic exponential increase or decline models, and so on. Such systems typically do not have an equilibrium density around which they fluctuate (unless we construct the function f in a very special way, to force such an "equilibrium" exogenously). Zero-order systems are not terribly interesting from the dynamical point of view, because any systematic dynamical patterns found in them are entirely due to the action of exogenous variables. The power of the dynamical systems approach would be largely misspent in applying it to such systems. However, zero-order dynamics provide a natural null model, against which other more complex alternatives can be tested.

First-order systems are governed by models of the form

$$\dot{X} = f(X, Z(t)) \tag{2.9}$$

where Z is an exogenous variable and does not depend on X. If Z is a stochastic variable, and f includes a negative feedback, then the dynamics are characterized by a stochastic equilibrium. X fluctuates in the vicinity of the stable equilibrium, and if X becomes too high or too low, endogenous dynamics push it back to the equilibrial level of fluctuations (in other words, the dynamic process is characterized by a return tendency). No cycles or any other kinds of complex dynamic behaviors occur in first-order systems, unless they are exogenously imposed (for example, Z oscillates periodically).

Second-order systems are governed by models like

$$\dot{X} = f(X, Y, Z(t))$$
$$\dot{Y} = g(X, Y, Z(t))$$

where Z is again an exogenous variable. More than two endogenous variables can be involved. Second-order systems are capable of all kinds of complex dynamics: stable equilibria, limit cycles, quasiperiodicity, chaos, multiple coexisting attractors, etc. Adding stochasticity expands the spectrum of possible behaviors even further. However, for the purposes of this book, I will call all such behaviors *second-order oscillations.* Perhaps the time will come when we have methods and data good enough for distinguishing between limit cycles and chaos in historical systems, but this time is not here yet. The fundamental importance of distinguishing between the three kinds of dynamics is that in zero-order systems all dynamics are driven exogenously, while in the first- and second-order ones some proportion of the variance in fluctuations is explained by the action of endogenous variables. Furthermore, different social mechanisms can often be classified as either fast or slow feedbacks, leading, correspondingly, to either first- or second-order dynamics. Detecting and characterizing such oscillation-inducing feedbacks is a major goal of the proposed research program in historical dynamics.

2.2 THE COLLINS THEORY OF GEOPOLITICS

One of the most powerful formulations of the geopolitical theory is found in the work of Randall Collins (1978, 1986, 1995); see Rozov (1997). Because Collins states his geopolitical principles clearly and succinctly, this verbal theory can be relatively easily translated into mathematical models. Furthermore, Collins and co-workers have also advanced formal geopolitical models, formulated as computer simulations (Hanneman et al. 1995). My plan in this section is to review the postulates advanced by Collins, and translate them into simple differential models. I will also do the same for the simulation model of Hanneman et al. (1995), thus bringing these developments to a common denominator. Another interesting model that is relevant to the issues at hand is the spatial simulation by Artzrouni and Komlos (1996).

2.2.1 Modeling Size and Distance Effects

As is natural, Collins' thinking has evolved over the last two decades, so the material below is based on his 1995 article, specifically on his Figure 1 there, which I redraw here as Figure 2.2. The main variable of interest is the state's territory size, or area. Temporal change in this variable occurs as a result of war success. The positive arrow from "war success" to "territory size" indicates that when the state is successful in war, it gains territory, while war failure implies territory loss. Territory size also positively affects "geopolitical resources" (more taxes and

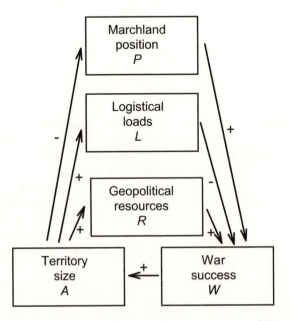

Figure 2.2 Feedback structure of the Collins geopolitical model. (After Collins 1995: Figure 1)

recruits for the army), which in turn positively affects war success. Increased territory size also means increased "logistical loads." The further that military power is projected from the home base, the higher the costs (Collins 1995:1558). Additionally, more state resources are tied up in policing the populace and extracting the resources. This connection between the state's size and logistical loads is often referred to as the "imperial overstretch" principle (Kennedy 1987). Increased logistic loads, in turn, have a negative effect on war success. Finally, "marchland position" favors war success, because states with enemies on fewer fronts expand at the expense of states surrounded by enemies (Collins 1995:1555). However, state expansion reduces the marchland advantage, as the state expands away from its initially more protected position.

We now translate this theory into formal models, starting with the loop involving geopolitical resources, and then adding the effect of logistical loads. Marchland position requires a spatially explicit approach and will be tackled in the next section. In developing the following models, I will make two general assumptions. First, and most importantly, I will assume that various feedbacks act rapidly with respect to territorial dynamics. Thus, I can use ordinary differential equations as the mathematical framework. Second, to make the model more concrete I will assume simple functional forms, usually linear ones. The effect of these assumptions on the results will be discussed below.

In the first model, there are three variables: territory size, or area A, geopolitical resources R, and war success W. I will assume that the rate of change of A is linearly related to war success: $\dot{A} = c_1 W$, where c_1 is a proportionality constant, translating war victory into square kilometers of territory gained. Resources should be roughly proportional to the area (in the simplest case, if population density is approximately constant, increased area implies greater population base to pay taxes and provide recruits). Thus, $R = c_2 A$. Finally, the relationship between resources and war success is a bit more complex. Resources translate into state power, but in order to gain victory, state power has to be greater than the power of the adversary. Assuming that the state we study (the *focal* state) exists in a homogeneous environment, characterized by a constant military power of rivals, we have $W = c_3 R - c_4$. The constant c_3 translates resources into power, while c_4 is the power of the adversary who must be defeated. The greater is the power of the focal state, in relation to the adversary power, the more successful it is in war, and, in consequence, the faster it increases its territory. Putting together these assumptions, and after some algebraic manipulations, we have the following model:

$$\dot{A} = cA - a \qquad (2.10)$$

where I defined $c = c_1 c_2 c_3$ and $a = c_1 c_4$, to gid rid of unneeded parameter combinations.

The dynamics of this linear model are very simple, and depend on the initial territory of the state (see Figure 2.3a). If the initial A is below the threshold $A_0 = a/c$, then the rate of change is negative, and A decreases to 0. However, if A starts above the threshold, then it grows exponentially (that is, at an accelerating rate) to infinity. In other words, we are dealing here with a zero-order type of

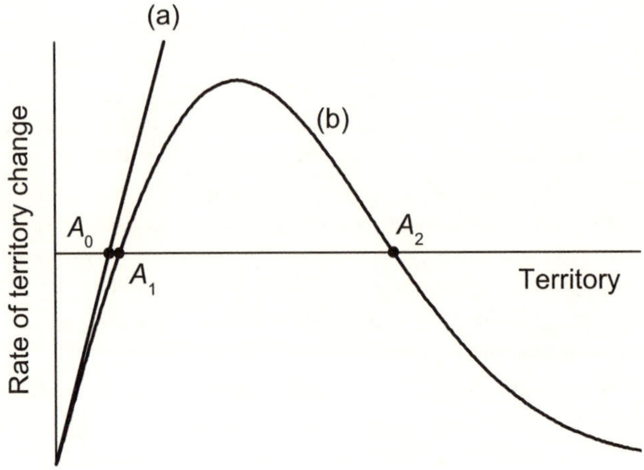

Figure 2.3 Relationship between the rate of territorial change, $\dot{A}$, and territory, A, in the two simple geopolitical models. (a) Model of territory size effects. (b) Model of territory size and distance.

dynamics. This is not at all surprising, because all arrows in the loop we modeled so far have pluses associated with them. In other words, we have just modeled a positive feedback loop, and obtained an entirely predictable result.

The loop involving logistic loads, on the other hand, involves one minus, and therefore it is a negative feedback loop. To model the effect of logistic load, let us follow Collins and assume that imperial overextension results from difficulties associated with projecting imperial power over distance. In other words, if state power at the center is P_0, then at distance r it is $P_0L(r)$, where $L(r)$ is the logistic distance multiplier, ranging from 1 at $r = 0$ to 0 at $r = \infty$. Boulding (1962:245–247) presents the argument that logistic distance multipliers should decline with increasing r as a negative exponential function: $L(r) = \exp[-r/c_5]$, with c_5 governing how rapidly power declines with distance. Since the relationship between area and radius is $A \sim r^2$, the logistic distance multiplier is $L(r) = \exp[-\sqrt{A}/c_7]$. Substituting this relationship in the model, we have

$$\dot{A} = cA\exp[-\sqrt{A}/h] - a \tag{2.11}$$

where parameter combinations were again replaced with single parameters. Figure 2.3b shows that state power, as measured by its ability to expand, is negative at low A (just as in the pure size model), and initially increases with A. However, eventually the effect of increased logistic load begins to be felt. At $A = 4h^2$ state power is maximized, and for $A > 4h^2$ it begins to decline. There are two equilibrial points, A_1 and A_2. A_1, similarly to A_0 in the size-only model, is unstable: if the initial condition is below A_1, then the state is eaten by its neighbors. A_2 is a stable equilibrium: below it, the state's ability to expand is positive and A increases; above it, the state expansion rate is negative and A declines (Figure 2.3b).

An alternative formulation is to assume that power declines with increasing distance as a Gaussian curve, $c_5 \exp[-r^2/c_6]$. The Gaussian curve appears convenient as a phenomenological description, because it is flat near the state center, where communications are best, and then declines at an increasing rate. Employing this assumption leads to a slightly different model: $\dot{A} = cA\exp[-A/b] - a$. The relationship between $\dot{A}$ and A in this model has the same qualitative shape as in Figure 2.3b, so the implications for territorial dynamics are exactly the same as in Model (2.11).

Note that in this model imperial overstretch does not lead to state collapse. Comparing the size-only model to Model (2.11), we see that the novel feature is the existence of the upper equilibrium A_2, which turns out to be stable. Thus, we now have a model of first-order dynamics; there is no possibility of boom/bust behaviors. How general is this result? Remember that we made two kinds of assumptions: fast feedbacks and simple functional forms. Taking the second assumption first, here is where our knowledge of dynamics (Section 2.1) begins to pay for itself. *No matter how nonlinear the various functional forms are, we will still end up with a one-dimensional ordinary differential equation model, which is not capable of generating boom/bust dynamics and second-order oscillations.* All we are likely to do is to create a few more equilibrial points, making the dynamics increasingly more metastable. If we add large enough amounts of noise, then we may be able to force the state trajectory to jump between a high and a low equilibrium. This would not be a terribly satisfactory model, because we then would have to understand just what were the exogenous forces that forced the trajectory from one basin of attraction to another. We would need to model these exogenous forces explicitly, and end up with a very different kind of theory from the one we are examining here.

The assumption of fast feedbacks is more crucial to the general theoretical results implied by Model (2.11). Clearly, adding delays, whether implicitly by using difference equations, or explicitly by making some variables, other than A, change on a slow time scale, will lead to models that are capable of oscillations. Let us consider whether adding such delays makes sense empirically. The historical record shows that the growth of empires occurs over time periods of many decades, and even centuries. Thus, A is a slow variable. The geopolitical resources may also come on line with some time lag (because it takes time to "digest" new conquests). However, R is involved in the positive feedback loop, and delays in R will only slow the state expansion, but will not cause an imperial collapse. The feedback loop involving logistic loads, L, on the other hand, should operate without an appreciable time lag. For example, the effect of distance, which is how we modeled logistics, is instantaneous: as soon as territory is conquered, the boundary moves away from the center, and the state immediately incurs the higher costs of projecting its power to the new boundary. Other factors, such as policing the newly conquered population, also should impose an immediate extra burden on the state.

The general argument of this section, then, can be summarized as follows. Imperial overstretch, at least as conceptualized by such geopolitical theorists as Collins and Kennedy, should not lead to state collapse. It is a first-order factor that acts to set a limit to further territorial expansion. Should the state, by chance, overstep this boundary, its power to defend the extra territory is immediately impaired. That territory may be reconquered by neighbors, or the state may abandon it as not worth the bother (as the Roman Empire did with Agri Decumates and Dacia). Such a retreat restores the ability of the state to defend itself. Thus, we need to look to other variables in order to understand the empirically observed examples of imperial collapse.

2.2.2 Positional Effects

In order to investigate positional effects properly, we really need a spatially explicit model, which in practice usually means computer simulations. Before jumping into simulations, however, it is often a good idea to generate some expectations with a drastically simplified version of the model that permits analytical insights. Even if these insights are shown to be completely wrong by the subsequent simulation model, we learn something (at the least, we learn that explicit space is the key element in obtaining correct results). For this reason, let us consider the following simple model. It is a modification of the size-distance geopolitical model [Equations (2.11)] which assumes that territorial dynamics occurs in one-dimensional space. I will again assume that the logistic distance multiplier is a negative exponential function of distance, but now that we have one-dimensional space, $A \sim r$. The resulting modified model is

$$\dot{A} = \gamma c A \exp[-A/h] - a \tag{2.12}$$

(note that there is no square root associated with A inside the exponential). The additional parameter γ takes values 1 or 2, depending on whether the state has enemies at both boundaries, or only at one. In the second case, the state delivers twice as much power at the single boundary ($\gamma = 2$). What is the effect of position (as codified by γ) on the resulting size of the state? To do a rough calculation, we approximate $\exp[x]$ with $1 + x$, and solve the resulting equation for the A_2 equilibrium (the upper stable one), obtaining $A_2 = 0.5h(1 + \sqrt{1 - 4a/ch\gamma})$. From this expression, we see that doubling γ does not result in doubling the equilibrium state size. To illustrate this with a numerical example, suppose that the equilibrium size of the state with enemies at both sides is only double the critical size below which the state collapses, $A_2 = 2A_1$. Then, having an enemy only on one side will increase A_2 by about 30%. If $A_2 = 3A_1$ then the increment resulting from the marchland effect is less than 20%. Thus, this simple model suggests that the marchland position should yield a rather modest increase in the equilibrium state size. Its primary effect is to give some protection to states that are rather marginal in size (in fact, the marchland effect reduces the critical state size, A_1, by 50%).

The Artzrouni and Komlos Model

I now turn to the spatial simulation of territorial dynamics constructed by Artzrouni and Komlos (1996) to investigate hypotheses explaining the formation of the European state system. These investigators represented Europe as a grid of unit squares, with linear dimensions of about 40 km. At time = 0 (which was assumed to correspond to 500 C.E.), the simulated space was filled with equal-sized states, each occupying 5×5 squares, and thus with a starting area of roughly 40,000 km^2 (see Figure 2.4).

The two variables that affect the power of states in the Artzrouni and Komlos simulation are the area A (measured as the number of unit squares that make up a country) and the perimeter C (the number of squares that have a foreign neighbor). The power is increased by greater A, but decreased by greater C, because longer boundaries require more resources to defend. Note that this is a different conceptualization of logistic loads from the one used in the previous section. The marchland effect was modeled by treating state boundaries along the sea and mountains differently from those where no natural borders are present. Artzrouni and Komlos assumed that a sea boundary is easier to defend. Therefore, in calculating the boundary length, each unit along the sea counted only as a fraction f of a unit along the land border. In addition, two European mountain chains, the Pyrenees and the Alps, were assumed to present impregnable natural barriers, so that unit squares abutting these areas were not counted as part of C. However, the Pyrenees and the Alps did not completely cut off their respective peninsulas from the continent (see Figure 2.4).

Artzrouni and Komlos assumed the following specific form for the power function of state i:

$$P_i = \frac{A_i}{\alpha + \exp[\gamma C_i + \beta]} \tag{2.13}$$

where A_i and C_i are the area and the perimeter of state i, respectively, and α, β, and γ are positive constants. This function, although conceptualized differently, results in the same general shape of the relationship between the state size and power as in Model (2.11). As we increase A from 0, P first increases with A, as a result of the positive feedback associated with increased geopolitical resources. Eventually, however, the negative feedback associated with increased logistic loads overpowers the positive one, and for very high A, P declines to 0.

The relative powers of states determine their success in war with neighbors. Each iteration of the model is made of one bilateral interaction (war). The simulation model chooses a country at random (call it i) and compares its power to the powers of all its neighbors. The simulation then determines which neighbor j differs the most in power from i (the j for which the absolute difference $|P_i - P_j|$ is maximized), and the two countries go to war. The more powerful country wins with probability $1 - 0.5 \exp[-K(P_i/P_j - 1)]$; otherwise, the weaker country wins. After the conclusion of war, all boundary squares of the loser contiguous to the winner are absorbed by the winner. The simulation then performs another iteration, choosing a country at random, etc. Each iteration corresponds to 1/3 year.

The Artzrouni and Komlos model has five parameters (f, α, β, γ, and K). The investigators used the method of trial and error to find the specific values of these parameters that would replicate the historically observed dynamic map of Europe as closely as possible. One particular realization of the simulation is shown in

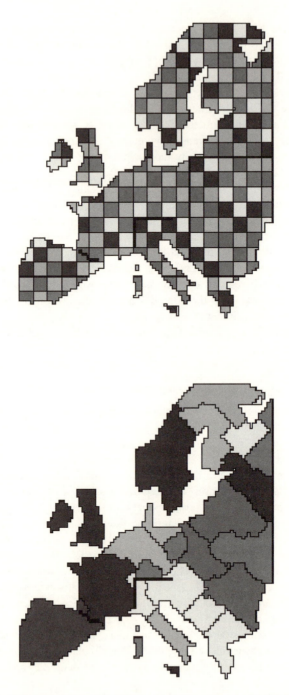

Figure 2.4 Territorial dynamics of the European state system as simulated by the model of Artzrouni and Komlos (1996). Top: initial map at 500 C.E. Bottom: model-predicted map at 1800 C.E. Thick black lines indicate the location of the Pyrenees and the Alps. (After Artzrouni and Komlos 1996: Figure 4)

Figure 2.4: the 234 initial countries at 500 C.E. are reduced to 25 by the end of the simulation. The outlines of coastal countries ("France," "Spain," and "Italy") take shape rapidly, while inland countries take longer to solidify. Additionally, there is much more variability in the final configuration achieved away from the coasts in different realizations. Thus, the marchland effect has two aspects. First, countries enjoying it achieve somewhat larger size compared to more centrally located ones (this can be seen by the large size achieved by "Spain," "France," and "Sweden/Norway" in Figure 2.4). Second, their boundaries reach stability much faster than the boundaries of inland states.

To summarize, the Artzrouni and Komlos simulation provides a confirmation of the postulated effect of the marchland advantage. Additionally, the simulation suggests that the boundaries of present states, especially those with long sea borders (Spain, France, Italy, and Greece), may be determined in a large degree by geopolitical mechanisms. However, Artzrouni and Komlos are very careful to stress that simulation parameters must be tuned just right for the simulation to reach the desired equilibrium. While the circularity involved in parameter calibration weakens the result, we should keep in mind that the simulation is very parsimonious, having only five free parameters. The sensitivity to one parameter, f, is of particular interest to the question of the marchland effect. If f is set too low, then the simulations usually yielded just one or two countries with maritime borders to the west of Europe that swept eastward across the continent. Their small effective perimeters kept their power high, allowing them eventually to annex all their neighbors.

Finally, the geopolitical simulation of Artzrouni and Komlos, similarly to analytical models advanced before, generates an essentially first-order behavior. Large countries conquer smaller and eventually expand until they reach the limits set by imperial overstretch, where their size is stabilized. In other words, the model does not predict that states reaching too high a size will collapse.

2.2.3 Conflict-legitimacy Dynamics

The geopolitical theory of Collins has three major principles (Collins 1986:168, 1995: Figure 1): (1) territorial resource advantage, (2) marchland advantage, and (3) overextension as a result of increased logistic loads. Our modeling in previous sections suggests that these postulates lead to first-order dynamics characterized by initially accelerating territorial growth that eventually reaches a stable equilibrium. Geopolitical models do not predict the collapse of large powerful empires (although small states may be destroyed before they manage to grow above a critical size). Yet, historical empires exhibit a different behavior, because they always eventually collapse. When a dynamical system exhibits opposite trends (growth versus decline) for the same values of variables in the explanatory set, this means that there is another hidden variable that determines the direction of change, which we have not yet included in the set. Thus, our modeling efforts have already paid for themselves: they showed that we need to look for explanatory mechanisms other than pure geopolitical principles, in order to understand the rise and collapse of territorial empires. It appears that Collins has also reached the same conclusion, judging by his extensive discussion of mechanisms of state breakdown in the 1995 paper. Specifically, Collins discusses two theories: (1) the demographic-structural model (Goldstone 1991b), and (2) ruler legitimacy as affected by geopolitical power-prestige (Hanneman et al. 1995). Dynamical systems theory suggests that the key property of the postulated mechanisms of collapse is the time scale on which they act (the concept of temporal scale is also discussed by Collins; e.g., Collins 1995: Figure 6). Thus, our task, which will be largely pursued beyond the confines of this chapter, is to translate various postulated nongeopolitical mechanisms into models, determine whether these models are in principle capable of generating second-order dynamics, and, if so, derive testable predictions from them.

Although the conflict-legitimacy model of Hanneman et al. is not based on a geopolitical mechanism (in the strict sense), I will review it in this chapter, because this model is already well developed (and can be quickly summarized) and is closely connected with the models considered earlier. Actually, Hanneman et al. develop not one model, but a series of models of increasing complexity. This is a methodologically sound approach; in fact, I am in complete agreement with the philosophy of modeling as set out by Hanneman et al. To their excellent recommendations (see also Hanneman 1988), I would add only that more attention should be paid to a parallel development and consideration of analytical models.

The core of the theory advanced by Hanneman et al. focuses on the interaction between power-prestige, state legitimacy, and international conflict. Hanneman et al. assume that the motivation of rulers to initiate external conflict is directly proportional to the difference between their current legitimacy and the goal of maximum legitimacy. For any given level of conflict initiated, the degree of success is determined by the proportional superiority of the power of the focal state, relative to that of its rivals. Change in the state prestige is proportional to war success, and legitimacy follows, with delay, from prestige (Hanneman et al. 1995: 17). Hanneman et al. do not explain why legitimacy should follow war success with a lag time. Yet, in their model they impose a substantial lag: whereas war occurs at every time step (they use a discrete-time framework), legitimacy follows with a lag of three time units. This would suggest that (crudely) on average it takes victory in three successive wars for the legitimacy of the state to increase substantially. I would argue, by contrast, that legitimacy operates on a much faster time scale. War victory is immediately followed by a rush of patriotism that floats up the fortunes of politicians, and, vice versa, war failure is immediately followed by disillusionment with the powers that be. If legitimacy were a slow variable, then there would be much less temptation for politicians to use "a small victorious war" to bolster their shaky legitimacy.

Hanneman et al. develop three models: (1) the core model that focuses on war legitimacy dynamics, (2) a more complex version that adds the costs and benefits of empire, and (3) the full model that further adds imperial capitalism and the military-industrial complex. Of particular interest to us is the second model because, for certain parameter values, it appears to predict repeated instances of imperial growth followed by breakdown. However, it appears that occurrence of these instances of state collapse depends in a critical way on the assumption of a lag time with which legitimacy follows war success. To check whether this is true, I translated the core of the Hanneman model into a differential equation model. In the Appendix (see Section A.1) I show that *the legitimacy-conflict model is described by a single-dimensional ordinary differential equation*. In other words, we again end up with a first-order model. This model can have multiple equilibria, and depending on the initial values of territory size and previous record of war success, the trajectory will be attracted to one or another of the stable ones. But the model is incapable of exhibiting boom/bust dynamics or sustained oscillations. The inescapable conclusion, therefore, is that the interaction between legitimacy, war success, and territorial expansion cannot generate sustained imperial decline. Thus, the imperial collapses occurring in the Hanneman model appear to be entirely due to the assumed delay with which legitimacy follows war success.

2.3 CONCLUSION: GEOPOLITICS AS A FIRST-ORDER PROCESS

I started this chapter by reviewing some elementary facts from nonlinear dynamics for the following reasons. Most social scientists are not closely familiar with dynamical systems theory, and I wanted to present a nontechnical summary of its insights most relevant to the issues dealt with in this book. One such particular insight is that there is a close relationship between the time scales at which negative feedbacks operate and the nature of the dynamics. If feedback mechanisms operate much faster than the dynamics of the focal variable, then the system cannot oscillate or even exhibit a single boom/bust behavior. If we do have an oscillatory system, then, more quantitatively, the speed with which a feedback acts determines the temporal pattern of the dynamics (for example, the average length of an oscillation, or a boom/bust cycle). This means that if a feedback loop operates on the scale of years, or even worse, weeks, then it is highly unlikely that it could cause oscillations, whose average period is measured in centuries. Centuries-long cycles are typically caused by feedbacks operating on the scale of human generations (decades or longer).

This insight is very relevant to the issue of what mechanisms underlie imperial boom/bust cycles. Empires grow and decline on the time scale of centuries (Taagepera 1978a, 1978b, 1997; see also Figure 4.4 in Chapter 4). Let us make a simple analysis of the imperial growth/decline data tabulated in the Appendix of Taagepera (1997). Taagepera defined the rise phase as the time it takes for a polity to expand from 20% to 80% of its maximum area (1997: 480). We can define the decline phase analogously, as the time needed to decline from 80% to 20% of the maximum, and the peak phase as the time from the end of the rise to the beginning of the decline. Table 2.1 gives the phase durations for the 31 polities from Taagepera (1997), that had four or more consecutive area observations (we need these data points to unambiguously define the phases). There is a large amount of variation in the durations of decline phases for these polities. In about half of the cases (14) the decline phase was on the order of one human generation (less than 0.3 centuries). The rest of empires exhibited longer decline phases,

Table 2.1 Durations (in centuries) of imperial phases (rise, peak, and decline) for large polities listed by Taagepera (1997: Appendix).

Empire	Rise	Peak	Decline
Sui/Tang	0.7	1.0	1.4
Sung	0.3	1.4	1.5
Kanyakubia	0.1	0.2	0.0
Tufan	1.7	0.7	4.3
Khmer	3.4	2.7	4.7
Liao	0.3	1.8	0.0
Jurchen	0.0	1.1	0.0
Frankish	3.2	0.3	1.4
Kievan Rus	1.2	0.5	1.0
Fatimids	0.6	0.1	1.0
Ayyubids/Mamluk	1.8	1.5	1.2
Caliphate	0.7	1.0	0.8
Samanid	0.8	0.6	0.4
Bujid	0.0	0.9	0.2
Ghaznavid	0.4	0.0	1.5
Seljuk	0.5	0.5	0.2
Khwarizm	0.8	0.1	0.2
Inca	0.2	0.4	0.0
Aztec	0.5	0.1	0.0
Lithuania/Poland	1.8	2.5	0.2
Golden Horde	0.0	0.7	1.7
Ottoman	0.9	3.4	0.1
Spain	1.4	0.5	0.0
Mongol/Yuan	0.5	0.5	0.9
Delhi	1.1	0.4	0.5
Ming	0.9	0.6	1.8
Mogul	0.7	0.9	0.8
Manchu	1.3	1.4	0.2
French	0.3	0.5	0.0
British	1.1	0.4	0.1
Portuguese	0.0	0.4	1.5

with 12 cases declining for one century or longer. Thus, Table 2.1 suggests that slow imperial declines are commonly found in the historical record.

My main argument in this chapter is that geopolitical variables (in the narrow sense) cannot explain the long-term (a century or longer) imperial decline phases. Such geopolitical variables as logistic loads and loss of marchland advantage begin operating essentially without a time lag. As soon as more territory is conquered, the state must shoulder the burden of defending it from external and internal (rebellion) threats. Similarly, as soon as the victorious state intrudes on a central location, any previous marchland advantage is diminished. It is true that the benefits of increased size can come with a substantial lag, because it takes time to organize production in newly conquered territory and to persuade the populace there to accept state authority. But this mechanism is part of the positive feedback loop; it is not what causes empires to decline. In an interesting extension of the usual geopolitical variables, Collins and co-authors proposed that the relationship between state legitimacy and war success may cause territorial overshoot, followed by collapse. However, our investigation of this idea suggested that this mechanism still leads to first-order dynamics (metastability), unless we impose an unrealistically (as I would argue) long lag on the response of legitimacy to war success. Furthermore, even if we stipulate such a long lag, only one of the models investigated by Hanneman et al. exhibited boom-bust cycles, and the collapse in this model was accomplished in essentially one time step. By contrast, historical data suggest that imperial decline often occurs on the time scale of decades or even centuries (Table 2.1). This empirical pattern is not explained by purely geopolitical theories.

The importance of time scales has not, of course, escaped previous theorists. Collins devotes several pages to discussing this issue (Collins 1995:1584–1586), Kennedy (1987) repeatedly stresses that the state's military strength and productive ability are correlated in the long term, and we certainly should not forget Braudel's (1972) *la longue durée*. However, the discussion of this issue typically does not get beyond verbal theories. It is precisely in these kinds of quantitative issues that nonlinear dynamics can be of great use, because formulating explicit models allows us to build in the empirically based characteristics of postulated mechanisms (including their rates of change) and predict the ensuing model dynamics (for example, the temporal durations of the rise and decline phases). Pushing through such an exercise can help us reject some rival hypotheses. Development of geopolitical models in this chapter is an example of this general idea.

If the time-scale argument advanced in this chapter is accepted, it does not mean that geopolitical mechanisms (in the narrow sense) are unimportant in the explanation of the imperial rise and demise. They are just insufficient, and we must look to other variables in order to build the required theory. One potential avenue that seems worth exploring is to abandon the view of polities as "black boxes" and look into their inner workings. This will be our goal in the next chapter.

2.4 SUMMARY

- There are three very general classes of dynamical behaviors. Zero-order dynamics, boundless growth or decline, arise in systems that are not affected by negative feedbacks. Examples include linear and exponential growth/decline processes. First-order dynamics characterize systems in which feedbacks act on a fast scale. First-order dynamics are equilibrial; examples include asymptotic and logistic growth processes. First-order dynamics may also be metastable (more than one stable equilibrium is present). Finally, second-order dynamics arise in systems in which dynamical feedbacks act with a lag. Examples of second-order behaviors include a single boom/bust dynamic and sustained periodic or chaotic oscillations.

- The geopolitical theory of Randall Collins postulates three main mechanisms explaining territorial dynamics of states: geopolitical resources, logistical loads, and the marchland position.

- The mathematical model incorporating only the positive feedback between territory and geopolitical resources exhibits zero-order dynamics. If the initial state territory is above a certain threshold, then it grows in an accelerating fashion. However, if the initial territory is below the threshold, then the state shrinks and eventually disappears.

- Adding to the model the negative feedback of the logistical loads leads to first-order dynamical behavior, metastability. Again, if the initial territory is below the threshold, the state loses ground and disappears. However, starting above the threshold, the territory does not increase without bound, as in the simpler model, but approaches an upper equilibrium. This equilibrium is stable with respect to small perturbations.

- In order to examine the positional effects I turn to a spatial simulation model developed by Artzrouni and Komlos. This model suggests that states initially enjoying marchland advantage (a higher proportion of boundary along a coastline) grow to larger sizes than inland states. However, the model does not exhibit any second-order oscillations: the loser states disappear, while the winners grow to the limits set by logistical factors, where their size is stabilized.

- Finally, I review the simulation model of conflict legitimacy dynamics developed by Hanneman and co-workers. I show that if we translate this model into differential equations, then we again obtain a first-order system that is incapable of second-order oscillations.

- An analysis of growth/decline data tabulated by Rein Taagepera suggests that long periods of imperial decline (more than a century) are frequently found in the historical record (12 cases out of 31). This finding strongly suggests that at least in some historical cases imperial dynamics were governed by second-order mechanisms. However, models based on purely geopolitical mechanisms do not predict such prolonged declines. Thus, we must investigate other mechanisms of imperial collapse.

Chapter Three

Collective Solidarity

3.1 GROUPS IN SOCIOLOGY

3.1.1 Groups as Analytical Units

In the previous chapter I suggested that we cannot understand the territorial dynamics of polities without studying their inner workings. This raises an important question: what are the elementary units in terms of which our theories should be constructed? The philosophical principle of methodological individualism maintains that ultimately sociological theories should be based on the properties of individuals. I agree with this approach in principle, especially if we stress the key word *ultimately*. However, methodological individualism, in my opinion, must be tempered with two important caveats. First, the idea that individuals are somehow more "real" than groups does not appear to be tenable. Human individuals cannot exist apart from a group and remain human (as real-life "Mowglis" attest). Furthermore, human groups are more than simple collections of individuals. Unlike animal groups, human groups are uniquely able to plan and purposefully carry out actions (Alexander and Borgia 1978; Melotti 1987).

Second, an attempt to follow the prescription of methodological individualism in one step does not appear to be a good modeling strategy (Section 1.2.3). Polities, especially such complex ones as empires, contain multitudes of individuals differing among themselves in a multitude of ways. Furthermore, an individual primarily interacts with a small subset of others, rather than directly with everybody else in the polity. In other words, large human societies consist of a number of groups, often hierarchically nested within each other. Thus, a much better modeling strategy would be to break the problem into two (or more) steps. First, we would like to understand how group dynamics arise from individual action, and then we can use group properties to model polity dynamics. "There is a distinctly sociological way of looking at the world. It holds that the key to understanding social life lies with the analysis of groups, rather than individuals." (Hechter 1987:2) An excellent example of such a hierarchical approach that introduces groups as intermediate actors between individuals and social dynamics is Jack Goldstone's (1994) analysis of revolutionary action. We also should keep in mind that eventually it will be necessary to progress to the next level and consider how polities interact within world-systems.

There are two characteristics that are particularly responsible for making human groups not just collections of individuals, but agents in their own right: the tendency to draw social boundaries and the capacity for group-oriented action even if it is individually costly.

Social Boundaries

Humans use many cues to demarcate group membership (Shaw and Wong 1989; Masters 1998). One of the most important recognition markers is language, especially dialect, accent, and speech patterns. For example, there is abundant experimental evidence from several societies that people are more disposed to cooperate with others who have the same dialect as themselves, even when dialectal differences are slight (Nettle 1999:57). Phenotypic similarity provides a number of potential markers: visible resemblance of facial and body form (and even odor); movement patterns, facial expression, and behavioral stereotypes; clothing and ornaments; and style and manners (the latter are especially important for signaling social class). Speech dialect and phenotype provide obvious, instantaneous information about group membership. Other categories of markers include kinship (presumed common descent; can be fictitious), religion (shared beliefs, norms, and rituals), and territory or proximity of residence (Masters 1998:456–457). The last category can also include shared membership in the same polity (nationalism or"regnalism"; see Reynolds 1997).

Capacity for Solidaristic Behaviors

A very powerful approach for inferring patterns of collective action from individual behaviors is the rational choice theory (Coleman 1990). The basic premise of this theory is that individuals are utility maximizers. The rational choice theory, however, has been unable to solve one very important problem in sociology: how societies can function without falling apart. An important theory (as formulated, for example, by Thomas Hobbes) maintains that society is based on the concept of social contract. However, it turns out that if people acted on a purely rational basis, they would never be able to get together to form society at all (Collins 1992:9). In fact, this "nonobvious sociological insight" (Collins 1992) approaches, in my view, the logical status of a theorem. For example, Kraus (1993) shows how the best developed theories of Hobbesian contractarianism all founder on the collective action problem, the free-rider predicament (Olson 1965; for a nontechnical review, see Collins 1992:13–19).

There appears to be only one solution to the puzzle of how societies can hold together (Collins 1992). Although people pursue their selfish interests most of the time, they also have feelings of solidarity with at least some other people. Such *precontractual solidarity*, in Durkheim's words, is the basis of societies (Collins 1992). States and armies break apart when people stop thinking of themselves as members of the group and think only of their own individual self-interest (Collins 1992:23).

Thus, the functioning of society can only be understood as a mixture of self-centered (rational) and group-centered ("extrarational") behaviors. In Collins' (1992:8) view, "the overall structure of society is best understood as a result of conflicting groups, some of which dominate the others. But conflict and domination themselves are possible only because groups are integrated at the micro level." This statement captures very nicely the essence of the approach that I develop here.

3.1.2 Evolution of Solidaristic Behaviors

The preceeding argument suggests that, in order to understand the functioning of societies and states, the rational choice theory must be supplemented by *norms* that promote group-maintenance behaviors. This observation, coupled with over-whelming empirical evidence for norms, leads to the question: where do norms come from? More precisely, we need a theory for how group-promoting norms could arise in the process of social evolution. Several mechanisms have been proposed, including reciprocity, punishment, kin selection, and group selection (Richerson and Boyd 1998).

Reciprocity as a mechanism for building trust and cooperation in long-continued interactions was proposed by Trivers (1971). Subsequently, Axelrod and Hamilton (1981) showed that a simple strategy, "tit for tat" (cooperate on the first round and then do as your partner did last time), provides a cooperative solution in the repeated prisoner's dilemma game. Thus, cooperation is possible between two rational individuals, provided that they interact over a long term. The problem is that the tit-for-tat strategy does not generalize to large groups, because it is very difficult to get reciprocity to increase when rare in a large group dominated by unconditional defection (Boyd and Richerson 1988).

Punishment has also been proposed as a mechanism to support norms. Axelrod (1997:44–71) used a series of computer simulations to investigate conditions under which norms can evolve and be stable. One possibility that he investigated is the employment of *metanorms*, or willingness to punish someone who did not enforce a norm. Axelrod found that a norm could become stabilized by a metanorm. However, this result was dependent on the population starting with a sufficiently high number of norm enforcers. If there were too few "avengers" to start with, then both the norm and the metanorm collapsed. A similar model was developed by Boyd and Richerson (1992), who showed that a division of labor can arise, with few, or even one, punisher preventing a large number of reluctant cooperators from defecting. However, there are some problems (Richerson and Boyd 1998). First, the number of group members that can be coerced by leaders is limited. Second, what is lacking in the punishment system is a mechanism to regulate individual behaviors in the group interest (if a leader is capable of coercing the whole group, then (s)he might be motivated to use the group in his/her interests). Finally, comparative evidence is not supportive of the idea that coercion can generate ultrasociality (Richerson and Boyd 1998:79).

Reciprocity and coercion are rational behaviors. But, as was noted above, norms promoting group-beneficial behaviors cannot arise as a result of a contract between self-interested individuals. Similarly, it is difficult to imagine how altruistic behaviors might arise if evolution acts only at the individual level (all formal models developed so far indicate that this is impossible). The only known theoretical mechanism for the evolution of altruism is multilevel selection (Sober and Wilson 1991), The noncontroversial example of multilevel evolutionary mechanism is kin selection, based on W. D. Hamilton's concept of inclusive fitness. A more controversial mechanism is group selection. Evolutionary biologists have gone through phases of first uncritically accepting group selection, and then re-pudiating the concept (Sober and Wilson 1991). Currently, there is a cautious but definite acceptance of group selection as a legitimate evolutionary mechanism, given certain conditions (which human groups satisfy; Sober and Wilson 1991). Unfortunately, many sociologists still think of group selection as a thoroughly discredited concept (e.g., Sanders 1999).

There seems no doubt that altruism can evolve in *small groups* by the mechanism of kin or group selection (Richerson and Boyd 1998). Furthermore, kin and group selection are not logically distinct categories (Sober and Wilson 1991) and can work synergistically (Jones 2000). Additionally, although altruistic norms cannot evolve purely by the mechanisms of reciprocity and punishment, these mechanisms can substantially enhance the likelihood of norms evolving in a group selection context, by reducing (although not completely eliminating) the free-rider problem. Another potential feature that could enhance evolution of altruism is leveling institutions, such as monogamy and food sharing among nonkin (Boehm 1997). Bowles (1999) lists yet other altruism-promoting characteristics of groups: segmentation, conformism, and parochialism.

While evolution of altruism in small groups is widely accepted by social biologists, and accounts satisfactorily for the small-scale cooperation in nonhuman primates, certain aspects of human ultrasociality remain puzzling (Richerson and Boyd 1998). There is some controversy about whether kin and genetic group selection, even when buttressed by reciprocity, punishment, and leveling institutions, could account for altruistic behaviors in large groups, where the recipient of altruism is not a relative, nor personally known to the altruistic donor. Sober and Wilson (1991) contend that, given the characteristics of human collectives, group selection is an entirely plausible mechanism. Boyd and Richerson think it is not enough, and propose their own theory, which invokes *cultural group selection* (original theory in Boyd and Richerson 1985; recent assessments in Richerson and Boyd 1998, 2001).

An important preadaptation for cultural group selection is what Boyd and Richerson call the conformist transmission of cultural traits, for example, "when in Rome, do as Romans do" (for a related concept of rational imitation, see Hedström 1998). Using this strategy can be advantageous, because the group is often "wiser" than an individual, having a longer collective memory and wider range of experience than any single individual could obtain alone. The side effect of conformity is that it reduces cultural variation within groups, while increasing variation between groups, a process that strengthens group-level selection compared to individual-level selection. Boyd and Richerson also developed a theory for the cultural evolution of symbolic and ideological markers of group membership (using models of "indirect bias"; see Boyd and Richerson 1985: Chapter 8) and for the evolution of moralistic punishment (Boyd and Richerson 1992).

Once symbolically marked adaptation for in-group cooperation stabilized by moralistic punishment evolved in small groups, such as bands of paleolithic hunter-gatherers, an important threshold in human evolution was crossed. Symbolic demarcation allows for large collectives to become designated as cooperating groups. "Success in intergroup competition came to depend on within-group cooperation; an evolutionary arms race arose. The scale of cooperation-to-compete might escalate until ecological, rather than evolutionary constraints bring a halt. Once the barriers imposed by kinship and reciprocity are breached by cultural group selection, it is not clear what the next natural evolutionary limit to scale of co-operation is" (Richerson and Boyd 1998:91–92). Thus, evolution of symbolically demarcated boundaries is an example of the "stairway effect" (Turchin 1977:102), in which an accumulation of small quantitative changes at some point allows a qualitatively large step to be made, rapidly followed by another, and so on. The critical theoretical problem is to understand the mechanism for widening the definition of the cooperating collective from a smaller-scale group to a larger-scale group. Repeated iteration of the mechanism leads to an ever-larger cooperative in-group, until some other force stops the process.

To summarize, evolutionary biologists are beginning to agree that the evolution of human sociality had to involve some kind of group selection. There are two versions of the argument, one emphasizing the biological ("genetic") aspect (Sober and Wilson 1991), and the other emphasizing the cultural aspect (Boyd and Richerson 1985) of group selection. In actuality, the two versions are not very far apart, the difference being mostly in the emphasis. Both arguments are buttressed by a battery of mathematical models and empirical evidence. For example, group selection has been shown to be a remarkably effective mechanism in experiments (Goodnight and Stevens 1997). Another example is the recent experimental demonstration of altruistic punishment in humans (Fehr and Gächter 2002). In their most recent review, Richerson and Boyd (2001) argue that the theory of cultural group selection passes a number of tests, such as those for logical coherence (checked with formal models), verification of the proximal (psychological) mechanisms assumed by the theory, tests for the existence of the necessary microevolutionary processes, and examinations of the large-scale comparative evidence, including patterns of adaptation and maladaptation.

3.1.3 Ethnic Groups and Ethnicity

One very important type of human collective is the ethnic group. All of the characteristics of human groups that we discussed above are expressed most vividly when applied to ethnic groups. Thus, the markers listed in Section 3.1.1—language, religion, phenotype, and territoriality—are all used in various combinations to draw ethnic boundaries. In fact, as was emphasized by Barth (1969), it is not the specific form of the demarcation markers that is important. The key aspect of ethnicity is "the ethnic boundary that defines the group rather than the cultural stuff that it encloses" (Barth 1969:15). According to Barth, ethnicity is a form of social organization and its main characteristic is self-ascription, as well as ascription by others. Different ethnic groups may use different kinds of markers, but the function is the same, to draw boundaries between "us" and "them." This insight has stood the test of time well (Vermeulen and Govers 1994).

Not only do ethnic groups tend to have the sharpest boundaries, they also tend to evoke the most intense feelings of solidarity. The ultimate form of collective solidarity, sacrifice for the common good, is relatively common in ethnic conflicts. By contrast, it is hard to imagine individuals sacrificing their lives for the sake of a professional organization or a corporation.

Ethnic groups appear to be quintessential human groups. The reason, most likely, is that ethnicity was the basis of social organization in humans during most of their evolutionary history. Hunter-gatherers living in bands were characterized by a very flat social hierarchy and very limited division of labor, and ethnicity (in the wide sense, see below) provided the main basis for group formation.

Ethnicity has been defined by Brass (1991:18) as a sense of ethnic identity that consists of the subjective, symbolic, emblematic use by a group of people of any aspect of culture, in order to create internal cohesion and differentiate themselves from other groups. Note that this definition of ethnicity (which I adopt in this book) does not specify the nature of the cultural markers that are used for ethnic boundary delineation. Thus, two religious sects that share all other cultural characteristics (dialect, phenotype, material culture, etc.) are considered as two separate ethnic groups if they use membership in a religious community as the way to distinguish "us" from "them." Thus, the Serbs, Croats, and Bosnians of the former Yugoslavia are clearly separate ethnic groups. Although they speak the same language, the religious markers (Orthodox, Catholic, and Muslim, respectively) play the dominant role in defining ethnic boundaries. The usage of "ethnic" and "religious" in this book thus differs from the lay meaning of the terms, which are often employed as alternative bases for classifying different groups. To avoid misunderstanding of what follows, this point is worth emphasizing: in my view the religious identity is just one of the many cultural markers used by groups to delineate ethnic boundaries, and it is a particularly important one for agrarian societies (especially for demarcating boundaries at the metaethnic level; see below).

3.1.4 The Social Scale

Even the simplest human societies known to anthropologists are characterized by a hierarchical structure with nested levels (Johnson and Earle 2000). Thus, family-level groups, such as Shoshone or !Kung, have two levels: the family or hearth group and the extended family camps or hamlets. The ethnicity of humans who lived (and still live) in agrarian societies can have many more layers. The simplest social organization reflecting this principle is the segmentary society, such as found in the Berbers of the central High Atlas of Morocco (Gellner 1969). Complex agrarian societies retain segmentary organization (although they can have additional sources of identities). For example, Sahlins (1989) identified the following circles of identity characterizing the inhabitants of early modern Cerdanya: village–quarters–Cerdanya–"Two Counties" (Roussillon and Cerdanya)–Catalonia–Spain. Thus, one important dimension along which ethnic groups can vary is the *social scale*. Most people think of themselves as having several ethnic identities, nested within each other. At the smallest scale, an individual is a member of a family and local community. Above that level identity may have regional, national, and finally "civilizational" (in the sense of Huntington 1996) components.

We need better terminology than "region," "nation," and "civilization," each of the terms carrying too much extraneous baggage with it. Unfortunately, the terminology has not yet settled down, at least in the English-language literature. Two imported terms are currently used: *ethnos* and *ethnie* (the latter will be discussed in a subsequent section). *Ethnos* is widely used in Russian ethnology (Gumilev 1971; Bromley 1987; Bromley and Kozlov 1989). The most common definition runs as follows: ethnos is a stable assemblage of people that historically developed within a certain territory; the members of the ethnos possess common, relatively stable linguistic, cultural, and psychological characteristics; furthermore, they are conscious of their unity as differentiated from other similar human assemblages (self-awareness), which is reflected in their ethnonym (Bromley 1987:14).

Of particular importance to our purposes here is the system-like nature of the ethnos concept. Thus, just as systems consist of subsystems, and themselves are part of a metasystem, ethnic groups of different scale, or hierarchical level, can be referred to as subethnos, ethnos, and metaethnos. Where we need more levels, we can always add categories like subsubethnos. In principle, we can designate any arbitrary level as "ethnos" and define other levels in terms of sub- and meta-prefixes. In practice, however, ethnos is typically used for that level of ethnic groups that roughly corresponds to modern nations. People belonging to different ethnoses tend to speak mutually unintelligible languages. Thus, Americans, French, Germans, Russians, and Egyptians are all different ethnoses. Examples of subethnoses are Mormons and Southerners ("Rebs") in the United States, and Bavarians, Saxons, and Schwabs in Germany. Different subethnoses within the same ethnos are often characterized by distinct speech dialects.

Metaethnic identity often arises as a result of past or present association within the same large state (or, rather, empire). Thus, Latin Christians of Medieval Europe were primarily inhabitants of successor states of the Carolingian empire (Bartlett 1993). Today, the inheritor of Latin Christendom is the European identity, based primarily on membership in the European Community (accordingly, Germans or French do not consider, for example, Belorussians as "fellow Europeans," even though Belarus is geographically a European country). Another important source of metaethnic identity is religion. Thus, an Egyptian is also an Arab, a Sunni Muslim, and, finally, a Muslim (so we need several metas to designate these identities). I hope that the advantage of viewing ethnicity as a systemic property is apparent from the preceding discussion: it prevents us from arguing about whether Arabs are an ethnos, a metaethnos, or something else.

Ethnos-based terminology also avoids arguments about whether there were nations before nationalism or not. Thus, an Athenian of the classic period was also an Ionian, and a Hellene. We know that ancient Greeks had a hierarchical sense of ethnicity, since they had two separate words to designate alloethnics: foreigners (*xenoi*) which was used for other Hellenes, and "barbarians" (*barbaroi*) which was used for non-Hellenes, even for members of other highly developed civilizations, such as the Persians. The Greeks also keenly felt such intermediate-level ethnic boundaries as the one between Dorians (to whom Spartans belonged) and Ionians (which included Athenians) (Smith 1986).

To sum up, ethnicity, in the broad sense that I use here, may range from solidarity felt toward a small circle of relatives, friends, and neighbors, at one end of the spectrum, to solidarity felt toward millions belonging to the same nation or even a supranational entity, at the other end of the spectrum. However, it must be stressed that the *strength* of collective solidarity usually varies with the scale of ethnic group. Thus, it is quite possible that solidarity may be very high at the subethnic level, and quite low at the next level up. A somewhat extreme but not unusual example is the situation in the France of the late sixteenth century, when Huguenots and Catholics engaged in an extremely brutal conflict. By this point in French history, Huguenot strongholds were primarily found in the south and southwest of France, while the Catholic League was strong in the north and east (Briggs 1998), so in this example regional and religious identities were tightly intertwined. This example also illustrates the dynamic nature of solidarity. Just a generation or two before, the French nobility was quite solidaristic in its struggle against the Habsburg hegemony, and many nobles fighting on opposite sides in the wars of religion were comrades in arms during the Spanish Wars (or their fathers were).

3.1.5 Ethnies

The second term, *ethnie*, was imported by Anthony Smith (1986) from the French. He defined ethnie as a named human population with myths of common ancestry, shared historical memories, one or more elements of shared culture, a link with a homeland, and a measure of solidarity, at least among the elites (Smith 2000:65). In my view, this definition is quite similar to Bromley's definition of ethnos, although the emphases, to be sure, differ (Bromley seems to put more stress on objective cultural characteristics). In any case, it is not important to resolve these definitional matters for the purposes of this book. Because of its current prevalence in the English literature, I will adopt Smith's term *ethnie*, but I will also employ the suffixes *sub* and *meta* for smaller- or larger-scale ethnic groups.

One aspect of Smith's theory that I find particularly useful is his analysis of interrelations between ethnicity and class (Smith 1986: Chapter 4). Smith distinguished two types of ethnies. The first is *lateral* or aristocratic ethnie, in which the sense of common ethnicity is largely confined to elites (nobles, clerics, and wealthier merchants). The second type is *vertical* or demotic ethnie, characterized by a much greater degree of "social penetration" of shared ethnic feeling. The important point is that lower strata of an ethnie can have a variable sense of solidarity with the elites. At one extreme are tightly vertically integrated ethnies like certain tribal confederations (e.g., Mongols under Chinggis Khan) and some city-states in ancient Sumer or classical Greece. At the other extreme are polities in which the elites are ethnically distinct from subjugated commoners (e.g, the Old Hittite Kingdom). Thus, the strength of collective solidarity can vary not only with the scale of the ethnic group (Section 3.1.4), but also with the socioeconomic stratum.

3.2 COLLECTIVE SOLIDARITY AND HISTORICAL DYNAMICS

As I stated at the beginning of this chapter, before we can understand polity dynamics we first need to analyze how various groups of people interact within a polity. There are two aspects of human behavior that make groups particularly effective agents in their own right: boundary demarcation and group-directed (altruistic or solidaristic) behaviors. As agents, groups can interact with other groups, and the interactions are often conflictual: "the best-organized group usually wins, and that means the group with the most internal solidarity" (Collins 1992:26; see also Richerson and Boyd 1998). Can we use this insight to help us understand why some states are more successful than others?

Respectable theories in historical sociology tend to avoid the subject of collective solidarity, and instead focus on coercion and economic relations, which of course are the bread and meat of the rational choice theory. One example of this bias is the (in other ways excellent) book by Tilly (1990), in which "coercion" and "capital" are actually the first words in the title. The impression that one gets from the professional literature is that war and economics are somehow "hard" subjects, while solidarity is "soft" and unscientific. The reason is probably due to the failure of earlier macrohistorians (Vico, Danilevsky, Spengler, Toynbee, Sorokin) to develop *scientific theories*, that is, theories that make nonobvious predictions that can be empirically tested. Quigley (1961:129) calls such historical explanations "softening of the fiber" theories. Tainter (1988:89–90) similarly dismisses them as "mystical explanations" that are "crippled by reliance on a biological growth analogy, by value judgments, and by explanation by reference to intangibles."

But what if "softening of the fiber" refers not to the moral degradation of individuals in declining empires, but rather to the loss of collective solidarity by these societies? In order to build a scientific theory of collective solidarity, we need to somehow *endogenize* this variable, that is, to postulate mechanisms that cause it to wax or wane in response to other dynamic properties of societies and polities. So far, no respectable sociological theory has managed to do this, in my judgment, although there are many hints scattered through the theoretical literature. For example, Hechter (1987) starts essentially with the same concept of collective solidarity that is being developed here. He makes this "groupness" itself a dynamic variable (Hechter 1987:8). However, he then makes a valiant attempt to develop a rational choice theory of group solidarity (Hechter 1987: Chapter 3), which is, however, doomed for reasons given in the previous section. Collins (1992: Chapter 1), in already cited passages, constructs a powerful argument in favor of collective solidarity as an important historical variable. In Chapter 2 he discusses one mechanism that can generate solidarity: Durkheim's theory of religion. However, Collins never connects solidarity with other historically important variables in a dynamical theory. Smith (1986:38) discusses how interstate warfare may ignite and maintain ethnic sentiment: "One has only to read Aeschylus' description of the Persian Wars in which his brother was killed and he himself fought, to grasp the communal significance for the ethnic identification of each individual, of collective resistance on the battlefield through the activation of comradeship, teamwork and *esprit de corps* in moments of crisis." Yet, again, warfare was almost continuous throughout history, but some polities grew and others declined even while under pressure from external aggression. We need something more to build a theory on. Tantalizing hints are also scattered throughout the historical literature. Here is, for example, McNeill (1963:809) discussing the rise of

Prussian industry in almost the same words as those of Smith: "a managerial elite with strong internal discipline and an *esprit de corps* quite different from the individualistic and nakedly pecuniary ethos common among British businessmen." I could go on. There are, however, two theories that have been developed to the point where they can actually yield testable predictions: Ibn Khaldun's theory of *asabiya*, and Gumilev's theory of *passionarity*.

3.2.1 Ibn Khaldun's Theory

The fourteenth-century Arab thinker Ibn Khaldun was probably the first sociologist in the modern sense (Gellner 1981). In his monumental work *The Muqaddimah: An Introduction to History* he advances a remarkable theory of political cycles. Ibn Khaldun developed his theory mainly to explain the history of the Maghreb (Northern Africa), but he also makes excursions to other areas known to him (e.g., Arabic Spain and the Middle East). Ibn Khaldun was not an ivory-tower academic. He was a practicing politician and almost lost his life in a failed coup. He also traveled extensively (even encountering and having a long conversation with Timur Lenk once). In short, Ibn Khaldun knew well the workings of the societies he studied from the inside.

Groups and Group Solidarity

Ibn Khaldun's main argument is remarkably modern (the following account partly relies on the introduction by the *Muqaddimah* translator Franz Rosenthal, indicated by lower-case Roman page numbers; upper-case Roman numbers indicate the volume). He begins by postulating that a human individual cannot live outside a group: it is absolutely necessary for man to have the cooperation of his fellow men (Ibn Khaldun 1958:I:90). Defense and protection are successful only for a closely knit group (Ibn Khaldun 1958:I:263). But a communal way of life is also necessary for acquiring different crafts and technical skills, and for intellectual intercourse. The next postulate is that different groups have different abilities for concerted action. Here Ibn Khaldun introduces the key concept of his theory: *asabiya*, which Rosenthal translates as "group feeling." Originally the word signified something like "making common cause with one's agnates" (Ibn Khaldun 1958:I:lxxviii). But in Ibn Khaldun's usage, asabiya is a wider concept, because it can also be shared by people not related to each other. Asabiya produces "the ability to defend oneself, to offer opposition, to protect oneself, and to press one's claims" (Ibn Khaldun 1958:I:289). Preponderance of asabiya renders one group superior to others (Ibn Khaldun 1958:I:lxxix).

Ibn Khaldun was clearly aware of the nested nature of ethnic groups, and that each level has its own asabiya associated with it. For example, he notes that, in order for the higher-level group not to fall apart, its asabiya must be stronger than the asabiyas of lower-level groups combined (Ibn Khaldun 1958:I:284). Additionally, he continuously stresses that the leading or ruling element within a group must be vested in a family or lineage that has the strongest and most natural claim to the control of the available asabiyas (Ibn Khaldun 1958:I:lxxx). Only the leader who controls an asabiya of sufficient strength may succeed in founding a dynasty.

Dynamics of Asabiya

Ibn Khaldun also develops a detailed theory explaining how asabiya is created, and also how it is lost. In general, asabiya arises from "the social intercourse, friendly association, long familiarity, and companionship" (Ibn Khaldun 1958:I:374). This is remarkably similar to the explanation of how social capital is acquired (Putnam 2000; for a comparison of asabiya and social capital, see Section 3.2.3). However, not all social conditions are equally conducive to the growth of asabiya. As I mentioned above, Ibn Khaldun's theory was developed for the specific situation of the Medieval Maghreb. Ibn Khaldun distinguishes two major ethnic groups inhabiting the Maghreb: the Berbers and the Arabs. These two groups differ not only ethnically, but also in the way their societies are organized: respectively, "desert" and "civilization." The distinction that Ibn Khaldun makes, however, is not between nomadism and sedentary life; he rather groups together nomads and sedentary backwoods people, and contrasts them with sedentary urban people as inhabitants of large population centers (Ibn Khaldun 1958:I:lxxvii). The sociological distinction is not qualitative, but quantitative, and refers to the size and density of human settlements, as well as the scale of polities. "Desert" is characterized by small-scale polities (chiefdoms, in the modern terminology). "Civilization" is organized in states and empires (except during the periods of state breakdown).

In Ibn Khaldun's view, the society type is the key to understanding why asabiya increases or declines. "Desert" life with its constant struggle for survival and, consequently, necessity of cooperation creates conditions for asabiya growth. "Civilized" society controls a large number of human beings. A large amount of human labor becomes available, and a certain proportion of it may be channeled into production of "conveniences" and luxuries (that is, not necessities). This development toward luxury carries a penalty in the form of causing degeneration. The ruling dynasty, and therefore the state (Ibn Khaldun does not make a distinction), is the principal victim of this tendency to luxury (Ibn Khaldun 1958:I:lxxxi–lxxxii). Ibn Khaldun (1958:II:119–122) essentially argues that access to luxuries causes increased intraelite competition and eventually intraelite conflict. As a result, asabiya rapidly declines. Ibn Khaldun even provides a quantitative assessment of the rate of decline: it takes four generations from the establishment to the disappearance of a dynasty, although it may continue into the fifth and sixth generations in a state of decline (I:281).

In addition to the decline of asabiya, there is another major factor that causes the disintegration of the state: economics. According to Ibn Khaldun, general prosperity leads to population growth, which in turn leads to scarcity, increased oppression by the elites, and eventually state collapse. This aspect of Ibn Khaldun's theory is further pursued in Chapter 7, in the context of the demographic-structural theory.

In summary, here are the main points of Ibn Khaldun's argument about the dynamic relation between asabiya and polity strength. Asabiya grows and is maintained at a high level in small-scale societies, where the capacity for collective action is the key to survival. Additionally, such societies produce only necessities, and therefore there is no corrosive effect of luxuries on asabiya. Ibn Khaldun's primary example of such "desert" societies are the Berbers of Maghreb, although he also cites other instances, e.g., several Arab tribes who invaded northwestern Africa in the eleventh century (I:283). Desert tribes with high asabiya conquer civilized people with low asabiya, and establish a ruling dynasty (a state) over them. Under conditions of civilized life, however, asabiya inevitably declines. In approximately four generations, asabiya becomes so low that the state collapses as a result of factional conflict. This is the point at which the civilized area becomes vulnerable to another conquest by desert tribes.

Assessment

There is much in Ibn Khaldun's theory that appears to be very useful to our objectives. First, the theory is very clearly formulated. Thus, it makes clearcut empirical predictions that can be tested. Additionally, if quantitative predictions are needed, then the theory can, rather easily, be translated into a mathematical model. Second, Ibn Khaldun describes explicit sociological mechanisms on which his theory of state collapse is based. This provides another way in which the theory can be tested.

There are also some weak points. In general, while Ibn Khaldun offered a brilliant account of one kind of society—an Islamic society of the arid zone—his account is not universally applicable even within Islam (Gellner 1981:88-89). It would be interesting to see if his theory can be extended to agrarian societies in general. More specifically, one could question Ibn Khaldun's emphasis on the importance of "luxury" in asabiya decline. Ibn Khaldun's is not the only theory that invokes this mechanism; many "softening-of-the-fiber" theories propose similar explanations. This is a question that should be resolved empirically, but to do that we need some explicit alternatives to test against. I try to construct an alternative explanation in Chapter 4.

3.2.2 Gumilev's Theory

Although the ethnogenetic theory of Gumilev (1971) is largely unknown in the West, it has generated a considerable controversy in Russia, at least among the lay public interested in macrohistorical questions. The reception among professional historians and ethnologists was cooler, for reasons that will become apparent shortly. Despite its serious scientific flaws, however, Gumilev's theory contains several interesting concepts, which can be of use to the historical dynamics project, and thus I briefly review it here.

The main kernel of Gumilev's theory is the explicit connection that he makes between ethnie and polity dynamics. According to Gumilev, each polity has its *core ethnie*, and it is the properties of core ethnies that drive the success or failure of their polities. The key concept of Gumilev's theory is *passionarity*. Individuals with high passionarity (*passionaries*) purse, with great energy, some goal that is usually extrarational. That is, passionaries are typically motivated not by personal gain, but by some higher goal (the goal may be selected either consciously or not). Although in his definition Gumilev does not directly address the collective solidarity aspect of passionarity, the language he uses in his examples is very evocative of asabiya. In particular, Gumilev repeatedly mentions the ability of passionaries to sacrifice themselves for the sake of the collective good. (This exposes one of the problems with Gumilev's theory: it is not developed very precisely. Instead, Gumilev relies on voluminous examples and evocative prose to get his point across.)

Different ethnies have variable proportions of passionaries. Additionally, the degree of passionarity of an ethnie changes with time. An ethnie with great numbers of passionaries will expand at the expense of other ethnies, in the process building an empire. Thus, high passionarity directly translates into a polity's capacity for territorial expansion, and vice versa.

The second key concept for Gumilev is *ethnogenesis*. He defines it as the process by which some or many members of an ethnie become passionaries. Unfortunately, the specifics of the mechanism that he offers rely on phenomena that are either currently unknown to science or flatly contradicted by it. According to Gumilev, the Earth is periodically struck by bundles of cosmic energy, which cause the mutation of passionarity. Gumilev identified a number (about ten) of such events that occurred during the known history of Eurasia. Each event gives impulse to multiple occurrences of ethnogenesis in bandlike regions several hundreds of kilometers long.

After the initial impulse, the passionarity of the affected group increases over the period of several centuries, reaches a peak, and then declines. Meanwhile, the group expands, first becoming a subethnie, then a full ethnie (in the process perhaps absorbing other ethnically related groups), and finally creating a metaethnic empire (unless it prematurely loses to an even stronger neighbor). Eventually, as passionarity continues to fade, the polity built around the core ethnie loses its cohesiveness and falls prey to a combination of internal warfare and external aggression. Using multiple examples, ranging across the whole history of Eurasia, Gumilev provides a detailed phenomenology of the rise and fall of ethnies and empires.

Assessment

Because I focused on what I perceive as major weaknesses in Gumilev's theory, my account did not really do justice to it. Gumilev has amassed an enormous amount of historical and ethnological material. Even when one disagrees with the mechanisms that he advances, it is difficult to escape the feeling that he has indeed identified some regularities in the historical process. I believe that there are several insights of Gumilev's that are of great interest. First, it is a fruitful hypothesis that there is a close connection between the fortunes of a polity and its core ethnie. This is a particularly important point, because Gumilev shows with much factual material that the modern relationship between nationalism and state has very close analogs in history. That is, ethnicity and polity are variables that may be dynamically connected.

Second, Gumilev's concept of ethnogenesis has a lot of merit. Most if not all currently existing ethnies started small and then expanded by a variety of mechanisms, including demographic growth and ethnic assimilation. Successful territorial expansion was very much a factor in this ethnic expansion. Something allowed these initially small ethnic groups to acquire a high capacity for collective action. Thus, another potentially fruitful hypothesis is that there is a close relation between the process of ethnogenesis and enhanced collective solidarity.

In contrast, Gumilev's concept of passionarity does not appear to be a fruitful concept to me; at least it does not add anything useful to Ibn Khaldun's asabiya. Furthermore, the temporal trajectory of passionarity increase followed by decrease, postulated by Gumilev, is too mechanical. Gumilev treats passionarity as an *exogenous* variable: it waxes and wanes according to its own internal nature, so to speak, and is not related in any obvious way to other variables in the system. Before this concept can be of use, it must be endogenized somehow. Interestingly, the few mathematical attempts to model Gumilev's theory that I know of specify passionarity as an exogenously driven variable.

3.2.3 The Modern Context

Durkheim's Mechanical and Organic Solidarity

The concept of asabiya (collective solidarity) that I discuss in this chapter does not "hang in the air." Instead, it appears to be related to several much more modern theories in sociology, social psychology, and political science. Within sociology the best-known theory of social cohesion has been developed by Durkheim (1915, 1933). Gellner (1981:86–98) provides a highly useful comparison of Ibn Khaldun's and Durkheim's theories, which I briefly summarize here. As is well known, Durkheim contrasted two kinds of solidarities: *mechanical* which was based on similarity between individuals and *organic* which was based on complementarity or mutual interdependence. Simple segmentary societies, such as the Bedouins of Ibn Khaldun, can possess only mechanical solidarity, while more complex urban societies characterized by greater division of labor have the potential to exhibit organic solidarity. In Durkheim's view, mechanical solidarity was an inferior form of social cohesion, compared to organic solidarity.

In Ibn Khaldun's theory the only kind of social cohesion is the one arising from what Durkheim would call mechanical solidarity. "Organic solidarity" for Ibn Khaldun was not solidarity at all, but a form of social dissolution. Civilized life with its complex division of labor was inherently inimical to social cohesion and given time would degrade the initially high asabiya of tribesmen moving to town (Gellner 1981:87).

In general, it is not clear whether such economic variables as the degree of division of labor have any relevance to the waxing or waning of asabiya. By contrast, *cultural uniformity* appears to be an important precondition of social cohesion. Ruling elites of such successful nation-states as France certainly thought so, and as a result employed rather draconian methods for imposing linguistic uniformity on their citizens (Weber 1976). In any case, the Durkheimian concept of organic solidarity appears to be primarily applicable to industrial societies. If so, then the distinction between organic and mechanical solidarity is largely irrelevant in our analysis of preindustrial agrarian polities. On the other hand, Durkheim's insight that religion is one of the most powerful forces that keep groups together appears to be highly relevant to the issues under investigation (see also Collins 1992).

Individualism and Collectivism

At first glance, it would appear that the direction within social psychology most relevant to social cohesion would be research on the individualism/collectivism dichotomy (Triandis 1995). A closer look, however, reveals that the two approaches apparently address different social scales. Actually, social psychologists studying individualism and collectivism do not explicitly discuss the scale of the group at which collectivistic behaviors are aimed. From the context of their studies, however, it becomes apparent that they typically focus on small-scale groups: families and local communities. However, although there is no explicit consideration of scale in the analysis, results obtained for small-scale groups are sometimes generalized to larger-scale societies. Furthermore, the primary variable of interest to psychologists is not the properties of groups made up from individualistic versus collectivistic individuals, but the inverse relation: the effect of the group on individuals. This is, of course, understandable since psychologists are primarily interested in individual behaviors, rather than the capacity of groups for collective action. Nevertheless, it decreases the relevance of their findings for issues of interest to us. Still, there is much of value in this area of psychology, not least of which is the empirical research on variation in individualism/collectivism in different cultures.

Social Capital

Of much greater relevance is the theory of social capital, which recently has garnered a lot of attention, thanks in part to several books and articles by Robert Putnam and associates (see, for example, Putnam 2000; for a closely related concept of *social trust* see Fukuyama 1995) Such aspects of social capital as mutual support, cooperation, social trust, institutional effectiveness, and, particularly, the implications of social capital for collective action suggest to me that social capital and collective solidarity are closely related concepts. "Social capital here refers to features of social organization, such as trust, norms, and networks, that can improve the efficiency of society by facilitating coordinated action" (Putnam et al. 1993:167). This is very close to my definition of asabiya as the capacity of a group for collective action. Thus, asabiya appears to be essentially the agrarian societies' equivalent of social capital (at least as the latter is defined by Putnam and co-workers). Several other features of social capital deserve a comment.

- There are two forms of social capital: bridging (or inclusive) and bonding (or exclusive) (Putnam 2000:22). Examples of bonding social capital include ethnic fraternal organizations and exclusive country clubs, while the civil rights movement and ecumenical religious organizations are examples of bridging social capital. This distinction appears to address the issue of social scale: bonding social capital characterizes smaller-scale groups, while the bridging kind characterizes larger-scale societies.

- Putnam cautions that social capital may have its "dark side." While it is generally good for those inside the network, the external effects of social capital are by no means always positive (Putnam 2000:21). One example is power elites exploiting social capital to achieve ends that are antisocial from a wider perspective. This is very similar to the already discussed idea of internally solidaristic groups coercing other, less cohesive groups.

- Societies belonging to different countries, and even regions within countries, vary in the amount of social capital. For example, Putnam et al. (1993) show that both the density of interpersonal ties and institutional effectiveness vary greatly between north and south Italy. Similarly, Fukuyama (1995) advances the argument that different industrial countries vary in the degree of social trust, and that this variation explains much about the economic effectiveness of their corporations.

Contrasting Social Capital and Collectivism

To illustrate why I think of social capital as a much more useful concept for our purpose than collectivism, it is instructive to contrast how the two concepts are applied when comparing two specific countries, the United States and Italy (with an emphasis on the Italian south—the *Mezzogiorno*). Triandis (1995:92–93, 97–98) classifies the Mezzogiorno society as collectivist and American as individualist. From the point of view of social capital, however, the picture is completely reversed: southern Italians have very little of it, while Americans have lots (Putnam et al. 1993; Putnam 2000). The sociological study of the Mezzogiorno goes back at least to Banfield (1967). Banfield described the extreme atomization of the southern Italian society, in which all cooperative efforts are limited to the smallest possible societal unit, the family. Relations to such kin as cousins, and sometimes even grown-up siblings, are rife with distrust and lack of cooperation. Community-level cooperative efforts are virtually impossible. Banfield called this type of society "amoral familism," and drew an explicit contrast with the vibrant civic culture of a small Midwestern American town.

In a later study that contrasted the Italian north and south, Putnam and co-workers (1993) described how lack of interpersonal association, trust, and cooperation in the Mezzogiorno leads to ineffective and corrupt local government. In contrast, the north has a much greater level of civic engagement, and correspondingly more effective government on the local level. A recent study (A'Hearn 2000) provides yet another confirmation of the original Banfield insight. I should also mention the work of Gambetta (1988, 1993:77), who cogently argued that the Sicilian mafia can be understood as a response to the lack of trust specifically affecting southern Italy, and that the endemic distrust is the crucial difference that explains why the mafia did not emerge elsewhere in the Mediterranean world.

The richness of American civic life was extensively commented on by de Tocqueville (1984). Putnam (2000) provides great factual material documenting the waxings and wanings of social capital in the United States. He also shows that American "rugged individualism" is a myth.

It is interesting that Triandis, in his discussion of the individualism and collectivism of Italians and Americans, cites the same two authors, Banfield and de Tocqueville, but comes to the opposite conclusions. This puzzle is resolved when we pay attention to the social scale. Triandis focuses on very small groups, essentially, family. Indeed, southern Italians are characterized by "tight" families, while American families are "loose." Putnam's focus of interest (and ours) is on larger-scale societies: regional and national. Thus, I am not trying to say that the work of Triandis and other social psychologists is wrong in any way. It is simply that their focus on very small-scale groupings makes their results less relevant to our concerns.

A Terminological Note

Collective solidarity, social cohesion, social capital, and asabiya are clearly closely related concepts. This raises the question of which term we should use in this research program. The problem with "social capital" is that it sounds jarring when applied to preindustrial or even prestate societies. Further, "capital" has the wrong associations. Capital should be something divisible, but social capital is a public good. In general, capital is too much an economic term, while collective solidarity is a very sociological concept. Finally, "social capital" is used in the sociological literature in at least two very different senses (Lin 2001: Table 1): one focused on the individual (Lin 1982; Burt 1992), the other focused on the group (Bourdieu 1980; Putnam et al. 1993). These are two very different notions. Contrast, for example, the "group-focused" definition of Putnam, given above, with the "individual-focused" one due to Lin (2001): social capital is "investment in social relations by individuals through which they gain access to embedded resources to enhance expected returns of instrumental or expressive actions." In light of the discussion in Section 3.1.2, these two kinds of social capital may actually act antagonistically: group-level capacity for action may occur at the expense of some individual interests, while individuals manipulating social networks for their advantage can harm group-level performance.

Collective solidarity and social cohesion also have some undesirable aspects. There is too much emphasis on interpersonal connection, rather than group-level emergent property. Thus, I decided to settle on asabiya as the term for the central concept in the theory that is developed: the group's capacity for collective action. Note the explicit reference to the group here: it does not make sense to speak of asabiya in general, or of the asabiya of a person (by contrast, one can speak of the solidarity that an individual may feel toward a group). The main kind of collective action we are interested in is coercive power: the ability of a group to defend itself and its resources (such as territory), as well as to extend its sway over other groups and their resources.

The usage of the term *asabiya* has several advantages. The most important reason is that it has very little theoretical baggage, because (unfortunately) few people are familiar with Ibn Khaldun's writings. Second, I would like to explicitly acknowledge the contribution of Ibn Khaldun's thinking to the theory of historical dynamics by using his terminology (and if we ever get to the point where we can actually quantify asabiya, I suggest that we do it in *khalduns*). Ibn Khaldun, of course, knew only a small subset of agrarian societies, and since we want to generalize asabiya to all agrarian polities, we had to stretch his concept considerably. As Gellner (1981), Lapidus (1990), and Barfield (1990) pointed out, Ibn Khaldun theorized how asabiya increased or decreased in small- and medium-scale societies. The specific historical cases that he discussed were the origins of regional states, rather than large territorial empires. In the historical dynamics research program, we want to generalize the notion of asabiya to apply to all kinds of agrarian polities.

Incidentally, there is a very interesting empirical pattern of medieval and modern Middle Eastern history: the deserts of North Africa and Arabia, and the mountainous zones throughout the whole region, which were inhabited by Bedouin nomads and sedentary tribes of the Berbers, Kurds, and Pashtuns, were divided into small regional states. By contrast, the Iranian and Anatolian plateau zones were generally under the control of great empires, which were inhabited by tribes organized into large confederations of Turco-Mongolian descent (Barfield 1990:157). This observation raises two questions: how did Turco-Mongolian polities manage to generate and maintain asabiya at such a large scale? And why do Arabian and Turco-Mongolian asabiyas exhibit this systematic difference throughout the period of many centuries? An attempt at answering these questions is made in Chapter 4.

Implications for the Research Program

Since my main focus is on preindustrial societies, I will restrict the term asabiya (the capacity of a group for collective action) to agrarian and extractive societies. If social capital is a closely related concept to asabiya, as I would argue, although one developed for industrial societies, then we can greatly benefit from theoretical and empirical research on this topic. The first important aspect of social capital is that political scientists have developed methods for measuring it. Measures can be made on both the individual and group levels. At the individual level, Putnam and co-workers quantify the density of networks within which people are embedded, the quality of interactions (cooperation, reciprocity), and mutual trust. At the level of societies, Putnam and co-workers have addressed institutional effectiveness, such as in the Italian example referred to above. Other theorists have connected the level of social trust to economic performance (Fukuyama 1995). If social capital is measurable, then by implication its equivalent for preindustrial societies, asabiya, may be measurable too.

As I argued throughout this chapter, one of the most important determinants of asabiya is the capacity of individuals to behave solidaristically, that is, to sacrifice individual advantage for the sake of the common good (however, this is not the only dimension of asabiya; for example, the capacity to self-organize, as in choosing and then obeying leaders, can also affect the capacity for collective action). The historical record provides several kinds of quantitative data that can be used to measure the degree of solidarism among individuals of a certain group, such as the willingness to provide recruits for the army and to pay taxes. The last variable, the tax rate to which the populace acquiesces, can be quantified for many different societies and historical periods. Several caveats should be kept in mind, mainly *who* is paying and for the benefit of *what group*. Thus, the tax rates imposed on the peasants may reflect more the degree of coercion that the elites can bring to bear on them, rather than any feelings of ethnic solidarity (although I would argue that we should not assume that lower strata will a priori lack any degree of ethnic solidarity with the elites). Similarly, alloethnic elites may be reluctant to contribute to an empire that recently conquered them. Tax rate as a measure of asabiya is probably least problematic when applied to the core ethnie's elites.

Furthermore, even groups of very high asabiya should not be expected to consist of pure unconditional altruists. In fact, the more commonly found altruistic strategy is to perform individually costly group-beneficial behaviors only if others are doing the same. An example of such behavior is the quasivoluntary compliance of citizens in paying taxes (Levi 1988:52). It is *voluntary* because taxpayers choose to pay rather than free-ride (and, therefore, it is not a rational, or self-interested behavior). It is *quasi*voluntary because taxpayers contribute only if they have reasonable assurances that free-riders will be punished. Nobody cares to be a dupe.

An interesting approach to measuring collective solidarity is suggested by Douglass North. Sociologists distinguish four general sources of power, based on the use and manipulation of norms and symbols (ideological), administrative structures (political), material incentives (economic), and coercion (military) (Mann 1986; Turner 1995). Collective solidarity clearly belongs to the first class. In fact, North explicitly defines ideology in solidaristic terms: "Ideology consists of the set of individual beliefs and values that modify behavior." Then he adds: "It can be measured by the premium people are willing to incur not to free ride" (North 1985:394).

3.3 SUMMARY

- Human groups constitute an intermediate level of organization between individuals and polities. Instead of attempting to connect polity dynamics directly to individual action, I build the theory in two steps: first inferring group dynamics from interactions between individuals, and then inferring polity dynamics from interactions between groups.
- Not all collections of individuals are true groups. Groups arise because their members draw imaginary boundaries separating in-group from out-group individuals ("us" versus "them"). Humans use a variety of recognition markers to distinguish between group members and outsiders, such as language, religion, and phenotype.

- Group members are capable of solidaristic behaviors that impose costs on the individual performing the behavior, but yield group-level benefits. (I distinguish *solidaristic* from *altruistic* behaviors: whereas the latter benefit other individuals, the former benefit the group as a whole.) Solidaristic and altruistic behaviors are not rational (they are "extrarational"), and are based not on calculated self-interest, but on norms. Thus, human motivation is only partly self-interested (although this might be a very large part, and in some individuals the only part).
- Theory suggests that solidaristic behaviors can evolve by a variety of multilevel selection mechanisms: kin selection and group selection acting on genetic and/or cultural traits. Group selection, especially its cultural variant espoused by Boyd and Richerson, has strong theoretical and empirical support, and provides the main mechanism for evolution of solidarism in large human groups.
- Several characteristics of human behavior and sociality promote the evolution of solidaristic behaviors. Leveling institutions (monogamy, food sharing) reduce within-group phenotypic variability, and consequently the strength of individual-level selection. Certain psychological mechanisms guard against free-riding (cheater detection circuits and norms to punish free-riders). Conformism is the mechanism that ensures that group members share norms and react similarly to the same behavioral stimulus (and also reduces within-group phenotypic variability).
- As a result of boundary demarcation, solidarism, and uniformity-causing behaviors, groups of individuals can act as independent agents in their own right.
- Different groups vary in their capacity for collective action. This capacity is a result of a complex mix of individual behaviors: the proportion of solidarists in the group and the strength of their solidarism, the denseness and nature of social networks within which individuals are embedded, the ability to detect and punish free-riders (including higher-level norms that detect and punish those who do not punish cheaters), and the self-organization capacity (for example, selecting and obeying a leader). The group capacity for concerted collective action is called collective solidarity or *asabiya*, using the terminology of Ibn Khaldun.
- Groups characterized by higher asabiya tend to survive, expand, and replicate themselves at the expense of groups with lower asabiya.
- One of the most important kinds of human collective is the ethnic group. The importance of ethnically based groups is, first, that they tend to invoke the highest level of group loyalty. Second, during most of human evolution groups were based on shared ethnicity.
- Individuals are embedded in a system of hierarchically nested ethnic groups—family, community, subethnie, ethnie, and metaethnie. Each group level has its own degree of asabiya. Thus, it is possible to have a high degree of collective solidarity at, for example, the subethnic level, but low solidarity at the ethnic level. The variation in collective solidarity with ethnic group level can potentially be quantified with "asabiya profiles."

I should stress here that, while Ibn Khaldun was concerned with asabiya of small- or medium-sized groups, I reformulate and broaden his concept to apply to groups of any scale, up to and including such huge metaethnies as Latin Christendom or Dar al-Islam.

- Groups in agrarian societies are formed on the basis of two main characteristics: ethnicity and socioeconomic stratum (most importantly, peasants and elites). I propose the hypothesis that the fortunes of a polity are primarily affected by the capacity of its elites for collective action. However, ethnic solidarity (or lack of it) between elites and peasants may also be very important in polity success or failure.

Chapter Four

The Metaethnic Frontier Theory

4.1 FRONTIERS AS INCUBATORS OF GROUP SOLIDARITY

Chapter 3 argued that the capacity for collective action, or *asabiya*, to use Ibn Khaldun inspired terminology, is an important variable that affects the ability of polities to defend and expand territory. Large territorial polities—empires—typically have a complex internal structure, and therefore polity-level solidarity is composed in a complex way from the asabiyas of various groups comprising it. As stated above, I focus on two main dimensions along which polities are structured. The first is the socioeconomic stratification, where we can distinguish elites who hold power from commoners concerned with producing goods. The second is the ethnic dimension, where we can distinguish core ethnies from the rest (alloethnies). For example, the core ethnies of the European Great Powers of the eighteenth century are Castilians in Spain, English in the British Empire, northern French (speakers of *langue d'oïl*) in France, Austrian Germans in the Habsburg Empire, Prussians in the Kingdom of Prussia, and Russians (*veliko-rossy*) in the Russian Empire. This scheme, of course, greatly oversimplifies the historical agrarian societies, but we must start somewhere.

Another simplifying assumption that I will make is that each empire has at its core a particular group, whose asabiya is of overriding importance to the empire's success or failure. One type of such an imperial core group is simply the elites of the core ethnie, who use their high asabiya to coerce compliance from both their own commoners and alloethnic elites (who, in turn, coerce alloethnic commoners). The second type is a more vertically integrated (or demotic, using Anthony Smith's classification) core ethnie, in which commoners of the core ethnie share a substantial degree of ethnic solidarity with their elites. The third type, alternatively, is characterized by lateral empire-wide integration of the elites (the aristocratic ethnie of Smith), who rule over ethnically heterogeneous commoners. Thus, I do not mean to imply that a core group must have hard boundaries. Rather, cores have fuzzy boundaries and internal structure, e.g., segmentary organization. Furthermore, although as the first step in theory building I tie polity success at territorial expansion to the asabiya of the core group, asabiyas of other groups, and their attitudes (cooperative, acquiescent, or antagonistic), will eventually also have to be included in the analysis.

Incidentally, it is possible for a polity to have two distinct cores, as in the sixteenth century Habsburg Empire of Charles V (Castilians and Austrian Germans), but such situations appear to be rather unstable. Thus, Charles V's empire, upon his resignation, was divided between the Austrian and Castilian branches of Habsburgs.

There is some amount of controversy about the relationship between nationality and the state, with some arguing that it is states that invent nationality, while others arguing that, on the contrary, it is nations that construct states around themselves. The approach I take in this book is that ethnie and polity exist in a state of dynamic interaction. The core ethnie provides the seed around which the polity crystallizes. But polity also affects ethnic dynamics. For example, being in the same polity sets up conditions for ethnic assimilation of alloethnic elites and commoners (this will be pursued in Chapter 6). Thus, the relationship between ethnie and polity is like that between a chicken and an egg; neither is primary, and both are components of an *ethnopolitical system*. Still, because both polities and ethnies have beginnings (and endings), we must confront the question of how ethnopolitical systems get started. The theory developed here provides an answer: an ethnic group characterized by high asabiya (1) expands the territory it controls, (2) increases the number of its members through population growth, colonization, and ethnic assimilation, and (3) advances up the social scale from subethnie to ethnie to, eventually, metaethnie. This proposition, however, raises another question: how do ethnic groups acquire high asabiya, and why do they eventually lose it? The development of a high level of asabiya that is capable of scaling up (from subethnie to ethnie, etc.) is a necessary condition for *ethnogenesis*, because otherwise small-level ethnic groups would never be able to evolve into a full-blown ethnie. Perhaps we should call this process "ethnopolitogenesis," because usually polity formation appears to be inextricably intertwined with ethnie formation.

4.1.1 Factors Causing Solidarity Increase

So far I have treated asabiya as an exogenous variable: it is something that is hypothesized to affect the territorial dynamics, but it is not yet clear what factors cause collective solidarity to increase or decline. Thus, the main objective in this chapter is to *endogenize* asabiya.

One possible approach to solving this problem is to think about specific social mechanisms that are used by groups to maintain high levels of collective solidarity. One of the most important of such mechanisms is clearly religion. Thus, Collins (1992) devotes a whole chapter to discussing Durkheim's theory of social rituals. But all societies have rituals and some form of religion, yet some societies are more cohesive than others. That is, identifying any specific cultural mechanism of creating and maintaining asabiya does not help us with the main question. Is it possible to abstract away from the cultural forms asabiya takes and focus somehow on its essence?

If we follow this tack, then we have only one general source of insights: the theory of multilevel selection. Let us see how far this approach could take us. The key prediction of the theory, as discussed in the previous chapter, is that group-level selection operates on *intergroup* variation, while individual-level selection operates on *intragroup* variation among individuals. The evolution of solidaristic (group-beneficial but individually costly) behaviors is enhanced by conditions that increase intergroup variation and decrease intragroup variation. What conditions are these? I can think of three.

Intergroup Conflict

The first factor that may affect the evolution of collective solidarity is the frequency and intensity of intergroup conflict. Two extremes may be imagined: one is location near the center of a territorially extensive empire during the periods when the empire is strong enough to maintain internal peace. The opposite end of the spectrum is the stateless environment—"the tribal war zone" (Ferguson and Whitehead 1992), in which each tribe is simultaneously a potential aggressor and a potential victim. Current anthropological evidence suggests that stateless societies were typically characterized by incessant warfare (Keely 1997).

The Ratio of Population to Resources

The second factor is the population density in relation to the carrying capacity of the local region. High population density pressing against the subsistence limit should cause persistent resource shortages, which promote intragroup competition and thus have a corrosive effect on group solidarity. Here we should distinguish the situations of mild and severe resource shortages. A mild resource shortage, or even an anticipated future shortage, may act to promote solidaristic action to solve the problem. Groups may employ some technology for food production intensification, or they may organize to deprive neighboring groups of their resources. However, as formal models of preindustrial population dynamics that combine Malthusian and Boserupian mechanisms indicate, economic change can win only a temporary respite from marginal immiseration (Wood 1998). When severe and persistent resource shortages develop, the ability of a group for collective action should be greatly diminished. It is particularly difficult to organize a successful military action: starving people do not make good fighters. As a result, intergroup competition should be reduced, while intragroup competition is enhanced, since it becomes much easier to think of another group member as a potential victim. Only highly solidaristic groups can resist the corrosive effect of severe and prolonged resource shortage without splintering.

By contrast, population density substantially below the carrying capacity means that there is a surplus of food in a typical year. Occasional subsistence crises are short in duration and can be buffered by communal action, such as surplus storing and food sharing. Thus, resource competition is reduced or entirely absent. As a result, intragroup variation in fitness is low, which promotes the evolution of group-directed behaviors. Note that when I speak of "carrying capacity," I mean the population density ceiling imposed by the ability to produce resources, mainly food. The actual population density equilibrium may be set at a fraction of the carrying capacity by factors other than food production, most notably by increased mortality due to conflict. Small-scale polities, in which all members are potentially exposed to the dangers of external warfare (intergroup conflict), should be particularly likely to have an equilibrium density much below carrying capacity. This idea is supported by formal models (Turchin and Korotayev 2003). Thus, the two factors, conflict intensity and population density, are related.

Ethnic Boundaries

The other feature that intergroup conflict and population density have in common is that they create conditions favoring asabiya increase in *small-scale* groups. Larger-scale groups can be created temporarily as a result of successful conquest by one particularly solidaristic tribe. But what mechanisms would maintain the cohesiveness of the larger group as one generation is succeeded by another? Apparently none. In the environment of a multitude of small groups, a large group should not be able to keep its cohesiveness for many generations, because this group will not be threatened by external forces (being the largest around). Internally divisive issues will eventually destroy the asabiya of the large group, unless it is "disciplined" by an external threat. Furthermore, in the tribal war zone it is common for the subgroups comprising the large group to be ethnically as similar to each other as they are to small groups outside the large group. The large group is likely to have a blurred symbolic boundary that separates it from other groups, with all the negative consequences for maintaining high levels of asabiya.

    Thus, it is hard to imagine how large groups can arise and maintain themselves in a homogeneous environment populated by many small groups, with an ethnic distance separating each pair of groups of roughly the same order of magnitude. But what if there is a major ethnic boundary? I will call it a *metaethnic fault line*, to emphasize the scale of ethnic distance separating groups on different sides of the boundary. A small group near such a boundary will be confronted with very different *others*, dwarfing in their "otherness" neighboring groups that are on the same side of the metaethnic line. Warfare across the metaethnic line is likely to be much more violent, with a higher level of atrocities and lethality (e.g., Dower 1986). This should lead to enhanced alliance formation among groups on the same side of the boundary. Alternatively, if small groups on the same side of the metaethnic frontier are unified by force, they are more likely to continue sticking together. Furthermore, any group demarcation symbols developed in opposition to the *others* across the boundary are likely to prove integrating with respect to ethnically similar groups on the same side of the boundary. In short, location near a metaethnic fault line creates conditions for the "stairway effect" in which symbols developed for marking boundaries of a small group are applied to successively larger-scale groups. Thus, my third proposed factor that enhances evolution of asabiya (for large-scale groups) is location near a major ethnic boundary.

4.1.2 Imperial Boundaries and Metaethnic Fault Lines

The three factors that I propose do not operate independently of each other. In fact, there is one set of conditions where they all work synergistically: frontier zones of large empires, and particularly empires with vigorous ideologies. During

the agrarian period of human evolution, the most internally integrative and exter-
nally divisive ideologies were, of course, the major religions of the exclusionary
kind (Stark 1996). Exclusionary religions are those that disallow simultaneous
membership in other religions or cults. Exclusionary religions often provide the
symbolic markers for metaethnic fault lines, and therefore imperial boundaries
and metaethnic fault lines often coincide (but not always, since religion can spread
beyond the imperial boundary).

I should emphasize that a combined imperial/metaethnic boundary typically
creates a frontier *zone*, that is, a two-dimensional area characterized not only by
its length along the boundary, but also by its width (and, in any case, boundaries
of preindustrial polities were much less like one-dimensional lines than they are
today). There are two kinds of frontier: between an empire and a stateless (but not
"chiefdomless") tribal zone, and between two empires. According to the argument
I advanced above, the tribal side of the frontier should provide ideal conditions
for (1) increase of asabiya intensity, and (2) increase in the asabiya scale (that is,
the social scale of the group that is integrated by asabiya). Because the tribal zone
is stateless, there is constant warfare among the ethnic groups inhabiting it, and
thus population density should be kept below the subsistence carrying capacity.

Frontiers on the imperial side are subject to much the same pressures. One potential difference is that vigorous empires prevent internecine fighting. However,
there is usually plenty of pressure and/or opportunities coming from the other
side of the boundary, so imperial frontiers should provide excellent conditions
for asabiya increase. If a very different imperial ideology (religion) is present on
the other side of the boundary (this is the case of the frontier between two empires), then such a situation provides a particularly strong incentive for asabiya
increase. Finally, in mature empires, in which central regions have lost much of
their collective solidarity (because of lack of conflict and high population density
there), frontier regions may acquire their own identity, separate from both the
parent empire and the enemy on the other side of the border. This process may
cause a new highly solidaristic group to arise, which will eventually establish its
own empire.

Additional Factors That May Affect Asabiya

Although I stress intergroup conflict, low population density, and metaethnic
boundaries as the main factors that generate increased asabiya, one can think
of additional variables that may or may not be important. First, group selection
theory suggests that it is much easier for collective solidarity to increase in small
compared to large groups. However, the various mechanisms characterizing human sociality, which we discussed in Chapter 3, should reduce the effect of group
size on asabiya dynamics. Furthermore, the size of the group with which individuals interact is correlated with the location along the imperial center–frontier
zone dimension, because densely populated cities with large groups of interacting
people are typically located away from the imperial periphery. Thus, on one hand,
it is not clear whether group size is a factor that can be isolated from the bundle of factors distinguishing imperial centers from frontiers. On the other hand,

there is some difficulty in defining just what the cooperating group might be in a city: Is it the whole city? A neighborhood? A guild? Since this issue raises more questions than it offers answers, I leave its resolution for the future.

The second factor, also suggested by the group selection theory, is the presence of leveling institutions, which has been proposed as promoting the evolution of collective solidarity. Central regions of mature empires usually acquire high levels of social inequality, implying high intragroup variance in fitness, which should be conducive to asabiya declines. Frontiers may or may not develop a high degree of egalitarianism, and perhaps one can capitalize on such variation for predictive purposes. Again, I leave this idea for future development.

The third factor is the differential in wealth and "civilization" across the frontier. An empire presents both a threat and an opportunity to the frontier tribes. Vigorous expansionist empires exert an enormous amount of pressure on the tribal society, generating a strong incentive for small-level groups to integrate into larger ones. But weaker stationary empires also play an integrative role, because they present an irresistible target for raiding, and large groups usually have a better chance of acquiring substantial loot. Additionally, empires are a source of technologies, ideologies, and trading goods, especially prestige goods that are impossible to obtain elsewhere. All this taken together suggests that a metaethnic fault line becomes a much stronger asabiya generator if it coincides with an imperial border.

A related mechanism is that metaethnic frontiers are places where very different cultures come in contact. Peoples, products, ideas, religious and other concepts and practices, human genetic material, microbes, and so on mingle on frontiers (Hall 2001). These cultural (and biological) elements may mutate and recombine in the contact zone, greatly increasing the overall amount of cultural variation on which group selection operates, and, therefore, increasing the rate of cultural evolution.

Specific cultural mechanisms enhancing asabiya, as well as maintaining it at a high level, clearly play an important role in historical dynamics. One example is the spread of a new religion, such as Christianity or Islam. Another example is the spread of nationalistic ideology in Europe in the nineteenth century (which played an important role in German and Italian unification). However, at this point it is not clear to me how we might endogenize such factors in a fruitful manner. Thus, reluctantly, I must model them as variables exogenous to the currently built theory (see also Section 4.1.3).

The Effect of Physical Geography

The physical environment, in particular, mountains and rivers, should clearly have a strong (and quantifiable) effect on the dynamics of collective solidarity. Mountainous terrain makes travel difficult, isolates small groups from each other, and inhibits the establishment of the dense interaction networks that are necessary for the maintenance of large-scale asabiya. Furthermore, a small polity occupying a highly defensible mountain valley has a good chance of avoiding conquest. As a result, a mountainous area, even with an intense metaethnic frontier, provides a poor environment for asabiya growth and scaling up. There is little incentive for small ethnic groups to unite for mutual protection, because each thinks it can do as well or even better in its own mountain fastness. It is difficult for an incipient empire to unite the area by conquest. Finally, even when conquered, it is difficult to fuse the numerous small ethnic groups into a single ethnie.

In contrast to mountains, rivers enhance the flow of people, goods, and cultural elements. A riverine environment, therefore, is an excellent place for an ethnic group to grow up in scale. Additionally, rivers often serve as trade routes. Access to prestige goods, with which rulers reward their followers, may provide an additional stimulus for state building.

The effect of seas on asabiya dynamics is less straightforward. On the one hand, seas can connect separate localities. Many sea coasts act very much like rivers (with one bank). Certain straits, such as the Dardanelles–Sea of Marmara–Bosporus system, can be thought of as simply saltwater rivers. On the other hand, seas can also divide. What is particularly nettlesome is that the same sea may play both roles during different historical periods. For example, the Mediterranean played an integrative role for the Roman Empire, but became a moat between Christendom and Islam during the Habsburg-Ottoman conflict era.

Conclusion: The Metaethnic Frontier Theory

Stimulated by insights from multilevel selection theory, I argue that areas where imperial and metaethnic frontiers coincide act as asabiya incubators. Frontier conditions impose an intense selective pressure under which weaker groups with low asabiya fragment and are incorporated into stronger groups. Groups with high asabiya expand and eventually become full-blown ethnies, unless they encounter and succumb to an even stronger group. It is important to emphasize that the mechanism of cultural group selection (Boyd and Richerson 1985) does not assume physical extinction of the individuals comprising the losing groups. Furthermore, the mechanism does not even require group extinction, because successful strategies can spread rapidly by imitation (Boyd and Richerson 2002).

I should also stress that no claim is made here that the metaethnic frontier mechanism is the only way of explaining how new ethnies and empires arise. The theory advanced here, however, should be particularly relevant to the "imperial" period of agrarian polities (roughly, –3000 to 1800 c.e.). Thus, the theory takes the existence of empires for granted—the question of the origins of the state is well beyond the scope of the historical dynamics program. (However, metaethnic fault lines can arise even in a stateless environment as a result of, for example, an invasion of alien tribal peoples. Thus, there are interesting implications from the theory for the origin of pristine states, although I cannot pursue them here.)

If the metaethnic frontier theory has validity, then it explains the cycle of empires as follows. We begin with a situation where at least one empire (the "old empire") is already present. Its frontier zones, especially where they coincide with metaethnic fault lines, create regions of intense cultural evolution leading to groups with increased asabiya. In the process of interpolity competition, one particular group with a combination of high asabiya, structures allowing it to scale asabiya up, and luck eventually emerges as the winner. This group can be either an offshoot of the old imperial ethnie, or a new ethnic group arising from the tribal side of the frontier. In either case, the group has a distinct identity, demarcated by a strong ethnic boundary, and a high degree of internal cohesion—in other words, this is a new subethnie (or small ethnie), and the preceding history can be thought of as its ethnogenesis. (Thus, ethnogenesis is not a single point in time, but a historical process that can take many generations and even centuries.)

As the new subethnie grows (both numerically and in the territory it controls), it assimilates other ethnically similar groups nearby, by either voluntary or (initially) coercive mechanisms. The ethnic boundary is expanded to encompass these groups, melding them into a single ethnie (although subethnic divisions may persist, it is important that the asabiya is high at the level of the whole ethnie). The positive feedback dynamic sets in, so that increased size enhances the ability of the ethnie to consolidate an area around it into a territorial polity. The new polity grows by conquest, first by consolidating ethnically similar groups, then at the expense of the rest of the old empire and the tribal zone. Eventually a new empire is created and expands to the limits set by geopolitical constraints. In the process, the ethnic group transforms itself into the imperial core group.

The new empire is initially governed by highly solidaristic elites and is successful in maintaining internal peace (all warfare is transferred to the frontiers). As a result, population density in the center increases to the limit set by the subsistence technology. Asabiya in the empire's center begins to decline, as a result of its inhabitants not being exposed to external threats, and as a result of increased internal competition. This process probably takes a long time (many generations, and perhaps even centuries). Meanwhile, a similarly slow process causes another round of ethnogenesis to occur in the frontier zone. Eventually a new ethnie (or, more likely, several ethnies) is born, bringing an end to the old empire, and the cycle starts again.

4.1.3 Scaling-up Structures

An important element of the theory is the ability of ethnic groups to scale up without splintering into subgroups. While the common general mechanism, as I postulated, is location near a metaethnic fault line, specific cultural structures that enable asabiya to scale up vary. Here I discuss three examples of such structures.

Religion

One of the most powerful mechanisms for the scaling up of asabiya is a religion that is (1) proselytizing and (2) exclusionary. The first property allows an expanding ethnic group, professing the religion, to increase its size by adding converts. The second property, exclusivity (Stark 1996), maintains a sharp boundary between the in-group and out-group: "who is not with us is against us."

The archetypal examples of proselytizing exclusionary religions are Christianity and Islam. Both religions, especially during their early periods, placed a big emphasis on the community of the faithful as opposed to the unbelievers. For

example, within the Islamic community, or *umma*, Muslims were expected to behave to each other altruistically (thus, one of the emphases was on charity). The
Muslim world (Dar al-Islam) was in opposition to the non-Muslims (Dar al-Harb,
literally "the House of War"), and Muslims were certainly not expected to behave
altruistically toward the nonbelievers: whereas enslaving Muslims was forbidden,
no such injunction existed against enslaving the infidels.

If we interpret the characteristics of such religions as Islam and Christianity in
terms of group selection theory, we see that they correspond very well to features
that promote selection at the group level:

- Sharp boundary between in-group and out-group
- Leveling institutions (charity; monogamy in Christianity)
- Strong norms and metanorms (enforcement of norms)
- Altruistic in-group behavior

Stark (1996) provides a sociological analysis of early Christianity, with an emphasis on its features that explain its spectacular rise.

Primogeniture

An example of a political structure that increases group cohesion is the institution of rulership, in which one group member becomes a symbolic focus for the
whole group. An example of a small-scale group of this kind is a warband with
its military leader. Many large empires started in this way; for example, the Ostrogoths (Burns 1984). However, the success of such groups is typically limited
in time and space, and they must evolve certain structures that will allow them
to overcome their scaling-up limitations. Extension of the temporal duration is
achieved by the cultural mechanism of *dynasty*. Some dynasties exerted an extremely powerful influence over very long periods of time, such as Chinggisids
and Sharifs (descendants of Muhammad). But the greatest danger to empires established by tribal conquest typically was the division of the acquired territory
among the multiple heirs. One cultural mechanism that prevented the splintering
of the realm was the rule of primogeniture.

It is interesting that history knows several cultural innovations that attempted
to prevent empire splintering, although they did not work as well as primogeniture. For example, during the Kievan period, Russian princes evolved an elaborate
mechanism by which the overall ruler (the Grand Prince) was succeeded by his
younger brother, who would move up to the main capital of Kiev, thereby freeing
a subordinate capital, which would be occupied by the next member of the hierarchy, and so on. This system, however, did not work very well, and quickly led to
a collapse into a feudal situation of multiple principalities, each governed by its
own dynasty. However, the process did not stop there. The practice of assigning
each heir his allotment lead to the progressive splintering of Russian principalities. Only when one of them, Moscow, adopted the rule of primogeniture, could
the trend toward disintegration be reversed.

Society-Wide Mechanisms of Male Socialization

In a cross-cultural study of warfare, Otterbein (1985) demonstrated that societies engaged in internal warfare (conflict among small-level groups) were dominated by small-scale "fraternal interest" groups composed of related males. Societies that emphasized socialization of males into military institutions that crosscut units of male relatedness, by contrast, were able to suppress internal warfare. Such societies were much more successful in external warfare (conflict among larger-scale groups). Examples of such cultural innovations include age sets and police societies among prestate people (Otterbein 1985), militia drilling in Greek city-states and seventeenth-century Europe (McNeill 1982:131), and obligatory nationwide military service in modern national states.

4.1.4 Placing the Metaethnic Frontier Theory in Context

The argument of the previous section has several intersecting points with theories previously advanced in sociology and history. I will not attempt a complete literature review here; my plan rather is to provide the context for the metaethnic frontier theory, and to highlight some of the similarities to, as well as dissimilarities from, the thinking of previous authors.

Ibn Khaldun's Theory

The basic premises from which I advanced the frontier model of ethnogenesis are very different from those of Ibn Khaldun, and it is not surprising that the mechanism I propose differs substantially from his. However, there are also some points of similarity. In fact, I believe that Ibn Khaldun's theory is largely a subset of the frontier model. (Here I focus on Ibn Khaldun's theory for the origin of dynasties; his theory dealing with the state collapse will be dealt with in Chapter 7.)

In Ibn Khaldun's theory for political cycles in the Maghreb, there are two ethnic groups, civilized Arabs living along the Mediterranean littoral, and desert Berbers living inland. Thus, there is an ethnic boundary dividing these two ethnies. The ethnic distance separating Arabs and Berbers, however, is not very large. Although Arabs lived in wealthy civilized states, these states were generally too weak to exert much pressure on Berber tribal communities. Additionally, both ethnic groups professed Islam, which is therefore a factor that unifies rather than divides them. Although several Berber dynasties were established by religiously motivated groups belonging to a different sect from the settled areas, such a sectarian difference is not as large as, say, the Muslim/Christian fault line. In short, the ethnic distance between Arabs and Berbers is moderate, and therefore we should expect that it would exert a moderate pressure for asabiya to scale up. And, indeed, the historical record shows that desert-originating dynasties in North Africa built only region-sized polities.

The contrast between the regional Maghrebin polities and large territorial empires build by Turco-Mongolian ethnies, to which I referred in Section 3.2.1, appears to be very interesting in light of the theory just advanced. Turco-Mongolian tribes, of course, originated from one of the most prominent and long-standing metaethnic fault lines in Eurasia, the Chinese–Inner Asian frontier. The ethnic gulf between the nomads of Central Asia and Chinese agriculturalists was very deep, since they did not share either religion or language (or economic way of life, obviously). Asian nomads faced (most of the time) a huge and powerful territorial empire, China. Thus, in order to successfully resist its pressure and have any chance of obtaining prestige goods from it by raiding or extortion, Turco-Mongolian nomads had no choice but to evolvè structures for large-scale asabiya. In this fashion, steppe polities were a reflection of agrarian polities on the other side of the frontier, as was brilliantly argued by Barfield (1989). But then we might ask, why did agrarian polities on the North African frontier reach only regional size, while on the Inner Asian frontier they typically expanded to imperial size? The theory advanced in this chapter suggests that the evolutionary pressure for scaling up affected not just the nomads, but both sides of the frontier. On the Inner Asia frontier, the scaling-up dynamic operated until checked by geopolitical constraints, resulting in huge empires on both sides of the frontier. In the Maghreb, by contrast, as soon as polities reached medium size, the ethnies across the frontier were no more alien than other ethnies on the same side. Thus, a more shallow ethnic divide should, and did, produce smaller-scale asabiyas and polities.

External Conflict–Internal Cohesion Theory

Social theorists have long known that conflict between groups tends to increase internal cohesion (Simmel 1955; Coser 1956). Conflict sets boundaries between groups and strengthens group consciousness (Coser 1956:34). Simmel and Coser also make the important observation that severe conflict can either break a group or increase its internal cohesion. The most important factor affecting the outcome seems to be the initial degree of group consensus. If a group is lacking in basic consensus, an external threat may lead to apathy, and the group disintegrates (Coser 1956:93). A group that enjoys some degree of initial cohesiveness, on the other hand, is likely to emerge from the conflict greatly strengthened. This observation is consistent with how I envision ethnogenesis in the frontier zone. Certainly not every ethnic group will immediately enjoy an increase in asabiya upon finding itself next to the frontier. Most groups will perish in the pressure cooker of a metaethnic frontier (note that, when a group disappears, it does not necessarily mean that all or even most of its members are physically destroyed). Other groups will survive but will be unable to scale up without disintegrating. Very few groups, by chance or conscious design, will be able to hit on the combination of norms and structures that will enable them to survive *and* expand.

Frontiers in History

There is an enormous literature on frontiers. Some directions, such as the "frontier thesis" of Turner (1921) and related literature, are not particularly useful to our purposes. Highly relevant is the observation made by McNeill (1963:60) about "a long line of lords marcher who created empires by successfully exploiting a strategic position on the frontier between civilization and barbarism." One example that McNeil cited was the Akkadian Empire. McNeill (1963:249) also pointed out that almost all the states that unified China in a single empire originated on the margins of the Chinese world (one exception was the Ming). The importance of the frontier between the agrarian China and steppe-dwelling nomads was stressed by Lattimore (1967), and more recently in an excellent study by Barfield (1989). Service (1975) made a similar observation about the frontier origin of Egyptian unifiers. Other examples of well-studied frontiers in history are: the Roman (Dyson 1985; Whittaker 1994; Williams 1997), medieval Europe (TeBrake 1985; Bartlett and Mackay 1989; Bartlett 1993; Abulafia and Berend 2002), and Europe's steppe frontier (McNeill 1964), as well as the Russian part of it (Wieszynnski 1976). Several general frontier studies are by Savage and Thompson (1979), Donnan and Wilson (1999), and Power and Standen (1999). I have already mentioned the civilizational fault lines of Huntington (1996).

From this highly incomplete list it is clear that there is a consensus that frontiers played an extremely important role in history. However, the reasons that made frontiers important are not completely clear. There seem to be two general explanations offered in the historical and sociological literature. The first one, the advantages of marchland position, was already discussed in Chapter 2. Note that this theory is in a sense the diametrical opposite of the theory that I advance. Whereas Collins argues that marchland position protects states from predation by neighbors, I postulate that frontier location, on the contrary, puts a lot of pressure on ethnic groups, so that only the most capable survive. Thus, in my theory, frontier location is destructive in the short run but constructive in the long run. Since the two theories offer different predictions, we have here the possibility for an empirical test (which is pursued in Chapter 5).

The second common explanation is based on diffusion of technology. For example, "the Akkadians were in a favorable position to unite barbarian prowess with civilized technique to form a powerful military force" (McNeill 1963:60). I have already commented on a related aspect, that metaethnic frontiers are characterized by a great amount of cultural variation, which, according to the theory of multilevel selection, should speed up cultural evolution. As to the purely technological aspect, I am somewhat dubious about its explanatory power regarding success at territorial expansion, at least in the long run. However, the final arbiter of this issue is data, and it should be possible to design an empirical test for distinguishing between these two hypotheses.

Semiperipheries in the World-Systems Theory

The world-systems theory was formulated by Wallerstein (1974, 1980, 1989), and later developed in various directions by other authors (for an overview, see the recent volume edited by Denemark et al. 2000), so that at this point in time it is more of a research program, rather than a single theory. One basic premise shared by researchers working within the world-systems paradigm is that the dynamics of any single polity or society are not endogenous, but are a consequence of complex interactions among local, regional, and global processes (Chase-Dunn and Hall 1997). An extremely important kind of spatial interaction is between core and periphery regions within the world-system (in fact, world-systems can be conceptualized as core-periphery structures; Hall 2001). Core/periphery differentiation exists when two societies systemically interact and one has higher population density and/or greater complexity than the other (Chase-Dunn and Hall 2000:91). Chase-Dunn and Hall further conceptualize the *semiperiphery* as those regions that are spatially located between core and peripheral regions, or between two competing core regions. Alternatively, semiperipheries may mix core and periphery forms of organization, or be intermediate in form between those forms found in the adjacent core and peripheral areas.

Chase-Dunn and Hall argue that "semiperiphery is fertile ground for social, organizational, and technical innovation and is advantageous location for the establishment of new centers of power. In particular, secondary state formation on the marches of empires has frequently been recognized as a semiperipheral phenomenon that is related to the rise and fall of empires" (2000:96).

There are some striking parallels between the Chase-Dunn and Hall theory and the one advanced in this chapter. However, I argue that the theory of semiperipheral marcher states has not yet been formalized to the point where it could be submitted to a rigorous empirical test. The first problem is that a region can be designated as semiperipheral either because of its spatial location, or because it has institutional forms intermediate between core and periphery. In other words, the definition is too broad, and too many polities could be classified as semiperipheral. The second and related problem is that the theory of Chase-Dunn and Hall does not resolve the issue of why some semiperipheral challengers succeed and others do not (Chase-Dunn and Hall 1997:98). By contrast, the metaethnic frontier theory makes much sharper predictions, and thus has a higher falsifiability potential. It essentially says that only those semiperipheries where imperial frontiers coincide with metaethnic fault lines should be the sources of aggressive challenger states. Furthermore, the more intense the ethnic differential and the longer the frontier occupies a region, the more likely it is that a challenger would emerge and be successful at building a large territorial empire. The empirical issue thus becomes whether the metaethnic frontier theory captures all cases of empires starting as semiperipheral marcher states, or whether there are semiperipheral states that gain their ability for territorial expansion by some other mechanism.

Ethnogenesis

While theoretical ethnology languished in the West after World War II, in the Soviet Union, by contrast, ethnology was a respected and productive direction of research. I have already discussed the original (although, in my opinion, deeply flawed) theory of ethnogenesis advanced by Gumilev (1971). But there was a great variety of other ethnological research in Russia, both theoretical and empirical. For a review of one influential school of research on ethnosocial processes, see Bromley (1987; Bromley and Kozlov 1989). Several studies examined the processes involved specifically in ethnogenesis (Alekseeva 1973; Alekseev 1986). Russian ethnology continues to evince a heightened interest in the problems of social and historical ethnology (Arutyunov 1989; Lurie 1998).

In recent years, researchers in western Europe and North America have also become interested in the problems of ethnogenesis. A particularly fruitful research program is taking shape in the study of the ethnogeneses of various Germanic peoples at the time of the later Roman Empire (Wolfram and Pohl 1990; Heather 1996; Hummer 1998). However, origins of other ethnies are examined with an increasing frequency (Roosens 1989; Emberling 1995; Hudson 1999; Moore 2001). Not all social scientists, however, are sanguine about the term "ethnogenesis," because of its connotation of "origin" (see the discussion by Ausenda in Hummer 1998:21).

The connection between frontiers and ethnogenesis has not escaped the attention of various authors. A very interesting study of the relationship between frontiers and ethnic identity is that of Armstrong (1982). A series of papers in the *Journal of World History* presented several case studies of frontier ethnogenesis (Chapell 1993a,b; Miller 1993; Mulroy 1994).

A very interesting perspective that merges the ideas of frontier ethnogenesis and core-periphery interaction is offered by Hall (2000, 2001). Hall defines a frontier as a region or zone where two or more distinct cultures, societies, ethnic groups, or modes of production come into contact. Contact often leads to conflict, and attempts by some groups to incorporate others across the frontier. Attempted incorporation and resistance against it exert tremendous pressure on both the incorporated people and the incorporating system. "These interactions also reshape the ethnic landscape. Frontiers are zones where ethnogenesis, ethnocide, culturicide, and genocide are common" (Hall 2000:241). Hall illustrates these processes with the example of Navajo (Diné) ethnogenesis. Navajo groups prior to the arrival of Europeans shared language, customs, and a vague sense of being the same people. However, Diné-wide institutions such as the Navajo Tribal Council developed as a result of frontier conditions. A consolidated Navajo ethnie began to form over the centuries of interaction between the Navajo and the Spaniards, and finally took shape under the American occupation (Hall 2001:260).

4.2 MATHEMATICAL THEORY

The theory that I advanced in the previous section is formulated verbally. It seems plausible that the waxings and wanings of asabiya could underlie imperial cycles, but we are dealing with dynamical systems, and intuition based on verbal reasoning can mislead. For example, it is possible that when we translate the verbal assumptions into a mathematical model, we do not get the expected boombust cycles, but some other dynamics. Thus, we need to make sure that our verbal reasoning did not mislead us.

Frontiers are inherently spatial quantities, and the mathematical theory that we will build must eventually include space in an explicit way. However, explicitly spatial models are more difficult to analyze and typically require numerical solutions or computer simulations. It is often useful to attempt to capture the main interactions postulated by theory with a simplified *pseudospatial* model that is much more transparent to analysis. This is the strategy that I pursue. First, I develop a very simple pseudospatial model and determine what it tells us about the dynamic relationship between empires and frontiers (Section 4.2.1). Second, I construct a spatially explicit simulation to make sure that the insights from the simpler model hold in a more complex setting (Section 4.2.2).

4.2.1 A Simple Analytical Model

In Section 2.2.2 I analyzed a simple geopolitical model (2.12) of territorial dynamics in one-dimensional space. Setting $\gamma = 1$ (since we are not interested in the effects of position) and employing the approximation $\exp[x] = 1 + x$, suggested in Section 2.2.2, we have the following equation for the territorial dynamics:

$$\dot{A} = cA(1 - A/h) - a \qquad (4.1)$$

The parameter c translates the state's resources into its geopolitical power, h is the spatial scale of power projection, and a is the geopolitical pressure from the hinterland (assumed to be a constant).

Model (2.12) assumes that a polity's power is proportional to the amount of its resources (cA). The "resources" primarily refer to the state's *human* resources, since it is the population that pays taxes and produces recruits who are necessary for territorial defense and expansion. As I argued in the previous chapter, however, the success of a state is a result of collective action. No matter how many subjects an empire has, if they cannot, or will not, work together, the imperial power is zero. Thus, the coefficient c is actually a function of collective solidarity.

Let S stand for the average polity-wide level of collective solidarity. I scale S to be between 0 and 1, with 0 corresponding to a completely atomized society that is incapable of collective action, and 1 corresponding to the maximum solidarity possible for humans. Next, I assume the simplest possible function relating the power multiplier to asabiya: $c(S) = c_0 S$. In other words, I have assumed that geopolitical power is proportional to the product of asabiya and the state's resources. Substituting this relationship in the equation, we have

$$\dot{A} = c_0 A S(1 - A/h) - a \qquad (4.2)$$

I now need to derive an equation for the temporal evolution of S. The first step is to choose a law of growth for it. We still lack a well-developed theory that would connect micro-level individual actions to macro-level dynamics of asabiya, so the next-best approach is to select among the simple models of growth such as the four discussed in Sections 2.1.1 and 2.1.2. The two boundless growth models (linear and exponential) are not good for our purposes, because it is unlikely that asabiya can grow without bound, and I have limited it from above by 1, anyway. Thus, the real choices are either the asymptotic or the logistic growth. The asymptotic growth implies that when S is at low level (near zero), it will grow linearly. This is also not a good assumption. As discussed in Section 3.2.3, most people are conditional altruists (if they are altruists at all). When they are in a minority, conditional altruists are likely to follow selfish strategies, because they do not wish to be taken advantage of by free-riders. It is only when there is a sufficient number of other (conditional or unconditional) altruists around that they will be likely to behave altruistically. This (admittedly crude) argument suggests that the initial growth of asabiya should be autocatalytic. In other words, if we wish to select one of the four simple models of growth, then it is the logistic that matches best the hypothesized dynamics of asabiya growth:

$$\dot{S} = r(A)S(1-S) \tag{4.3}$$

Note that I have already made the relative growth rate r a function of A. Figuring out the form of this function is our next task.

In the verbal theory advanced earlier in this chapter, I argued that asabiya is expected to grow in locations near the imperial boundary and decline in the empire's center. Let us assume, for simplicity, that the relative rate of growth of asabiya is a linear function of distance from the border (Figure 4.1). We see that the space is divided into three areas: the "hinterland" outside the empire, the "frontier" where asabiya tends to increase, and the "center" where asabiya tends to decrease. The parameter r_0 is the maximum relative growth rate, which takes place right at the border ($x = A$), and b is the width of the frontier region [where $r(x) > 0$].

The average polity-wide asabiya is

$$r(A) = \frac{1}{A} \int_0^A r(x)\, dx = r_0 \left(1 - \frac{A}{2b}\right) \tag{4.4}$$

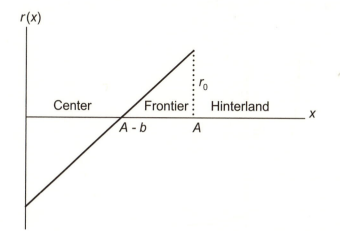

Figure 4.1 The relative growth rate of asabiya, $r(x)$, in relation to the imperial boundary. Symbols: A is the polity size, b is the width of the frontier zone (thus, the "Center" extends from $x = 0$ to $x = A - b$, while the frontier is between $A - b$ and A), and r_0 is the maximum relative growth rate of asabiya, taking place at the boundary $x = A$.

Substituting this formula into the equation for $\dot{S}$, we have

$$\dot{A} = c_0 A S \left(1 - \frac{A}{h}\right) - a$$

$$\dot{S} = r_0 \left(1 - \frac{A}{2b}\right) S(1 - S) \qquad (4.5)$$

The state variables are constrained as follows: $0 < S < 1$ and $A > 0$.

Analysis of this simple model is very straightforward, and can be accomplished graphically by looking at the isoclines in the phase space. The isocline for the first equation in (4.5) is the curve showing all combinations of A and S values for which the change in A is zero. The significance of the isocline is that it divides the phase space (which graphically represents all possible combinations of A and S values) into parts where A either grows or declines (and on the isocline itself, where $\dot{A} = 0$, A does not change). The isocline for the second equation is defined analogously, by setting $\dot{S} = 0$. Plotting the two isoclines (Figure 4.2), we see that they intersect at only one point. In other words, the model admits a single nontrivial equilibrium point. The stability of the equilibrium is determined by the position of the $\dot{S} = 0$ isocline in relation to the minimum of the $\dot{A} = 0$ isocline. Thus, the stability is determined by only two parameters: h and b. If $2b > h/2$ (the intersection point is to the right of the minimum), then the equilibrium is stable to small perturbations. The mechanism works as follows. Increasing A also increases the area in the center, and causes the average asabiya to decline, which pushes the empire boundary back. On the other hand, decreasing A causes S to increase, which pushes the border forward. I should add that, in addition to the equilibrial dynamics, it is also possible for the polity to fail, if the initial combination of S and A is too low. Roughly speaking, if $A(0)S(0) < a/c$, then the expansion never starts, and the fledgling polity is destroyed by the pressure

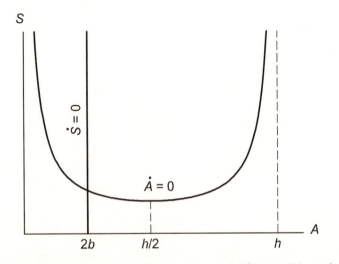

Figure 4.2 Isoclines of the asabiya-territory model (the unstable case).

from the hinterland. This is not a novel feature of the asabiya–territory model, but a characteristic of the original geopolitical model (see Section 2.2.1). In fact, the case of $2b > h/2$ is not qualitatively different from the geopolitical model without asabiya.

If $2b < h/2$, then the equilibrium is unstable. The population dynamics are characterized by a single boom/bust cycle [assuming that initial power $A(0)S(0)$ is over the threshold]. Initially, both A and S increase, but when A exceeds $2b$, S starts declining. The territorial expansion stops because the empire runs into logistic limitations, and S continues to decrease, because the central areas of the empire dominate the periphery. Low S eventually means that the empire cannot counter the geopolitical pressure from the hinterland. As a result, A begins contracting, first slowly, and then at an accelerating rate. The collapse rate accelerates because the empire has progressively decreasing resources. At some point, S begins to increase again (when A falls below $2b$), but by that point it is too late: the positive feedback dynamic (decreased A–decreased resources–even faster decrease in A) overwhelms any increase in S, and the empire collapses (A hits 0). An example of these dynamics is shown in Figure 4.3.

This analysis illustrates the value of translating verbal theories into mathematical models. Even though we made a number of greatly simplified assumptions, so that our model is at best a caricature of reality, nevertheless, the model turned out to be capable of more complex behavior than we could have guessed beforehand. Most importantly, although the model confirms that the postulated mechanism can lead to imperial boom/bust cycles, it also indicated that other kinds of dynamics are possible for different parameter values. Most importantly, if the empire's "reach" (as quantified by parameter h) is not much longer than the frontier width (b), then the expected boom/bust cycle will not materialize. Instead, the empire

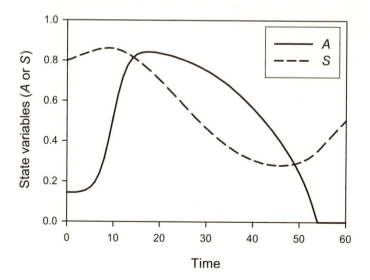

Figure 4.3 Dynamics of Model (4.5) for the case of unstable equilibrium. Parameter values: $r_0 = 0.1$, $c_0 = 1$, $h = 1$, $b = 0.2$, and $a = 0.1$.

will reach a state of equilibrium (just as in the original geopolitical model without asabiya dynamics). Furthermore, b must be substantially less than h. While the precise quantitative result, $b < h/4$, is likely to be affected by the structural assumptions of the model (for example, the linear relationships assumed for various functions), the qualitative insight is probably robust. Frontier areas must be small in relation to the empire size, determined by logistic constraints; if they are not, then no boom/bust dynamics ensue.

The other interesting insight is that the model does not appear to admit repeated boom/bust cycles or sustained oscillations. The key factor preventing a resurgence of a collapsing empire is that the outside pressure never relents (it is parameterized by a constant a). In reality, the pressure from outside is likely to come from other polities that will have their own logistic limitations. Thus, if we model the rival states explicitly, perhaps we will see another possible dynamic behavior that cannot be generated by the very simple model we developed here. This is a conjecture that I will pursue in the context of the spatially explicit simulation (next section).

Finally, yet another advantage of translating verbal theory into simple mathematical models is that we can quickly check the effects of various assumptions. For example, in the derivation of the model I assumed that asabiya grows logistically. What is the effect of using another growth model, for example the asymptotic one? It turns out that this assumption does not substantially affect the qualitative results. Most importantly, the isocline structure is precisely the same as in the model with the logistic S.[1] Similarly, making $r(x)$ a nonlinear function of space in Figure 4.1 does not affect the isocline structure. Finally, Sergey Nefedov (personal communication) investigated the effect of *not* using the approximation $\exp[x] = 1 + x$ in deriving the equation for A, and found that the qualitative result is unchanged, but the quantitative condition for the boom/bust cycle becomes $2b < h$ instead of $2b < h/2$ in Model (4.5). Thus, the insights from the model appear to be quite robust with respect to various modifications.

4.2.2 A Spatially Explicit Simulation

Our next step is to make the frontier model spatial and determine how this change affects the predicted dynamics. The details of the simulation model are banished to the Appendix (Section A.2). Here I give a brief overall description of the model, focusing on ways in which it differs from the nonspatial model (4.5). The most important addition is the explicit spatial dimension. The elementary spatial unit in the model (a "cell") corresponds to a small regional polity (a chiefdom) or a province within a large territorial empire. Cells are arranged on a rectangular grid.

Asabiya is tracked at two spatial levels: each cell has a value of asabiya, and each empire is characterized by its own value of asabiya, which is the average of the asabiyas of all cells belonging to the empire. The asabiya of a cell grows logistically (to the upper limit $S = 1$) if the cell is a "frontier" one: that is,

---

[1]For the mathematically inclined readers: remember that I imposed the condition $0 < S < 1$, so we do not care about the $S = 0$ isocline

situated next to a boundary between two empires, or between an empire and the "nonimperial hinterland." If a cell is not on a frontier, then its asabiya declines exponentially to 0. This is a slightly different implementation of the effect of the frontier on asabiya dynamics than that depicted in Figure 4.1. First, rather than declining linearly with distance from the border (as in the analytic model), the relative growth rate of asabiya is Z shaped: it is flat (and positive) within the frontier region, then abruptly declines to a flat (negative) value within the interior. Second, the width of the frontier region, b, is fixed at the size of one cell.

The dynamics of territorial expansion is modeled in a way analogous to equation (4.5). Each empire attempts to expand by attacking cells bordering it. The success of expansion is determined by the relative powers of the attacker and defender. Power is directly proportional to imperial size, A, and average asabiya, $\overline{S}$, but discounted by distance between the empire's center and the site of conflict, d: $P = A\overline{S}\exp[-d/h]$. The parameter h measures how fast power attenuates with distance [see equation (2.11) in Section 2.2.1]. The attacker wins if the power it brings to bear on the conflict site exceeds the power of the defender by a certain threshold (Δ_p). Note that this is a more realistic description of the process of expansion, because the powers of polities bordering the empire are modeled explicitly, rather than implicitly (with a constant, a) as in Model (4.5).

Dynamics Predicted by the Model

The dynamics of the model are illustrated by a typical realization (Figure 4.4a). The simulation was initiated with Empire 1, located in the upper central region of the arena, while the rest of the cells were assigned to nonimperial hinterland. Empire 1 grew rapidly for about ten time steps, until it occupied half of the available space, and then stabilized due to logistic constraints. During this first period of relative stasis, a stationary imperial frontier was established, which caused an increase of asabiya in the frontier zone just outside the empire. Soon after time step 20, a bunch of trajectories suddenly appeared, as a result of asabiya in the frontier zone increasing to the point where small polities began conquering each other. Only four polities (Empires 2, 9, 11, and 16) survived of this initial bunch, and grew first to consolidate the area around them, and then at the expense of Empire 1, causing its eventual extinction. During this process all area was divided between the four empires (no hinterland was left). A second period of relative stasis ensued, succeeded by an abrupt growth of Empires 9 and 16 at the expense of the other two. However, Empires 2 and 11 were not extinguished. After the third period of relative stasis, when the asabiyas of the two large empires declined while the asabiyas of smaller empires grew, another period of rapid change caused Empires 9 and 16 to collapse, while Empires 2 and 11 grew to take over most of their territory. Interestingly, one portion of the arena turned stateless as a result of Empire 9 collapsing, and this area was not conquered by the remaining empires. The fourth period of stasis was ended by the appearance of a new empire (17) arising in the stateless area. This eventually led to the collapse of one of the older empires, and a period of back-and-forth dynamics between the two remaining polities.

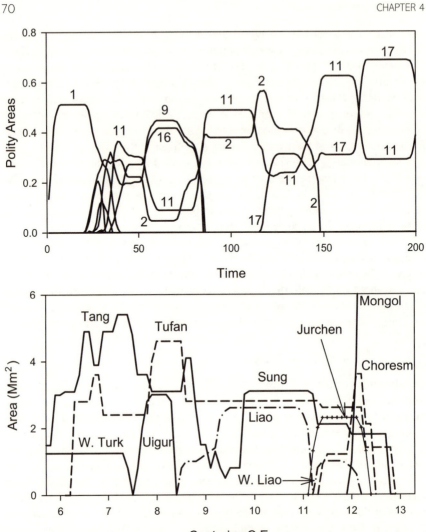

Figure 4.4 (a) Dynamics of the spatial asabiya-area model. Each curve depicts the territorial dynamics of simulated empires (polity area is expressed as a fraction of the total arena occupied). Model parameters are $r_0 = 0.2$, $\delta = 0.1$, $h = 2$, $S_{crit} = 0.003$, and $\Delta_P = 0.1$. Numbers associated with the trajectories are the imperial indices of the polities. (b) Expansion-contraction curves of areas for polities in East and Central Asia, 600–1200 C.E. (Data from Taagepera 1997: Appendix)

The model-generated trajectories look quite similar to the trajectories of historical polities (compare to Figure 4.4b). One striking similarity is how periods of rapid change are succeeded by periods of relative stasis. Another similarity is how situation dependent are the dynamics of polities. In particular, the maximum quasistable area during each stasis period is quite variable, despite all empires be-

THE METAETHNIC FRONTIER THEORY

ing subjected to the same logistical constraint function. This variability is, first, due to history resulting in a variable proportion of high-asabiya cells producing different average asabiya at the empire level. Second, since the location of boundaries reflects the balance of the opposing forces exerted by neighboring polities, the ultimate size of the empire depends very much on the relative powers of neighbors.

The qualitative similarity between historical polity trajectories and the simulated ones does not, of course, constitute any "proof" that the theoretical and empirical dynamics are driven by the same mechanism. In general, for any potential pattern there are an infinite number of mechanisms that can produce it: the mapping between mechanisms and patterns is many to one. Thus, in order to build empirical support for the frontier hypothesis, we will need to subject it to rigorous empirical testing (this will be our task in Chapter 5). Nevertheless, the observation that several features of the model's output match the observed dynamics is, at the very least, an encouragement to further theory developing and testing. Remember that the dynamic patterns in Figure 4.4a were not built in as model assumptions. On the contrary, they are an emergent macroscale feature of the assumptions about specific microscale mechanisms. Furthermore, the match between the observed and predicted dynamics goes beyond the superficial resemblance. Consider, for example, the political dynamics in Central–East Asia during the twelfth century. At that time there were two large empires (Sung and Tufan) with stationary borders throughout most of the century. Then a bundle of four "challenger" polities arrived on the scene: Western Liao, Jurchen, Khwarism, and Mongol. All challengers arose in the northern frontier zone. By the end of the thirteenth century, only one of the challenger polities survived (Mongol); the other three, as well as the two older empires were destroyed by it. This is very similar to what happens in the simulation during time steps 20–30, when a bundle of challenger polities arise in the frontier zone surrounding Empire 1, with most of them (as well as Empire 1 itself) eventually consumed by the four winning empires.

Trajectory Instability of Model Dynamics

One interesting feature of the model is that its output is very erratic looking. In fact, if we repeatedly simulate the model starting with exactly the same initial condition (the initial location and asabiya of Empire 1), each run will produce wildly different outcomes. Because the rules of change are largely deterministic (the only way stochasticity enters in the model is in the order in which cells become potential attackers, as well as in the order in which neighboring cells are attacked), this observation suggests that the model behaves chaotically. To check on this, I removed all stochasticity from the simulation (by fixing the order of attackers and directions to attack). The purely deterministic model still produced very erratic-looking trajectories (although now, of course, each run was exactly the same as the previous one). However, a small change in the initial conditions (for example, adding or subtracting a single cell from the initial state of Empire 1) again produced rapidly diverging trajectories. Thus, it appears that the simulation is indeed characterized by chaotic dynamics (that is, sensitive dependence on initial conditions; Ruelle 1989).

In retrospect, the finding of chaotic dynamics in the spatial version of the metaethnic frontier model is not surprising. Complex dynamics are promoted by nonlinearities and high dimensionality in dynamical systems. Several features of the frontier model introduce severe nonlinearities. One is the size-threshold effect (see Section 4.2.1): small polities are highly liable to extinction, but as soon as they grow over a certain size they become much more resistant to external pressure. The second threshold is S_{crit}, the critical value of average asabiya, below which an empire cannot sustain its cohesion. Yet another important factor is the logistic growth assumption underlying the asabiya equation. Logistic growth at low values of the state variable is essentially exponential, and thus is characterized by sensitive dependence. This means that two cells within a frontier zone that differ slightly in their initial asabiya (due to historical effects) will actually diverge in their asabiya values, even though they are subjected to exactly the same dynamic rule.

The high dimensionality of dynamics is imposed by space. Each cell is characterized by two state variables: its imperial index and its asabiya. Thus, the dimensionality of the dynamic process is twice the number of cells within the arena (for example, it is 800 for a 20 × 20 arena). This means that there are typically several empires contending for territory at any given time, and that each empire's internal composition is highly context and history specific. This situation dependence was already remarked on above.

To sum up, nonlinear functional forms and high dimensionality due to the spatial nature of the simulation conspire to make its dynamics highly chaotic. If the frontier model actually captures some important aspect of reality, then the prospects for long-term prediction of the trajectories of agrarian polities are not good. It is true that the spatial frontier model is extremely simple, even simplistic, but more complex models typically tend to have even more chaotic dynamics.

The Effect of the Logistic Load Parameter on Stability

The analysis of the nonspatial frontier model suggested that the key factor determining stability in that model was the ratio h/b (increasing the spatial scale of power projection, quantified by h, in relation to the frontier width, b, resulted in a destabilization of the equilibrium polity size). In the spatial simulation, the width of the frontier is fixed at 1, but we can vary h and observe the effect on predicted dynamics. The nonspatial model suggests that decreasing h should eventually stabilize the dynamics, while increasing it should further destabilize the dynamics. Numerical exploration of the spatial simulation showed that this is indeed the case. When h is reduced to, for example, 1 (compared to the reference value of 2), the simulation output ceases to generate oscillations. Instead, after some transient dynamics, a number of medium-sized polities arises, each occupying between 7 and 16% of the total area (30–70 cells).

Increasing h serves to destabilize the dynamics, in accordance with predictions of the nonspatial model. For example, if we set $h = 3$, then, after some initial oscillations, one polity will eventually take over the whole simulation arena.

Lacking any frontiers, all cells will eventually decline in asabiya to 0. When the average empire asabiya declines below the threshold S_{crit}, the empire collapses, but since it collapses everywhere uniformly, no new boundaries arise, and the system persists in its stateless condition for ever.

The Reflux and Breakthrough Effects

One further pattern predicted by the spatial simulation is worth discussing at this time. In examining the spatial dynamics of the simulation output, I noticed that challenger empires arising in the frontier zone initially tend to expand away from the older empire, into the hinterland, or even at the expense of other, smaller challengers near them (Figure 4.5).

In retrospect, it is very clear what is going on here. A challenger polity typically cannot successfully attack the old empire, because the empire is still very strong due to its large size and perhaps still not insubstantial average asabiya. Meanwhile, the asabiya in the nonfrontier hinterland is low and expansion there is easy. Furthermore, as the challenger empire expands into the hinterland, its center of gravity moves away from the old empire, and thus the pressure it can exert on the old empire decreases with time. Further expansion within the hinterland is stopped only by logistic constraints (or by reaching the edge of the simulation arena). I term this expansion pattern away from the frontier zone the *reflux effect*.

Under certain conditions, the reflux does not occur. Specifically, this happens if a challenger arises late in the game, when the average asabiya of the old empire is so low that it cannot resist pressure from the challenger. In this case, we often observe a "breakthrough" effect: a long period of quasistasis, during which the asabiya of the old empire is slowly declining, while the asabiya of the challenger polity grows. Then suddenly the difference between the powers of the antagonists goes over the threshold Δ_P, and the challenger takes over the border cells of the empire. This takeover catastrophically lowers the average asabiya of the old empire (since the only cells where asabiya is high are on the frontier), and leads to rapid expansion of the challenger into the interior regions of the old empire (and, frequently, to the collapse of the old empire, if its average asabiya, when deprived of border regions, goes below the threshold S_{crit}).

The reflux effect is a very typical feature of the dynamics predicted by the spatial simulation. It is also an emergent feature, because it was not built in at the micro level. This striking prediction of the model provides us with a way to test it, by looking through the historical record and determining whether reflux events are present in it.

Caveats

Finally, I need to discuss the limitations of the frontier model, as well as how we could modify the model to address them. First, the simulation models distance effects using the simplest possible approach, by assuming that the power that an empire can bring to bear on a particular cell at its boundary declines exponentially

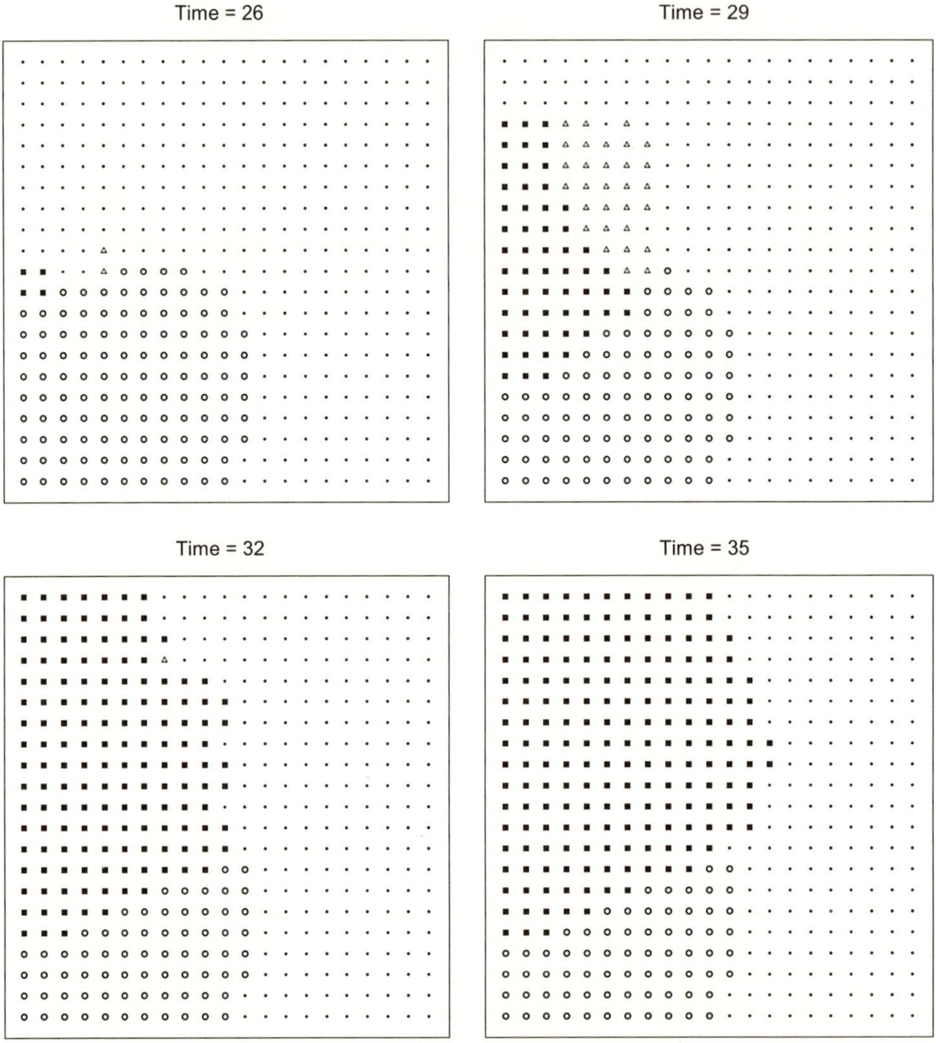

Time = 26

Time = 29

Time = 32

Time = 35

Figure 4.5 The reflux effect in the spatial frontier model. In each of the four snapshots, dots indicate the hinterland regions, circles are regions belonging to Empire 1, squares to Empire 2, and triangles to Empire 3. In the first snapshot (time = 26), Empires 2 and 3 have just appeared in the frontier zone of Empire 1. At time = 29, both new empires expand into the hinterland. Subsequently, Empire 2 conquers Empire 3, and expands to the limits imposed by logistical constraints (time = 35).

with increasing distance from the imperial center. It would be very interesting to explore some more mechanistic assumptions. For example, one could explicitly model the movements, locations, and supply of army units. Such an approach would impose a more realistic constraint on the ability of the empire to expand (in the current simulation, the empire can in principle expand in all directions simultaneously). Another important geopolitical aspect is barriers to movement like mountains and water bodies. Investigating such aspects would be a very important project but would lead us well beyond the confines of the present book, and thus must be left to the future.

The second aspect of the simulation that greatly oversimplifies the reality is its lack of attention to ethnic dynamics of populations inhabiting various polities. Rather, the simulation equates ethnicity to membership in the polity. Thus, all imperial borders are assumed to represent metaethnic divides. Conversely, the simulation assumes that as soon as a cell is taken over, its inhabitants immediately transfer their loyalty to the conquering empire (or, alternatively, are immediately replaced with colonists). This is a very serious flaw, because ethnokinetic processes such as ethnic assimilation clearly take time. This aspect of the problem is pursued in Chapter 6.

The third large area in which the theory needs more development is the dynamics of different social strata (most importantly for our purposes, commoners and elites), including their population dynamics, as well as upward/downward mobility. This is also a serious omission, because the degree of collective solidarity that ties different strata together in a polity is an important variable in itself. Furthermore, population dynamics is an important determinant of economic power of the state. Some initial steps in developing theory addressing these issues are made in Chapter 7.

4.3 SUMMARY

- The main objective of this chapter was to *endogenize* the concept of asabiya (capacity for collective action). This means that we need to advance a theory specifying variables that cause asabiya to increase or decline.
- We turn to the theory of multilevel selection for theoretical insights as to what conditions favor evolution of collective solidarity. Multilevel selection theory states that selection for group-beneficial but individual-costly behaviors is promoted when intragroup variation in fitness is minimized, while intergroup variation in fitness is maximized. This argument suggests at least three variables that should affect evolution of asabiya.
- The first variable is the degree to which the environment of a group is pacified. Because the primary source of intergroup variation is conflict between groups, location in a stateless environment should promote asabiya increase, while location near the center of a large polity (far from boundaries where warfare mainly occurs) should promote asabiya decrease.
- The second variable is population density in relation to the carrying capacity. Density pushing at the subsistence limits promotes intragroup competition, and causes asabiya to decline. Low population density implies low intragroup competition, and conditions favoring the increase of asabiya. Note that this variable is correlated with the first, since mortality rates in stateless environments tend to be higher than in the centers of large polities, resulting in population densities substantially below the carrying capacity.

- The first two variables primarily affect the conditions favoring increase in the asabiya of *small-scale* ethnic groups. The third variable, location near a major metaethnic fault line, creates condition for the widening of asabiya profiles. The general mechanism is the expansion of the symbolically demarcated ethnic boundary to encompass a larger-scale group, in opposition to the very alien group (or groups) situated on the other side of the metaethnic fault line.

- Metaethnic fault lines may coincide with imperial boundaries, creating regions that I call metaethnic frontiers. Metaethnic frontiers are regions where all three factors (intergroup conflict, population density, and deep ethnic divides) work synergistically. Thus, the theory developed in this chapter makes the prediction that metaethnic frontiers are asabiya "crucibles."

- Conditions most favorable to asabiya increase should be the frontiers of a major empire, particularly if it is also a carrier of a universal religion, abutting stateless hinterlands. Imperial frontiers can exert a "push" or "pull" (or both) on the tribal zone. When empires are vigorous they exert expansionary pressure on the ethnic groups inhabiting the hinterland. When empires are weak, they tempt border tribes with rich booty. In either case, "barbarians" living on the imperial frontier have an added stimulus to generate a better capacity for collective action.

- Another kind of situation that should also be conducive to asabiya increase is the frontier between two large empires that espouse different exclusionary religions (for example, Christianity and Islam). In this case, it is the groups inhabiting the frontier regions of the empires that are under pressure to increase and scale up their asabiyas.

- Metaethnic frontiers are zones where groups come under enormous pressure, and where ethnocide, culturicide, and genocide, but also ethnogenesis, commonly occur. Intense intergroup competition eventually results in one group with high asabiya, scaling-up structures, and simple luck emerging as a victor. In the process, the group acquires a distinct identity, demarcated by a strong ethnic boundary, and a high degree of internal cohesion—in other words, it becomes a new ethnic group (an incipient ethnie). Thus, the process leading to the formation of this new ethnopolitical system can be thought of as ethnogenesis. Note that the theory views polity formation and ethnogenesis as two aspects of the same dynamic process.

- Formalization of this verbal theory into a simple analytical model suggests that the dynamics of polity size and asabiya should go through a single boom-bust cycle. However, this dynamic occurs only if the extent of the frontier zone is small compared to the upper limit on the polity extent imposed by logistic constraints. If this condition is violated, then polity dynamics are not qualitatively different from the simple geopolitical model of Section 2.2.1.

- To check on the analytical results, I constructed a spatially explicit simulation of a world-system of polities whose territorial dynamics are driven by geopolitical forces and asabiya. Asabiya increases in the frontier regions, and declines in central regions. The simulation indicates that for a wide variety of parameters, polities go though repeated boom-bust oscillations. However, these oscillations are not cyclic, but highly chaotic.

- One of the key periods in the life of a polity is its beginnings. The asabiya of its core ethnie must somehow increase above that of the surrounding ethnic groups in order for the focal group to expand. The process that increases a group's asabiya and launches it on the polity-building and expansionary course is *ethnogenesis*.

Chapter Five

An Empirical Test of the Metaethnic Frontier Theory

5.1 SETTING UP THE TEST

The theory developed in Chapter 4 predicts that large territorial empires should originate at metaethnic frontiers. My goal in this chapter is to test this prediction empirically. The theory is universal, in the sense that its prediction applies to any agrarian polity, anywhere in the world. A test encompassing all known history, however, is not feasible given resources currently at my disposal, so it is necessary to select a discrete area and period as a first step. I chose to focus on Europe during the first two millennia C.E., because the history within these spatiotemporal boundaries is reasonably well known (and is easily accessible in Western language literature).

One disadvantage of using Europe as a testbed of general theory is the argument that Europe may have a number of unique features distinguishing it from the rest of the world; special characteristics that explain its spectacular rise during the modern era (e.g., Jones 1981; Landes 1998). However, explanations of the rise of Europe based on such "European exceptionalism" have been severely criticized (Blaut 1993, 2000). Furthermore, current scholarship (summarized by Frank 1998; Pomeranz 2000) suggests that Europe began diverging from other world regions only after 1800. In any case, it is not necessary for me to choose a side in this debate. My working assumption at this time is that the metaethnic frontier theory is equally applicable to Europe and other world regions. Here I report on the results of testing the theory on European material, while future publications will report on tests of the theory in Central/East Asian, South Asian, and Southwest Asian regions (research in progress). In other words, I treat this as an empirical issue. In Charles Tilly's words, "the European historical experience, for all its special features, is long enough, well-enough documented, and a large influence on the rest of the world that any systematic conclusions which hold up well in the light of that experience would almost automatically become plausible hypotheses to be tried elsewhere" (Tilly 1975:13).

Geographically, Europe is a western peninsula of Eurasia, and thus the boundary separating it from the rest of the Old World is somewhat arbitrary. I use the standard geographic boundary between Europe and Asia (Urals Mountains, Ural River, Caspian Sea, the Great Caucasian mountain chain, Black Sea), but with two exceptions. I will omit the area of Northern Caucasus, because its history is poorly known for most of the period of interest. However, I include the Anatolian peninsula (Asia Minor), because excluding it would force me to treat several important European Great Powers (the Byzantine and Ottoman Empires) as exogenous intrusions. Another area where drawing a sharp boundary is problematic is the Iberian-Moroccan junction. I chose to treat Moroccan polities (most notably, Almoravids and Almohads) as exogenous intrusions.

Because my focus is on agrarian polities, the temporal end point I use is 1900 C.E. Although several states in northwest Europe had made the agrarian-industrial transition by this time, this development affects only a small part of the spatiotemporal domain. I chose 500 C.E., which roughly coincides with the fall of the western Roman Empire, as the starting point for the consideration of polity dynamics. Because frontiers affect ethnopolitical dynamics with a long time lag, I started my frontier database at 0 C.E. I readily admit that the spatial and temporal bounds that I chose are somewhat arbitrary and other choices could be made. However, I would argue that the important principle here is that all regions and all polities falling within the specific spatiotemporal bounds should be used in the empirical test. In this way, the outcome of the test cannot be criticized as resulting from conscious or unconscious selection bias. As to specific spatiotemporal bounds, they simply need to encompass sufficient number of regions and polities so that we can do statistics.

5.1.1 Quantifying Frontiers

Frontiers are hard entities to pin down (Hall 2000), both in time and space. They move around and have fuzzy spatial extent. Yet, in order to devise a statistical test, we have to discretize them. The first step is to divide space into discrete geographical units. I divided the total area into some 50 "cultural regions," mostly characterized by areas of between 0.1 and 0.2 Mm^2 (Figure 5.1). When drawing the borders between the geographical units I attempted to take into account major fixed terrain features (mountains, coastline) and ethnic divisions (language, religion). In addition to spatial divisions, I also need temporal ones. Because we are dealing with very slow processes, I divided time into intervals of one century.

Let me reiterate that any scheme that would translate temporally dynamic and spatially fuzzy things like frontiers into discrete spatiotemporal units must be procrustean, to a greater or lesser degree. I have no doubt that better schemes than the one proposed here can be devised. Yet one needs to start somewhere. This is what I do here, while hoping that in the future the approach will be improved or a better alternative will be proposed.

With over 50 cultural regions and 19 centuries I have close to a thousand area-centuries, which are my main data units for analysis of shifting frontiers in Europe 0–1900 C.E. The next step is to assign each unit a quantitative score reflecting the intensity of cross-ethnic interaction in it. I assume that the interaction intensity has four components, based on differences in religion, language, way of life, and the pressure of warfare. I give religious difference a score with four levels:

- The highest score, 3, is given to areas where Islam and Christianity interact with each other, or with paganism.
- The next score, 2, is given to major religious divisions within Christianity or Islam (e.g., Catholics versus Orthodox after 1000 C.E.; Shiites versus Sunnis).

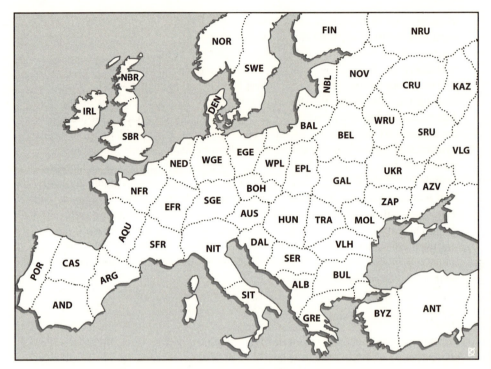

Figure 5.1 Cultural regions used as geographical units in the statistical analysis of the relationship between metaethnic frontiers and polity size.

- Sects within the same religion are scored as 1. Examples include Catholics versus Protestants, or Latin and Greek Christians prior to 1000 C.E. I also scored differences between various pagan religions at this level, because these religions, unlike Christianity and Islam, tend not to be exclusive and proselytizing.
- Finally, no religious difference is scored as 0.

Linguistic distinctions are scored 0 (none), 1 (different languages within the same linguistic group: Romance, Germanic, and Slavic), and 2 (different linguistic groups). I do not give an extra point for different linguistic families (Indo-European, Ugro-Finnic, etc.) because I assume that once languages diverged to the point of complete mutual incomprehensibility (which certainly happened by the time the two languages belong to different groups), the speakers will have no way of knowing that they belong to the same linguistic family. My reasons for giving an intermediate score of 1 to speakers of clearly related languages (such as Catalan and Castilian, or Occitan and French) are as follows. First, a speaker of the northern French (*langue d'oïl*) will recognize Occitan as a related language, and may feel a greater degree of kinship to an Occitan speaker than to a German. Second, historically the gradations between languages belonging to the same group were typically not abrupt. Thus, it would be difficult to draw clearcut boundaries during the Middle Ages separating Romance speakers from each other. The same was true with respect to the area inhabited by Germanic languages and dialects, or the area including speakers of east and west Slavic languages.

The greatest difference in the economic way of life (score 2) is between settled agriculturalists and nomadic pastoralists. This distinction codes for a whole bundle of cultural differences, including very different behavioral norms, as well as attitudes to each other. Score 1 distinguishes agriculturalists with urbanized culture and literacy (at least, among some social stratum) from "backwoods" cultivators.

Finally, the intensity of warfare index codes for the demographic impact of war across the metaethnic divide. The highest score of 2 reflects intense warfare (up to and including genocide) that results in detectable depopulation of the area. Score 1 is given to persistent raiding for loot and captives that does not cause a significant drop in the population numbers. Finally, the score of 0 corresponds to either relatively peaceful interaction, or "mild" warfare, practiced by the elites, and not affecting the demographics of the productive class.

The total score for frontier intensity is obtained by summing the religion, language, way of life, and warfare intensity indices. It varies from 0 to 9. Note that, because religion has an extra intensity level, compared to other indices, this approach gives it a somewhat bigger weight in the final score. I believe that this is appropriate, given the important role of religion in erecting and maintaining metaethnic divisions.

Details of translating historical information into frontier scores are given in Appendix B. Briefly, I examined the history of each cultural region, and determined whether at any given point in time it had a state boundary running through it, or next to it. If the region was in the interior of a large empire, it was assigned the frontier index of 0. Similarly, a region would be assigned an index of 0 if it was situated in a stateless environment (that is, chiefdoms and smaller-scale polities). If a region was on a state boundary, then I scored the four components of ethnic interaction intensity, as described above, and summed them for a total frontier score. If there were two or more frontiers running through the same region, I used the highest score (the assumption being that frontier intensities do not add up).

5.1.2 Polity Size

In the test I am setting up, the frontier intensity is the independent (predictor) variable. For the dependent (response) variable, we need some measure of imperial success. One appropriate measure, as discussed in Section 1.2.1, is simply the territorial extent of polities. Accordingly, I quantified the imperial success as the maximum extent of territory controlled at the peak. One disadvantage of this measure is that it does not distinguish between empires that reached the peak quickly, and as quickly collapsed, from more durable polities. It is clear that a longer-lived polity was probably based on a greater degree of asabiya, since surviving for many centuries means that the polity has encountered and overcome a number of challenges. By contrast, an evanescent empire may have just been lucky, by capitalizing on temporary weaknesses of its rivals. One way to distinguish between these two cases is to build duration into the index. For example, we can integrate the area under the territorial curve of a polity. I plan to pursue this idea in future (work in progress), but for now I will be content with a simpler measure based on the maximum territory.

The metaethnic frontier model predicts where *large* territorial polities should arise. The distinction between large polities and the rest is, of course, arbitrary, but I need some cutoff point, simply in order not to have to deal with a myriad of small polities, such as lesser Imperial states in the early modern Europe. I set the threshold at 0.1 Mm^2 (1 Mm = 1,000 km; thus 1 Mm^2 = 10^6 km^2), which is comparable to the area of smaller-sized geographic units in Figure 5.1. In other words, I do not care to consider polities that occupy only a fraction of a geographic unit.

In addition to the cut-off point for polity size, I also need a cut-off for cumulative frontier intensity. After all, the theory does not predict that just any state boundary would serve as an asabiya generator. A frontier must be *intense* and its influence on the area *long in duration*. The second attribute is important because asabiya increases on a long time scale. Thus, a frontier that rapidly moved through an area is unlikely to cause any ethnogenetic events. More likely, the area will be incorporated into the advancing empire, and as the frontier moves away, the forces acting on the population of the area will cause asabiya to decline, rather than increase. To incorporate both of these attributes, I required that a frontier, in order to be classified as "asabiya generator," should have an intensity of 5 or higher (note that 5 is the midpoint of the frontier intensity scale), and should persist in the given cultural area for three centuries or longer.

We are now ready to specify the prediction of the theory in terms that can be immediately testable. Cultural regions where the frontier intensity is 5 or higher for three or more centuries are expected to be the sources of territorial polities with maximum areas larger than 0.1 Mm^2. By "sources," I mean regions where large polities originated, which are inhabited by the polity's core elites, and where they typically have capitals. We can test this prediction by classifying all units in a two-way table as (1) with or without metaethnic frontiers, and (2) with or without a polity over 0.1 Mm^2 at some later time (this will be specified below). The theory predicts that the cells "no frontier and no empire," and "frontier and empire" should have more entries than randomly expected. Some entries in the "frontier, but no empire" cell are also expected. The most common reason for this happening, as predicted by the model of Section 4.2.2, is that some other region nearby, and also on the frontier, may get its empire going first, and conquer the region we are observing before it has the chance to develop its own empire. Another potential reason is that in the real world the increase of asabiya leading to the foundation of an aggressive empire must be a stochastic process, so variable periods of time may pass before it is complete. Nevertheless, if a region is situated on a frontier for a long period of time without being taken over by another empire, and does not develop its own empire, then this is an anomaly, as far as the theory is concerned.

The entries in the "no frontier, but empire" category, however, present the greatest empirical challenge to the theory, because according to it, there should be no such observations. Adopting the Lakatosian perspective, we will treat such observations as anomalies. If there are too many anomalous observations, then the theory collapses, especially if there is an alternative that can explain the observations better. The value of anomalies is that they often suggest how an alternative theory can be constructed.

5.2 RESULTS

I now proceed to presenting the results, starting with Europe during the first millennium C.E., and then Europe during the period up to 1900 C.E. The description of intermediate steps in the analysis and data tables has been banished to Appendix B.

5.2.1 Europe: 0–1000 C.E.

During the first half of the millennium the political geography of Europe was dominated by the Roman Empire. The frontier of the Roman Empire was largely stationary, although with some oscillations. There were advances into Germania, northern Brittania, and Dacia that were not sustained for long periods of time. During the calamitous third century, the frontier was overwhelmed by barbarian invasions. But, generally speaking, the frontier affected broadly the same swath of regions running southeast from present-day Netherlands to Romania. The regions classified as "frontier" during 0–500 C.E. are SBR, NED, NFR, EFR, WGE, SGE, BOH, AUS, HUN, TRA, VLH, BUL, BYZ, MOL, and ZAP (see Figure 5.1).

The presence of a single empire during this period makes construction of the statistical test straightforward. I simply use the frontier regions during the first half millennium, and observe whether there is a correlation with large polities originating from these regions and reaching their maximum size during the second half millennium (500–1000 C.E.). The temporal separation is determined by the direction of causation (frontiers must temporally precede empires). The separating date, 500 C.E., is convenient because it is very close to the date of collapse of the western Roman Empire. The results are summarized in Table 5.1.

The overall pattern documented in Table 5.1 confirms the predictions of the metaethnic frontier theory: the overwhelming majority of cases are concentrated in the categories "no frontier, no empire" and "frontier and empire." The statistical test indicates that the probability of this outcome occurring by chance alone is vanishingly small. Now that we have an overview of the pattern, let us delve into some specifics.

A Quick Overview of the Ethnopolitical History of Europe during the First Millennium

The Roman frontier in Europe had three fairly distinct segments: two in the flat terrain separated by one in a rugged area. The first flat segment stretched along

Table 5.1 Results of the empirical test of the frontier model: (a) Europe 0–1000 C.E. Test of independence (Sokal and Rohlf 1981:737): $G_{adj} = 27.1$, $P \ll 0.001$. (b) Europe 1000–1900 C.E. Test of independence: $G_{adj} = 22.0$, $P \ll 0.001$.

	(a) 0–1000 C.E.	
	No frontier	Frontier
No empire	34	4
Empire	1	11

	(b) 1000–1900 C.E.	
	No Frontier	Frontier
No empire	19	6
Empire	3	22

the Rhine north of the Jura and Vosges mountains, where it runs through the north European plain (I will return to this area in Section 9.1.1). The rugged segment of the frontier was situated north of the Alps. It was crosscut by the foothills of the Alps, as well as by smaller chains of mountains and hills: the Jura, Bavarian/Bohemian forest, the Sudetes, and the Tatras. The last flat segment, along the Danube river, itself consisted of two pieces: the Hungarian and, beyond the Transylvanian Alps, the Wallachian plain. The Wallachian plain merges smoothly into the coastal lowlands of the Black Sea, running from Constantinople/Stambul to the Dnieper and beyond (the latter area will be discussed in Section 9.2.1). This whole segment of the frontier, including the Hungarian plain, can be thought of as a western extention of the great Eurasian steppe.

In Section 4.1.2 I advanced the hypothesis that rugged terrain has an inhibiting effect on asabiya increase. Thus, we should expect large polities forming along the flat segments of the Roman frontier. This is precisely what happened. The largest European polity of the first millennium (for a complete list of polities, see the Appendix) was the Frankish Empire, whose territory reached a peak of roughly 1.8 Mm² during the reign of Charlemagne. Smaller Germanic states and chiefdoms, forming in the same general area, include the Burgundian Kingdom and the Duchies of the Alamanni, Thuringians, and Saxons. Across the English Channel, a similar development took place, albeit on a smaller scale, with Wessex, Mercia, and Northumbria eventually merging into England.

The second largest empire in Europe (or, more precisely, in western Eurasia) during the first millennium was Byzantium (1 Mm² in 970 C.E.). The Byzantine empire presents a fascinating historical puzzle, usually posed as follows: why did the eastern Roman Empire survive the collapse of the western Empire, and then thrive for another thousand years? The metaethnic frontier theory proposes a solution to this puzzle. Beginning in the third and until the tenth century, the area around Byzantium-Constantinople became the imperial frontier. Once the invader from the north crosses the Danube, there are no significant geographic barriers between it and Constantinople. Furthermore, the area around Constantinople is vulnerable to sea-based raiding. As a result, it was repeatedly raided and invaded, and Constantinople was besieged by a succession of barbarian hordes, such as the Goths, Huns, Slavs, Avars, Bulgars, and Arabs. Furthermore, from the fourth century and until the conversion of the Bulgars in 863–900 C.E., the frontier coincided with a metaethnic fault line between Christianity and Paganism.

As I discussed in Chapter 4, a new empire can be born on either the imperial or the tribal side of the old empire's frontier. In the case of the lower Danube frontier, both sides gave rise to empires. Turkic-speaking nomads and Slavic-speaking agriculturalists merged into a new Bulgarian ethnie north of the frontier, while another new ethnie, the Byzantines, formed south of the frontier. The case for the Byzantines as a new ethnie, I believe, is quite strong. Certainly, the Byzantines were distinct both linguistically and religiously from the Romans of the classical age, but the cultural changes went ever deeper, including a striking transformation from the naturalism and rationalism of Hellenism to the transcendentalism and mysticism of the fifth and sixth centuries (McNeill 1963:451). Of course, the Byzantines continued to call themselves "the Romans," but so did many other people—from "the Holy Roman Empire of the German nation" to the modern Romanians and the (gypsy) Roma and even the Rum Seljuks. Note that I am not suggesting that this ethnic transformation occurred overnight, or even within the course of a single century. The eastern Roman Empire was subjected to an extreme pressure from barbarians in the north and the Muslims in the east for at least half a millennium. But the Byzantines survived and when the pressure abated in the middle of the ninth century embarked on sustained territorial expansion of their own (Whittow 1996, Treadgold 1997).

So far I discussed polities that formed in situ on the former Roman frontier. One feature fairly unique to the particular period, however, is the number of polities for whom the location of ethnogenesis was quite distant from the location of the polity that was eventually established. Thus, Visigoths and Ostrogoths originated north of the Black Sea, yet established states in the Iberian and Appenine peninsulas, respectively. Langobards initially coalesced in Pannonia (HUN), but eventually established a state in northern Italy. The Hungarian plain, in fact, saw a truly bewildering succession of state-building ethnies: the Dacians before the Roman conquest, then the Huns, Gepids and Langobards, Avars, and finally Magyars. The reason for such a rapid ethnic turnover, most likely, is the location at the western end of Eurasian steppe, making this plain the last stop of invading nomadic hordes.

Cases Not Fitting the Predictions of the Metaethnic Theory

Four regions fell into the category of "frontier, but no empire." In each case, the reason is incorporation into an empire based in a neighboring region. NFR and AUS were incorporated into the Frankish Empire, TRA was part of the Avar Khanate, and BUL was an integral part of the Bulgarian Khanate (whose center was initially in VLH and later shifted south to BUL). In addition, AUS is disadvantaged with respect to its neighbors, since it sits on the rugged segment of the Roman frontier (it has a mountain chain, the Alps, running right through its middle).

The single case in the "no frontier, but empire" category is the Duchy of Aquitaine. As discussed in the previous section, any instances falling into this category are considered as anomalies from the point of view of the frontier model. However, Aquitaine does not present a strong challenge to the theory. This polity was formed after the collapse of Merovingian Frankish Empire, and can be considered as a relict (along with Neustria and Austrasia). It was reincorporated into the Carolingian Empire during the eighth century. Thus, this polity may not even merit inclusion into the analysis, but I decided on the conservative course of action.

In summary, the results of the analysis of Europe during the first millennium C.E. provide strong support for the frontier model. The statistical test indicates that there is a high degree of correlation between the frontier and the genesis of large states (Table 5.1). Actually, the pattern is so clearcut that almost no statistical test is needed. Essentially all large polities that are found on the map of Europe during the 500–1000 C.E. were organized by peoples who went through ethnogenesis on the frontier of the Roman Empire. The only exceptions are two exogenous polities (the Avars and Omayyads) and a possible anomaly (Aquitaine). By contrast, the heartlands of the Empire (notably Italy and Spain), as well as tribal hinterlands far from the frontier (northern and eastern Europe) were conspicuous in the absence of in situ-originating polities. This general pattern is precisely what the frontier model predicts.

5.2.2 Europe: 1000–1900 C.E.

After the Roman Empire collapsed, the geography of frontiers in Europe became much more complex. First, there were more frontiers. During the period 500–1500 C.E. slightly more than half (28 out of 50) of cultural regions were classified as frontier ones (a frontier of intensity five or higher located in the region for three or more centuries). Second, frontiers were much more dynamic than during the Roman era. We can distinguish three general classes of frontiers.

The first set of frontiers, which dominated western Europe throughout much of the period, are the Carolingian marches (Bartlett 1993). Into this class, I include frontiers of the predecessor polity (Merovingian Empire), as well as successor polities, collectively referred to as the Latin Christianity (Bartlett 1993). The frontier in northwestern France faced Bretons and later Norse; the Spanish march guarded against the Muslims of Cordoba Emirate, a later site of the Reconquista. The Austrian march initially was the site of Carolingian operations against the Avar Khanate. Later, it faced the brunt of the Magyar incursions. After the Hungarians converted to Latin Christianity, this frontier lost its intensity (but was reactivated in the sixteenth century as a result of the Ottoman advance).

Finally, the Saxon march during the pre-Carolingian times was directed toward pagan Germans. After Charlemagne's conquest of Saxons, this frontier bifurcated, with one prong moving east, and eventually transforming itself into German *Drang nach Osten*. The second prong moved north through Scandinavia, first affecting Denmark (whose very name reflects its position on the Danish march), and then Sweden and Norway. The northern prong fluctuated between "push" and "pull" influences. At the height of its power, the Carolingian empire exerted military (this mostly affected the Danish) and ideological pressure. Persistent proselytization attempts, however, triggered a backlash from native paganism, especially in Sweden, which was finally Christianized only during the twelfth century. After the Carolingian decline, the frontier recoiled, with Scandinavians even colonizing parts of northwestern France. However, in the end Christianity won, and the eastern expansion resumed. In the northern Baltic, the Danish and Swedish advance sometimes competed and sometimes cooperated with the German expansion along the southern shore.

The second set of frontiers can be collectively called "the Great Steppe frontier" (McNeill 1964). One end of this frontier is located in present-day Hungary (Great Alfold plain), which is the westernmost extension of the Great Eurasian Steppe. From HUN it runs first east (TRA, VLH, MOL) and then northeast (ZAP, UKR, SRU, KAZ), following the transition between forests and grasslands. The steppe frontier had a greater degree of stationarity, compared to the Carolingian marches and their offshoots, because it was (and still is) anchored by the physical geography of eastern Europe. Nevertheless, this frontier swayed back and forth as time progressed. During the Kievan Russia period, the frontier was pushed south and east. After the Mongolian invasion, the frontier was pushed far back north. Finally, the frontier again advanced south during the Muscovite period, and finally was closed down by the Russian Empire in the late eighteenth century (with the conquest of the Crimean Khanate).

The third class of frontiers includes several "leftovers" from the Roman frontiers. The frontier between Germanic invaders and the indigenous people of Roman Britain is one example. This frontier lost its intensity by the end of the seventh century, with Anglo-Saxon conversion to Christianity. It then regained intensity after the invasion by another set of Germanic pagans, these ones from Scandinavia.

At the other end of Europe, the frontiers of the Byzantine Empire are another example of a "Roman leftover." The Balkan frontier lost its intensity by the tenth century, when invading Slavs and Bulgars had been largely converted to Christianity. The eastern frontier, however, remained a major fault line throughout the period. In the seventh century, Byzantium lost its Middle Eastern and African possessions to the Caliphate. As a result, Anatolia became one of the most intense interfaces between Christianity and Islam. The Arab expansion put an enormous amount of pressure on Byzantium. The Byzantines survived and two centuries later began their own advance. Unfortunately, the Byzantine Empire experienced a disastrous reverse at the battle of Manzikert in the late eleventh century, and the advance turned into retreat. In the fourteenth century, the advancing Ottomans reached the Balkans, and eventually as far west as the Hungarian plains. Thus, the Ottoman frontier connected and coincided with the Great Steppe frontier, especially if we take into account that the Crimean Khanate was an Ottoman dependency throughout most of its existence. Incidentally, the Anatolian Plateau can be considered as another extension of the Great Eurasian Steppe frontier.

This is a very schematic sketch of the frontier history of Europe, which focuses only on intense and long-lived metaethnic fault lines. There were many other population movements (Gaelic Scotti into Scotland, Basques into Aquitaine, Muslims into Southern Italy and especially Sicily, Vlachs into Moldavia, Greeks from Egypt and Syria into Byzantium after the Muslim conquest, and later to Greece, etc.) but according to my calculations these occurrences were either too local or did not result in an intense *and* prolonged frontier (see the Appendix for details).

To construct a test of the frontier model, I classified all fifty regions as "frontier" if during 500–1500 C.E. they had a frontier satisfying my intensity and length requirements (five or higher intensity and three or more centuries). Otherwise, the region was classified as "no frontier." I then identified all large polities (achieving an area of at least 0.1 Mm^2 at some point in time) that occurred in Europe (including Asia Minor) during the period of 1000–1900 C.E. I then eliminated some polities so that I would have at most one per cultural region, retaining the one that achieved the greater peak area. For example, the region KAZ was the locus of two polities (Volga Bulgars and the Kazan Khanate). I eliminated the Kazan Khanate and retained the Volga Bulgars, since the latter controlled a greater area at its peak. I also eliminated two polities that were of clear exogenous origin, the Cumans and the Teutonic order. The latter originated within Europe, but if any region can be assigned as its origin, it is EGE, which also generated a larger polity, Brandenburg-Prussia-Germany. There was also one polity that I classified as a relict, the Astrakhan Khanate, which was the largest piece left when the Golden Horde collapsed in the fifteenth century. Finally, each region was classified into the same four classes as in the previous section. The results are shown in Table 5.1b.

As we can see, the general pattern is consistent with the predictions of the frontier model. It is gratifying that all the Great Powers (England-U.K., Castile-Spain, France, Brandenburg-Prussia-Germany, Austria, Lithuania-Poland, Byzantium, the Ottoman Empire, and Muscovy-Russia) originated from regions heavily influenced by frontiers. Equally revealing are areas that never experienced intense frontiers, for example, AQU-SFR and EPL-BEL-WRU. These regions were always objects of geopolitics, never its subjects.

There are also six anomalous cases, in which the frontier presence did not result in a large polity. Four regions (AND, NED, VLH, and SRU) were incorporated into empires originating from neighboring regions. One interesting case is SGE, which had a polity originating in it, Switzerland, that did not make the size threshold. The Swiss case is interesting because initially, during the fourteenth-fifteenth centuries, the Swiss expanded their polity quite aggressively. But after the middle of the sixteenth century expansion ceased, even though there were apparently plenty of opportunities to expand north into the lesser imperial states. A possible explanation of this failure is the negative influence of the rugged topography on the scaling up of asabiya (Section 4.1.2). Another rugged region, ALB, may have failed to develop a strong polity for the same reason.

The greatest challenge to the model, however, is presented by the three cases of no frontiers, but empires. The first, medieval Poland (0.3 Mm^2 in 1020 C.E.), is not a strong anomaly, because it apparently formed very much under pressure from the Frankish march, similarly to the nearby Bohemia. However, its conversion to Christianity was quite rapid, so that it experienced a high-intensity frontier only for two centuries (and thus failed to be classified as a *prolonged* frontier). The second case is the Duchy of Burgundy. Burgundy arose as a scavenger state following the fourteenth-century French collapse. Its dukes then embarked on a program of territorial expansion, mainly relying on dynastic marriages. At its peak in 1480 C.E. it was about 0.13 Mm^2, which is just over the threshold size. The Burgundian state, however, turned out to be quite fragile, and collapsed in the late fifteenth century. Nevertheless, I believe that it presents a genuine anomaly for the frontier model, since instability was a general feature of most agrarian polities.

The last case, Savoy-Sardinia-Italy, appears to be the strongest anomaly. Incidentally, it is also one of the best examples of the reflux effect, since the state originated in Savoy, which is now part of France, and was successively pushed by its stronger neighbor over the centuries toward the east. Nevertheless, there is nothing even remotely resembling a metaethnic frontier in the Savoy case. And even though Italy has never managed to achieve Great Power status (some authors, however, do give it this status for the period 1870–1914), it has not collapsed, and even managed to acquire colonies in Africa. Thus, all hallmarks of empire are present (albeit not a very strong one), but the frontier model clearly does not apply. This anomalous case, therefore, is a clear indication that the frontier model cannot pretend to be a universal explanation of how all states arise.

5.3 POSITIONAL ADVANTAGE?

So far I have been comparing the predictions of the frontier model to an implicit null hypothesis that polity size and frontiers are statistically independent of each other. A stronger test is to contrast the performance of the frontier model with an explicit alternative (Section 1.2). One possible alternative theory has already been discussed in Section 2.2.2. Recollect that the Collins geopolitical theory postulates a positional advantage (a "marchland effect") to polities expanding from an area that is easy to defend. We can use the empirical machinery developed in this chapter to test the effect of marchland position.

As a first step in addressing the effect of protected position, I will focus on the proportion of the boundary of the polity that is coastline (Artzrouni and Komlos 1996). A more sophisticated analysis would also include the effect of mountainous terrain. However, estimating the effect of topography on the defensibility of a border is not straightforward. For example, we cannot just use the average elevation in the area, since low-elevation but very rugged hills can present a more significant barrier to invading armies than a high-elevation plateau. Thus, I will leave such refinements to future work, and for now use a cruder index that incorporates only the effect of large bodies of water (seas, straights, etc.) on the defensibility of a border.

To come up with a rough index of positional vulnerability, I approximated each cultural region by a rectangle and scored how many sides of the rectangle were inland versus coastlines. The index, therefore, ranged from 0 to 4, with 0 corresponding to an island region, and 4 to a landlocked region. There was only one region with the vulnerability index of 0 (IRL), nine regions with index 1, six with index 2, sixteen with index 3, and eighteen with index 4. I combined regions with indices 0–2 into one class, to obtain three vulnerability classes with roughly the same number of cases in each (16, 16, and 18).

Because the vulnerability index is a static measure, I combined my two data sets on polity sizes (before and after 1000 C.E.) into one. If a region had two polities, I retained the largest. I then classified each region according to the maximum polity area it achieved. In order not to depend too much on the specific threshold size, I used two: 0.1 and 0.3 Mm^2. This approach yielded three size classes of polities: small (0–0.1 Mm^2), medium (0.1–0.3 Mm^2), and large (> 0.3 Mm^2).

Examining the results, sorted by vulnerability and polity size classes, we see that there is no apparent connection between the two (Table 5.2). Thus, the inescapable conclusion is that geographical position does not affect the eventual polity size either positively or negatively. This conclusion must be tempered by the crudity of the procedure I used to generate data in Table 5.2. However, some further qualitative consideration suggests that, if a more sophisticated test finds a relationship between marchland advantage and geopolitical success, it will be weak. A major geographical feature of Europe is the plain running from southwestern France through northern France, Germany, Poland, Belarus and Ukraine, and Russia. There are no significant mountain chains interrupting this plain. Existence was always precarious here (as the example of Poland shows most graphically). Yet, most of the European great powers originated precisely in this swath of territory (France, Frankish Empire, Holy Roman Empire, Prussia-Germany, Lithuania-Poland, Kievan Russia, and Muscovy-Russia, to name just the largest ones). With so many counterexamples, it is unlikely that positional advantage would help explain historical dynamics in Europe. At best, it is a factor of secondary importance.

Table 5.2 Results of the empirical test of the positional effects model.

Vulnerability	Polities			
Index	Small	Medium	Large	n
0–2	5	5	6	16
3	7	3	6	16
4	6	7	5	18

5.4 CONCLUSION: THE MAKING OF EUROPE

In a paper on the history of European state-making written a quarter of a century ago, Charles Tilly asked, "At each point in time from 1500 forward, what features of a political unit would have permitted us to anticipate whether it would (1) survive into the following period as a distinct unit; (2) undergo territorial consolidation, centralization, (3) become the nucleus of a national state?" (1975:40). This is precisely the kind of question that motivates the theory developed in this book. I cannot claim that the metaethnic frontier theory gives a precise and accurate answer for the territorial dynamics of every European state. However, I believe that the theory explains the *general pattern* of European political development—"the making of Europe" (Bartlett 1993).

A particularly lucid exposition of this general pattern is found in the work of Stein Rokkan (1975; Rokkan and Urwin 1982). Rokkan pointed out that geopolitically the early modern Europe can be divided into a series of bands, in which aggressive state-building regions alternated with politically weak, fragmented areas. In the middle there is a belt of territorially fragmented but economically vibrant city-states that runs from the North Sea and the Baltic south along the Rhine and into Italy. To the west of this "trade-route belt" there is an area of strong conquest centers ("the seaward empire nations"): Denmark, England, France, and Spain. Further to the west lies a band of politically weak territories ("seaward peripheries"): Iceland, Scotland, Ireland, Wales, and Brittany. On the other side of the central trading belt, the situation is a mirror image of the west. First, there is a band of "the landward empire nations": Sweden, Prussia, Bavaria, and Austria. Next comes a band of "landward peripheries": Finland, Bohemia, Poland, and Hungary. Thus, "paradoxically the history of Europe is one of center formation at the periphery of a network of strong and independent cities" (Rokkan 1975:576).

The theory advanced and tested in Chapters 3–5 suggests that there is nothing paradoxical about this striking pattern. The explanation has two aspects: the spread of state by "contagion" via the metaethnic frontier mechanism, and a slow (centuries-long) decay of asabiya in imperial cores. However, in order to understand which regions develop strong states and which fragment and are conquered after 1500, we must go back to the Carolingian Europe, which itself is explained by the Roman Europe (and, incidentally, the rise of Rome can also be traced to the dynamics of the Mediterranean region of the early first millennium B.C.E.). The Rhenish frontier of the Roman Empire, for reasons amply discussed in Section 5.2.1, became the core region of a series of Germanic empires: the Merovingians, the Carolingians, and the Ottonians. Thus, the central belt of highly urbanized and politically fragmented polities is comprised of two former imperial cores (the classic Roman and medieval German).

The key period for the making of modern Europe was the post-Carolingian ninth and tenth centuries (Bartlett 1993), when Latin Christendom was assaulted on all sides by the Vikings, Saracens, Magyars, and Polabian Slavs. A set of defensive frontiers—the Carolingian marches—formed to respond to these threats.

The attention of new polities forming on the marches was directed outward.[1] West and southwest of the Carolingian core, strong conquest polities arose on the Breton and Spanish marches, and in England, once it was brought into the Latin Christian world by the Norman conquest. In the north, the Scandinavian world was incorporated by conversion, rather than conquest, and its main direction of expansion was east, simply because there were few opportunities in the western (Iceland) and northern (Lapland) directions. Finally, east of the core two conquest centers developed: one on the Saxon-Slavic frontier (*Drang nach Osten*, eventually leading to the formation of Brandenburg-Prussia), and the other on the Bavarian-Magyar frontier (eventually leading to the Habsburg Austria).

In summary, I argue that the metaethnic frontier theory provides a coherent explanation for the spatiotemporal pattern of political development in the post-Roman Europe. It also gives a more accurate representation of the pattern. For example, Rokkan rather arbitrarily assigned Denmark to the seaward, but Sweden to the landward empire-nation belts. By contrast, I interpret the political evolution of Europe as centrifugal from the Carolingian-Ottonian core, in all directions but the southern one (where another old imperial core was located). Finally, the explanation advanced above has the virtue of generality. In his account Rokkan (1975:596) emphasizes the uniqueness of the European configurations. I suggest that what was unique about Europe was the particular combination of initial and boundary conditions (using the mathematical language), rather than the general mechanism. In other words, the specific course of events in Europe was contingent on the Roman Empire starting where it did, on the timing and locations of extra-European invasions, and on physical features such as the rivers and mountains, which affected where frontiers formed. But the general explanation, based on the link between frontiers and collective solidarity, should work outside of Europe. At least, it seems to be a plausible working hypothesis (Tilly 1975), worthy of investigation in other world regions.

5.5 SUMMARY

- The metaethnic frontier model predicts that large territorial polities originate in areas subjected to a prolonged influence by intense metaethnic frontiers. In this chapter I empirically tested this prediction for Europe (plus Asia Minor) during the first two millennia C.E.
- I divided the total testing area into fifty "cultural regions" of between 0.1 and 0.2 Mm^2 in area. In each region and for each century from 0 to 1900 C.E., I calculated a "frontier index," consisting of four components, based on differences in religion, language, and economic way of life across the ethnic divide, and on the intensity of warfare. An index of 0 is assigned to regions through which no frontier passes during the given century, while a score of 9 is assigned to very intense, major metaethnic fault lines. I classified regions as "frontier" ones if they had a relatively intense (intensity score 5 or more)

---

[1]Thanks to Jack Goldstone for suggesting this formulation.

and stationary (three or more centuries) frontier. The rest of the regions were classified as "no frontier" ones.

- I first examined the relationship between frontiers and large polities in the period ending 1000 C.E. There was a strong correlation between an intense and prolonged frontier in a region during the period of 0–500 C.E. and the maximum territory the polity originating from the region achieved during 500–1000 C.E. A statistical test rejected the null hypothesis of no association with $P \ll 0.001$.

- A similar result was obtained for a comparison of frontiers during 500–1500 C.E. and maximum polity sizes achieved during 1000–1900 C.E. Again, the null hypothesis was rejected at the $P \ll 0.001$ level. In particular, I found that all the European Great Powers (England, Castile-Spain, France, Brandenburg-Prussia-Germany, Austria, Lithuania-Poland, Byzantium, Ottoman Empire, and Muscovy-Russia) originated from areas subjected to intense and prolonged frontier influence. The only exception was Savoy-Sardinia-Italy.

- I also examined an alternative hypothesis, based on the geopolitical notion of "marchland" positional advantage. I constructed an index of vulnerability for each region, based on the proportion of its boundary in coastline versus land. I found no association between the vulnerability index of a region and the size of polity that originated from it.

- These results provide a great degree of empirical support to the metaethnic frontier model, which outperformed both the null hypothesis of complete randomness, and an explicit rival hypothesis connecting positional advantage to geopolitical success. However, the test also revealed several anomalous cases, of which the most significant is the Italian one. In other words, although the frontier model predicted correctly the majority of large territorial polities (at least for Europe 500–1900 C.E.), it did not predict a few others. This observation suggests that there may be other mechanisms, in addition to the frontier one, that explain the genesis of large territorial polities.

Chapter Six

Ethnokinetics

6.1 ALLEGIANCE DYNAMICS OF INCORPORATED POPULATIONS

The previous two chapters analyzed the initial stage of a polity's expansion, during which newly incorporated groups are rapidly integrated into the core ethnie. One assumption of that theory was that the population inhabiting newly added areas immediately transfers its loyalty to the conquering empire. This is not necessarily an unrealistic assumption. Under certain circumstances, notably when newly incorporated elites are ethnically similar to the polity core, lack of strong ethnic differences may allow them to merge with the core elites without any substantial time lag.

Such a state of affairs, however, cannot last long. Sooner or later, a successfully expansionist empire will annex a territory inhabited by ethnically very different people (*alloethnics*). In fact, one definition of an empire is a polity encompassing more than one ethnie. Once a polity becomes multiethnic, its ability to function and expand will be strongly affected by the loyalties of incorporated ethnies. The asabiya profiles of annexed ethnies will probably show a substantial decline between the regional level (inhabited by each ethnie) and that of the empire. This has two consequences. First, because members of annexed ethnies feel little loyalty to the empire, they will be reluctant to contribute resources to it. Thus, annexation of an alien ethnie will increase the geopolitical power of the empire much less than adding an equivalent number of ethnically similar people. (If the state coerces alloethnics to contribute the same amount as members of the core ethnie, the overall contribution to the state power is still going to be diminished, since coercion is expensive.) It is especially difficult to obtain willing and loyal recruits for the army from alloethnies, so many empires choose to recruit only from the core ethnie (examples, the Roman Republic, but not Empire; the Russian Empire).

Second, ethnically different people are much more likely to rebel against the empire. If their ethnie-level asabiya is high, it will be relatively easy for their elites to overcome the collective-action problems associated with starting a successful uprising (for a general review of this issue, see Goldstone 1994). Thus, the empire will have to devote a considerable amount of resources to either buying the alloethnic elites off, or suppressing their rebellions.

In short, ethnic divisions have the potential to severely reduce the geopolitical power of the state. However, ethnicity is not a static variable, and ethnic composition of a polity continuously changes. Ethnic composition changes, first, as a result of demographic mechanisms (differential rates of population increase) and, second, as a result of ethnosocial mechanisms (Bromley 1987), such as ethnic assimilation and mobilization. Thus, whether alloethnic elites will assimilate to the core ethnie or not, and how fast this process proceeds, should have a great effect on the fortunes of the empire.

The overwhelming majority of medium- to large-sized polities in history were polyethnic (McNeill 1986; Hall 1998). Because geopolitical power depends so much on the ethnic composition of a polity, we need to develop some quantitative understanding of how and why the ethnic composition of polities evolves with time. Thus, the main purpose of this chapter is to develop dynamic models of ethnosocial change. I call such models *ethnokinetic*, because mathematically they are very similar to models of chemical kinetics. My primary emphasis is on ethnic assimilation, because of its postulated importance to the empire's power base. I should also remind the reader that, because I use the broad definition of ethnicity, I do not reduce assimilation to just *linguistic* assimilation. Granted, language or dialect is a very important cultural marker of ethnicity. However, during the period of interest, religion often provided an even more relevant (meta)ethnic marker. Thus, the two social processes of particular interest for purposes of this chapter are linguistic assimilation and religious conversion as examples of how ethnic identity may be changed. My empirical examples below will be drawn from instances of religious assimilation.

6.2 THEORY

6.2.1 Nonspatial Models of Assimilation

The Noninteractive Model

I begin with the simplest possible formulation of an ethnokinetic process. First, I assume that there are only two groups: the *core* and the *periphery* ethnies. Second, the population growth rates of the two ethnies are the same. This means that the relative proportions of core and peripheral ethnics change with time only as a result of individuals switching ethnic allegiance (identity). Third, peripheral ethnics switch their ethnicity and become members of the core ethnie with a constant probability per unit of time. These assumptions lead to what I call the *noninteractive assimilation model* (*noninteractive* because the probability of switching ethnic identity does not depend on what others are doing). Very similar models were proposed by Hopkins (1973) and Cederman (1997), although these authors modeled not two, but several classes of individuals (classified according to whether they were assimilated or not, and mobilized or not).

Obviously, the assumption of two distinct ethnies, with individuals making an instantaneous switch between them, is a great oversimplification of the reality. However, there were some instances in history for which this simple model may provide not a bad approximation. I refer to those historical ethnies who defined their ethnic boundary primarily (or even exclusively) in terms of religion. "Switching of ethnic identity," then, refers to the religious conversion. Two historical examples in which the entry into the core elite was relatively open to individuals willing to convert to the state religion were the Ottoman Empire and Muscovite Russia. More complicated situations, involving language barriers as well as multidimensional ethnic boundaries, are discussed in Section 6.5.

Let C be the proportion of population in the core ethnie, and $P = 1 - C$ be the proportion of population in the peripheral ethnie. The probability of ethnic switch from periphery to core is p. Then, the differential equation describing the dynamics of ethnic composition at the macro level is

$$\dot{C} = pP = p(1 - C). \tag{6.1}$$

We have already encountered this simple model of *asymptotic growth* in Section 2.1 [see equation (2.3)]. At low values of C, this variable grows approximately linearly, and eventually it approaches the equilibrium point $C^* = 1$ in an exponential manner (refer to Figure 2.1c).

When deriving equation (6.1) I assumed that only members of the periphery could switch ethnic identity. We can allow for an inverse process, in which members of the core ethnie switch identity ("going native," so to speak; for example, Old English in medieval Ireland; Kidd 1999:146). Suppose the probability of switching from the peripheral to the core identity is p_0, while the probability of the reverse switch is p_1. This modification leads to a very similar model of asymptotic growth: $\dot{C} = p_0 P - p_1 C = p_0 - (p_0 + p_1)C$. However, at equilibrium, the proportion in the core ethnie is not 1 but $C^* = p_0/(p_0 + p_1)$. This equilibrium, however, is approached in the same fashion as in the simpler model: initially linearly, then asymptotically.

The Autocatalytic Model

Although the noninteractive model has been used to investigate ethnic assimilation (e.g., the multiclass modifications of Hopkins 1973 and Cederman 1997), I believe it is deeply flawed. It is not a matter of it being overly simple, because the alternative I am about to discuss is equally simple (actually simpler, as it has one fewer parameter). The problem is that the noninteractive model assumes a sociologically implausible scenario. Societies are not composed of atomized individuals; instead, each individual is embedded within a social network (or multiple networks) of other individuals. What we know about the spread of rumors, innovations, and perhaps ethnicity suggests that these cultural elements spread by contact, from one individual to another along the social networks (Rogers 1995). Taking religious conversion, individuals simply do not convert to a new sect spontaneously, upon reading about it in the newspaper, for example. On the contrary, as sociologists of religion have demonstrated (Stark 1996; Stark and Bainbridge 1996), conversion, like contagion, travels along interpersonal links. "The basis for successful conversionist movements is growth through social networks, through a *structure of direct and intimate interpersonal attachments*" (Stark 1996, emphasis in the original).

How can we translate these assumptions at the micro level into a model describing dynamics of conversion at the macro level? The rigorous approach would require an explicitly spatial approach (where "space" may refer to social rather than physical space). We discuss such an approach in the next section. Here, however, I seek to capture the difference between a noninteractive and a network based assimilation (or conversion) processes with a simple model, so space has to be implicit in it. Let us, then, simply assume that the probability of conversion is proportional to the numbers already converted, and explore the consequences of this assumption.

To make things slightly more complicated, I will allow ethnic switching in both directions. Let the probability of an individual switching from the peripheral to the core identity (per unit of time) be $p_0 = r_0 C$, and the reverse probability $p_1 = r_1 P$ (the probability of switching into an ethnie is proportional to the fraction of population belonging to the ethnie; the proportionality constants r_0 and r_1 are *relative* rates of switching). The rate at which peripherals are switching to the core, then, is the product of the probability of switching multiplied by the proportion in the periphery. The rate of switching from the core is determined analogously. Thus, the rate of change of C is

$$\dot{C} = r_0 CP - r_1 PC = (r_0 - r_1)C(1 - C)$$

Defining $r = r_0 - r_1$ and substituting it in the equation above, we have

$$\dot{C} = rC(1 - C) \tag{6.2}$$

We see that this derivation led us to the logistic equation—another elementary model of growth discussed in Section 2.1. This model is even simpler than the full noninteractive model that had two rate parameters, p_0 and p_1. In this model, we need to know only one parameter, the difference between the two relative rates, r.

The dynamics of equation (6.2) differ from the noninteractive model in one important respect: when C is at low levels, it will grow at an accelerating rate. The reason for the accelerating pattern of growth is that the more people have converted or assimilated, the more probable it is that any particular individual will switch identity. Such a dynamic pattern is analogous to autocatalytic reaction in chemical kinetics, in which the presence of a compound increases the rate at which it is created. Accordingly, I will refer to equation (6.2) as the *autocatalytic* model.

Another way in which the noninteractive and autocatalytic models differ is that the equilibrium that C approaches in the autocatalytic model is 1 (assuming that $r > 0$), whereas in the noninteractive model the equilibrium can be substantially less than 1. This difference alone should make us suspect the noninteractive model. Why should core individuals continue switching to the peripheral identity when the core identity has reached overwhelming proportions? Yet that is precisely what the noninteractive model suggests. Clearly, core individuals switching to the peripheral identity should occur only in locations where $P \gg C$, as happened in the Anglo-Irish example mentioned above.

The Threshold Model

Making the probability of switching a function of proportion in the core ethnie was a step in the right direction. However, we assumed that the relationship between p and C was linear ($p = rC$), and it is a good idea to investigate what will happen if we relax this assumption. A particular class of nonlinear behaviors, threshold models of collective behavior (Granovetter 1978; Schelling 1978), has been extensively discussed in the sociological literature. Particularly important to the issue at hand is that it has also been applied to the problem of switching ethnic identity (Laitin 1998).

We can model threshold behavior by modifying the previously assumed linear relationship between p and C to a nonlinear one of the form $p = rC(C - C_0)$. The new parameter, C_0, is the threshold proportion. When $C > C_0$, the rate of switching to the core identity is positive, because the core ethnie has achieved the "critical mass." When $C < C_0$, the rate of switching is negative. That is, more individuals are switching from core to peripheral identity than vice versa (in other words, I interpret p as the difference between the probabilities of switching in either direction). The notions of critical mass and threshold behaviors are amply discussed by Schelling (1978) and Granovetter (1978), among others, so I do not discuss them further here, referring the reader to these authors instead.

Substituting the assumed form of p in the model, we have the following equation

$$\dot{C} = rC(C - C_0)(1 - C) \tag{6.3}$$

The threshold model belongs to the class of *metastable* dynamics (Section 2.1.2). It has three equilibria: two stable $C = 0$ and $C = 1$, and one unstable $C = C_0$. The outcome of the ethnic assimilation process is entirely dependent on the initial conditions. If C starts above C_0, then the trajectory eventually approaches 1. In other words, all the population of the empire acquires the core identity. Alternatively, if C starts below C_0, then the peripheral identity will win in the end, and all core ethnics lose their original identity. This is an interesting prediction of the threshold model, and it seems to fit the many historical cases when a small group of invaders conquered a much larger ethnically different population. Often the invaders would proceed to convert to the dominant religion of the conquered people and switch to speaking their language (examples are the Visigoths, Langobards, Bulgars, and Normans).

There is one feature of the threshold model that is problematic: its dynamics are determined by whether the *global* frequency is above or below the threshold, yet it is more plausible to assume that an individual probability of switching identity should be affected by the *local* composition of society. The autocatalytic model as an approximation of the social network process also suffers from this criticism, although, as we shall see below, it still appears to be not a bad approximation, even in an explicitly spatial setting (under certain conditions). Adding explicit space to the threshold model, on the other hand, may substantially change its predicted dynamics. This is the next issue that we need to investigate.

6.2.2 Spatially Explicit Models

As I have repeatedly stressed in this book, there are many advantages of developing mathematical models. One such advantage is that when we derive a specific
model for some issue, we may find that it is mathematically exactly the same as
some equations developed to model a completely different problem. This means
that we do not have to develop an analytic apparatus from scratch, but can profit
from what others did before. This is the case with ethnokinetics. The kind of
models that we formulated in the previous section have been extensively used
in modeling chemical kinetics, spread of rumors and innovations, dynamics of
epidemics, and so on. As I argued in the previous section, one key element that
we need to investigate theoretically is the addition of explicit space. Fortunately,
there is a very rich theory for the dynamics of both chemical and population
processes in space (reaction-diffusion theory and epidemiological models), and
we can use the insights from these mathematical theories for our purposes (for
a good review of the mathematical theory, see Murray 1993). In the following
I will mainly rely on results from the theory of epidemics in space, because
its mathematical formalism fits most closely the kinds of processes we need to
understand.

Social Space

When I say that we need to add "space" I do not necessarily mean physical
space. Rather, what we need is some notion of social space, in which distance
between individuals is measured by the frequency and intensity of their social
interactions. The social space has many dimensions, but sociologists often reduce
them to two principal classes: the vertical and horizontal (Sorokin 1927). The
vertical dimension refers to the position in the social hierarchy (stratification).
Thus, a peasant may have a lot of interactions with the village head, who in turn
interacts with the local noble, and so on to the polity ruler. Two people inhabiting
the same location may be very socially distant from each other (for example, a
prince and a pauper). The horizontal dimension arises as a result of patterning
in day-to-day activities such as working, raising children, or simply conversing
to neighbors (Black 1998). There is a strong spatial component present in the
horizontal dimension. Thus, a typical peasant will interact mostly with people in
the same village, to a certain extent with inhabitants of nearby villages, and very
little (if at all) with anybody in a different province.

Social space has some peculiar topological characteristics (Black 1998). First, it
is often anisotropic, because downward interaction may be stronger than upward
interaction. For example, the decision of a king to convert to Christianity has a
much stronger effect on the probability that a peasant will convert than vice versa.
Second, higher ranked persons tend to belong to wider-scale social networks. For
example, a noble of middle rank will likely have a closer connection to another
noble in a nearby province than two peasants separated by a similar geographic
distance. Finally, certain geographic features, such as mountains, tend to attenuate
social distance. Perhaps a better measure would be not the physical distance,

but distance measured in travel time. Horizontal anisotropy may also arise, for example, along rivers (it is much easier to move down river than against the current).

There is an important concept from epidemiology that can be useful in conceptualizing spatial models of linguistic assimilation and religious conversion. I refer to the *contact distribution*, which in epidemiology is defined as the probability of disease passing from one individual to another as a function of distance separating them. We can reinterpret the contact distribution as the intensity of social interaction between two people located at different points in the social space. In the context of religious conversion, the analogy is complete because we can interpret the contact distribution as the probability of religious conversion spreading from one individual to another. This formulation allows one, in principle, to model a variety of complicating effects, including heterogeneous space (e.g., mountains and other barriers), and anisotropy (such as larger-scale contact distributions characterizing higher-ranked persons). I will not pursue these complications here, because a model including all these realistic features would have to be solved by simulation on the computer. Instead, I will focus on how space can modify the frequency-dependent aspects of ethnokinetic processes. This topic is where we can profit from the analytical results made available by the epidemiological theory. I consider, first, the spatial extension of the autocatalytic model and, second, the threshold model (the noninteractive model is not affected by space, because each individual changes identity spontaneously and independently of what others do). In the following account I provide no mathematical equations, because the interested reader can find them in the appropriate special literature. An introduction to the ecological aspects of spatial contact processes and models of spread can be found in my book on quantitative analysis of movement (Turchin 1998:70–72, 329–348). More technical accounts are in Murray (1993) and Mollison (1995). I do not need to delve into the mathematical results because all I do is take the already developed theory and reinterpret it in terms of social contacts and social influence on identity switching.

The Autocatalytic Model in Space

To make the autocatalytic model spatially explicit, first we redefine the frequency of individuals with the core identity, $C(t)$, into a spatially varying variable, $C(x, y, z, t)$. Here x and y may stand for physical space coordinates and z for position in the social hierarchy; t is time as usual. As an illustration, $C(x, y, z, t)$ might be the proportion of Christians among small merchants in a particular town at a particular point of time. Second, we define the contact distribution: $V(s)$ is the intensity of social contacts between two individuals separated by social distance s. Note that in this model I assume that the contact distribution does not vary with space, rank, or time. As stated above, however, such modifications can be made, and the resulting model investigated numerically. Third, I assume that the probability of an individual switching identity is a function of the identities of other individuals in the social vicinity, weighted by their social distance to the focal individual. To illustrate how the model works, suppose the contact distribution is rectangular in shape, as in Figure 6.1a. This means that there is a certain

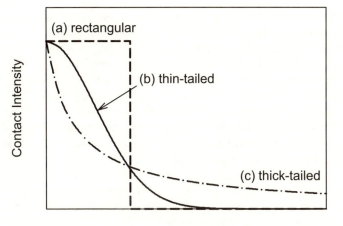

Social Distance

Figure 6.1 Different shapes of the contact distribution: (a) rectangular, (b) "thin-tailed," and (c) "thick-tailed."

circle of relatives and friends with which the focal individual interacts socially, and the intensity of interaction is the same with each individual in the circle. Outside the circle, however, the intensity of interaction is zero. Then, the probability of converting will simply be proportional to the fraction of individuals within the circle who are already converts.

The rectangular contact distribution is not a realistic shape for human social interactions, because some humans are likely to have very distant acquaintances, even though their interactions with them may not be very intense. Thus, the contact distribution should not end abruptly, but there must be some "tail" extending quite far for a few individuals (for example, long-distance merchants). The mathematical theory of spatial contact processes distinguishes two important cases: the "thin-tailed" case when the tail of the contact distribution declines exponentially (or faster) with social distance, and the "thick-tailed" case when the tail declines more slowly than exponentially (Figure 6.1). As we shall see below, these two classes of tails imply very different spatial dynamics.

When the contact distribution has a tail, it means that the focal individual makes a decision about conversion not only based on what others in the immediate social vicinity do, but also taking into account what the society at large does. However, the influence of socially distant individuals is much less than the influence of the close circle of friends and relatives. The diminution of influence with increasing social distance is measured with how fast the contact distribution drops off to zero.

The case of thin-tailed contact distributions is mathematically well understood. If the probability of switching identity is directly proportional to the weighted average of identities held by others (the weights are given by the contact distribution), then this spatial contact process is well approximated by a reaction-diffusion model in which the local source/sink term is logistic, and spatial redistribution is simple diffusion. This model has been thoroughly investigated, starting with the seminal work of Fisher (1937) and Kolmogoroff et al. (1937) on the spatial spread of advantageous genes. A well-known application in social sciences is the model of spread of neolithic farmers in Europe (Ammerman and Cavalli-Sforza 1973). The dynamics of the model are as follows. Suppose we start with initially a small number of converts to the new religion (such as a group of disciples forming around a prophet or messiah). Locally, the conversion process will follow the S-shaped logistic curve, initially growing exponentially and then saturating when all local people are converted to the new religion. The spatial spread will also initially accelerate, but rather rapidly a well-defined front of advance is established, and this front expands with time at a constant velocity. As a result, the total *area* where the majority of people are converted expands linearly in time. Thus, after an initial acceleration the number of converts will grow linearly with time until the whole available space is taken over.

This orderly front advance observed for thin-tailed contact distributions is in great contrast with what happens if the contact distribution has a thick tail. An initially small group of converts will grow locally according to the logistic curve, as in the previous case. However, as the number of converts builds up, it becomes increasingly more likely that one of them will have a long-distance acquaintance who will be converted. The most likely mechanism for a proselytizing religion is that the initial religious commune would send missionaries out. Such long-distance jumps of the conversion process will prevent formation of an orderly front. Instead, we will observe a number of secondary foci of spread forming around the original focus, then tertiary foci will appear as a result of missionaries sent from the secondary foci, and so on. The whole spatial process will spread in an accelerating fashion, and the global number of converts will exhibit an S-shaped growth pattern. The more thick tailed the contact distribution, the more closely the global spread process will approximate the logistic.

Threshold Model in Space

The spatial threshold model behaves in a very different manner from the autocatalytic model (for mathematical details, see Lewis and Kareiva 1993). First, and rather obviously, the initial local proportion of converts must exceed the threshold C_0, otherwise the new cult will die out. Second, and less obviously, the size of the area initially occupied by the cult (the "beachhead") must exceed a certain threshold. Otherwise, the "diffusive losses" across the boundary will overwhelm the conversion rate within the area occupied by the religion, and it will fail. The third and most important difference is that the threshold model can exhibit only linearly advancing fronts, no matter what the shape of the contact distribution. This feature arises because any converts that get out too far in advance of the main front suffer from the threshold effect: they are locally swamped by nonbelievers.

The other interesting prediction made by the theory is that in well-connected space coexistence of two identities is impossible. Suppose a spatial front between two identities was somehow established. Then it will always advance in one direction or another. In the specific form of the threshold model proposed above

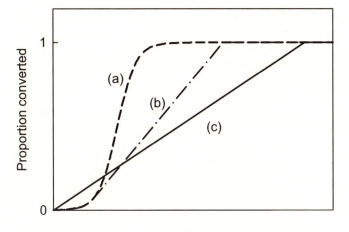

Time

Figure 6.2 Schematic patterns of spread predicted by spatial contact models: (a) autocatalytic process and thick-tailed contact distribution, (b) autocatalytic process and thin-tailed contact distribution, and (c) threshold process.

[equation (6.3)], the direction of advance depends on whether $C_0 > 0.5$ or not. If yes, then the core identity will lose; otherwise, it wins (Lewis and Kareiva 1993). However, if social intercourse across the boundary is substantially less than on each side, then stable coexistence is possible (e.g., Levin 1976).

Summary: The Three Types of Growth in Spatial Contact Models

To summarize, the spatial models reviewed in this section predict three distinct patterns of conversion or assimilation process. These patterns are schematically illustrated in Figure 6.2a. The fastest spread occurs in the autocatalytic model with thick-tailed contact distributions. In this case, the process of conversion begins to grow at an accelerating rate in the locality of the initial group of converts. Before this process can reach the phase where it is locally saturated (as a result of locally converting most of the population), the conversion process jumps to several other locations, which fuel further growth, and also generate further foci of spread. As a result, the conversion dynamics are explosive. The thicker is the tail of the contact distribution, the faster all points in the total area we model are reached. If the tails are essentially flat on the scale of the whole area, then the spatial process will be indistinguishable from the nonspatial logistic dynamics.

By contrast, if the tail of the contact distribution attenuates rapidly (the thin-tail case), then we should first observe a "latent period" during which no spread occurs (this is the time when local numbers of converts are building up), followed by an accelerating growth period. Eventually, a spatial front between the converted and unconverted areas is established. This front advances at a constant velocity, which results in a linear spread until the whole area is eventually converted [curve (b) in Figure 6.2].

Finally, if the conversion process is characterized by a threshold, then the shape of the contact distribution does not matter. If the conversion process is viable (which requires a sufficient initial mass of converts, not too high a conversion threshold C_0, and not too great losses of converts by diffusion), then a spatial front between the converted and unconverted areas becomes rapidly established. The front then advances linearly, but more slowly than in the autocatalytic case. The reason for the slower rate of spread is because, in order for the front to advance, the numbers of converts at the boundary must build up past the threshold C_0. In the autocatalytic case, by contrast, the conversion process can spread even when locally at low density. Thus, in the threshold case, the front is "pushed" by high numbers of converts behind it. In the autocatalytic case, the front is "pulled" by the interactions of low numbers of converts with the unconverted populations ahead of it.

6.3 EMPIRICAL TESTS

The three models of Section 6.2.1 provide a reasonable starting point for empirical tests of the ethnokinetics theory. I will focus on testing the nonspatial models because currently I do not have access to any spatial data sets on conversion or assimilation that could allow testing of spatial models. It is true that spatial models predict somewhat different global patterns of the temporal course of assimilation (as depicted in Figure 6.2), and theoretically one could capitalize on that to devise an empirical test. Several practical problems, however, prevent a straightforward implementation of this idea. First, the patterns depicted in Figure 6.2 are highly stylized. To obtain more precise quantitative predictions it would be necessary to numerically solve spatially explicit models based on various assumptions about the process of identity switching and the shape of the contact distribution. Second, all three trajectories in Figure 6.2 predict roughly S-shaped dynamics. Given realistic data, affected by various degrees of process and observation noise, it will be difficult to distinguish between the theoretical alternatives in practice. In other words, I argue that approaches attempting to distinguish between spatial models on the basis of data on global patterns of ethnic change will be characterized by low statistical power. We need explicitly spatial data to test explicitly spatial models.

In contrast to spatial models, global curves of ethnic change should provide us with an excellent opportunity to design an empirical test for nonspatial models (the noninteractive, the autocatalytic, and the threshold processes). Nevertheless, one must choose the response variable carefully in order to maximize the statistical power of the test. A *response* or dependent variable in statistics is something that is predicted on the basis of *predictor* or independent variables (Box and Draper 1987). We distinguish between alternative models by determining how well they predict the response variable. The model that predicts the response variable the best is the one that is best supported by the data. The obvious, but not necessarily optimal, choice of a response variable for contrasting the predictive abilities of the three models would be the trajectory $C(t)$, the proportion in the core at time t. Consider, for example, the trajectories predicted by the noninteractive and the autocatalytic models (see Figures 2.1c and d). Given non-plentiful data and large amounts of noise (which is the realistic assumption in historical applications), it will often be difficult to determine whether the curve has an initially accelerating phase or not. By contrast, if we look at the predictions that different models make about the rate of change of C, the contrast between the models is very stark (Figure 6.3). The noninteractive model predicts the linear relationship between $\dot{C}$ and C (Figure 6.3a), while the autocatalytic model predicts a humped curve (Figure 6.3c). A simple contrast between the slopes of the relationships for $C < 0.5$ (negative versus positive) is sufficient to determine which model is closer to reality. The prediction of the threshold model is also very striking: a *negative* rate of change for $C < C_0$ (Figure 6.3e). Another useful contrast between the autocatalytic and threshold models is in their predictions for *relative* rates of change, $\dot{C}/C$ (Figure 6.3d versus f; examining the relative rate of change for the noninteractive model, panel b, is not very instructive, but is included for completeness).

The take-home message here is that, while we should certainly examine empirical time trajectories and compare them to trajectories predicted by models, in order to more fully utilize the data we should also plot them (and fit models to them) in the way depicted in Figure 6.3. Doing so allows us a closer approach to the mechanisms that may underlie the observed trajectories, because we examine the structure of the dynamical process at the level of the differential equation (by plotting the observed rate of change versus the state variable), rather than at the more phenomenological level of the time solution of the equation.

I now apply these ideas to three data sets, dealing with conversion to Islam, Christianity, and Mormonism. Our goal is to determine which of the three alternative models provides the closest match to the empirical patterns.

6.3.1 Conversion to Islam

The Data

The first case study is based on the remarkable database developed by Richard Bulliet. One of the characteristic cultural products of Islamic society has been the literary genre of the biographical dictionary (Bulliet 1979:9). The numerous biographical compilations, which contain many hundreds of individual entries, provide unique sources of quantifiable data for medieval Islamic societies. Bulliet analyzed the almost six thousand biographies contained in Iranian biographical dictionaries and discovered a very interesting pattern. There is an almost complete absence of Persian names among the subjects of biographies, who belonged to the religiously eminent upper class, and were characterized by a universal custom of giving their sons Arabic names. Yet Persian names appear in the genealogies of the biographical subjects. Over two-thirds of genealogical sequences are initiated by a Persian name, followed by a shift to exclusively Arabic ones (Bulliet 1979:18). Bulliet hypothesized that the Persian name that initiates the sequence is that of the first family member to become a Muslim (this proposal can be confirmed in certain cases by independent information). Thus, it is likely that the

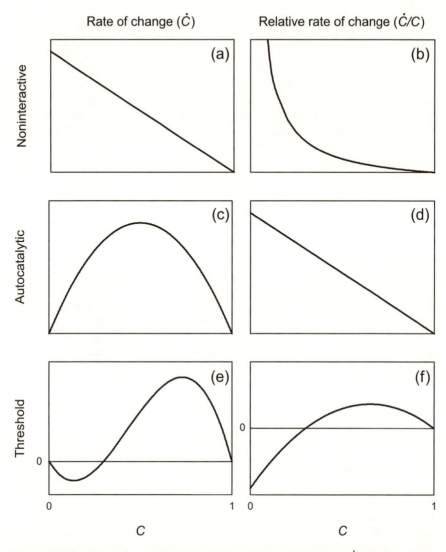

Figure 6.3 Predicted relationships between C and the rates of change $\dot{C}$ (panels a, c, and e) and the relative rates of change $\dot{C}/C$ (panels b, d, and f) for the noninteractive model (panels a and b), the autocatalytic model (panels c and d), and the threshold model (panels e and f).

subgroup of genealogies that begin with a Persian name can provide reliable data on the approximate date of conversion of specific Iranian families. There were 469 genealogies that fell into this subgroup. Bulliet divided the Muslim calendar into 25 year periods, and calculated the expected proportion of conversions falling within each period (see Bulliet 1979: Chapter 3 for further details).

Large numbers of genealogies are also available for Iraq, Syria, Egypt, and Spain. It would be very useful to perform the same analysis for these areas, as a way to check on the results from Iran. Unfortunately, the occurrence of non-Arabic names in Iraq, Syria, and Egypt is very rare. All these areas became Arabic speaking in time, and Iraq and Syria were inhabited by speakers of languages related to Arabic even prior to Islamic conquest. In Spain, fortunately, the situation is different (Bulliet 1979: Chapter 10). Bulliet identified 154 Spanish genealogies beginning with non-Arabic names from five biographical dictionaries. Performing the analysis along the lines of the Iranian genealogical database, he calculated the proportion of families converting during each 50-year period (a longer period has to be used since there are fewer data points than in the Iranian case). We can use these data as an independent check on the Iranian data, because Muslim Spain was a region isolated both geographically and in time (it was conquered some seventy years after Iran).

The Analysis

Plotting the proportion of Iranian families converting to Islam during each 25-year period against the midpoint of the period, we obtain the estimated curve of conversion to Islam in Iran (Figure 6.4a). Visual inspection of the data strongly suggests a logistic-like process. This impression is confirmed by fitting the temporal solution of the logistic:

$$C(t) = \frac{1}{1 + [(1 - \gamma)/\gamma] \exp[-rt]}$$

where the fitting parameters $\gamma = C(0)$ is the initial proportion of converts at time $t = 0$ and r is the relative rate of conversion [the same parameter as in equation (6.2)]. This two-parameter curve explains a remarkable 99.98% of the variation in the response variable, $C(t)$. This is an excellent fit, even by the standards of the physical sciences. By contrast, the noninteractive model explains only 79.2% of the variance (note that taken by itself this would be a very respectable result, but in comparisons of alternative models with data as the arbiter, it is the relative fit that matters; that is, which model performs better and by how much).

Almost identical results are obtained in the analysis of the Spanish data (Figure 6.4b). The logistic curve explains 99.7% of the variance. Interestingly, the fitted value of the parameter r is substantially lower than that for Iran (r is 2.8 century^{-1} for Iran, but only 1.5 century^{-1} for Spain). Again, the noninteractive model fits the data substantially worse (76.6% of the variance explained).

Further evidence in favor of the autocatalytic model (as compared to the two alternatives) comes from examining $\dot{C} - C$ phase plots (Figure 6.5a). The positive slope of the curves in the region of $C < 0.5$ is obvious and needs no statistical test. Furthermore, there is no evidence for negative rates of change, which would be predicted by the threshold model. Thus, of the three simple alternatives considered in Section 6.2.1, the autocatalytic model provides by far the best description of empirical patterns. On the other hand, plotting the data in the phase space has revealed some interesting features of the conversion process that were not apparent in the trajectory plot. In particular, the curves appear asymmetric (skewed to the right), while the logistic model, of course, predicts a completely symmetric

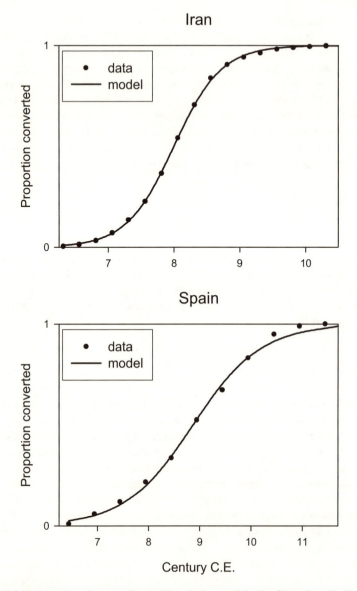

Figure 6.4 Trajectories of conversion to Islam in Iran and Spain. (Data from Bulliet 1979: Table 2 and Graph 20)

parabola. To delve further into this issue, let us look at the relationship between relative rates of change and proportion converted indicated by the data (Figure 6.6a). We see that, while quantitatively there is quite a large difference between relative conversion rates (the Iranian process went almost twice as fast), both curves have qualitatively same nonlinearities. The observation that the nonlinearity is almost identical in both cases suggests that this is not simply a sampling

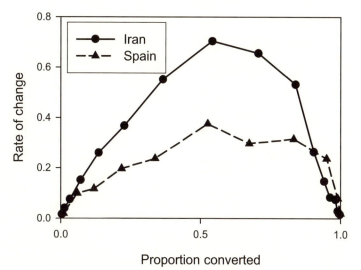

Figure 6.5 Iran and Spain data plotted on a $\dot{C} - C$ phase plot. Units of the rate of change $\dot{C}$ are in proportion converted per century.

issue (of course, these are only two replicates). On the other hand, it is still emi-
nently possible that the observed nonlinearities are some artifact of the procedure
used by Bulliet to extract conversion dates from the genealogies. Let us speculate
what possible mechanisms may underlie the nonlinearity if it is real (this is a way
of generating hypotheses for future research). First, the nonlinearity is certainly
not suggestive of any threshold effect, because that would introduce a nonlinearity
of opposite curvature (see Figure 6.3f). Furthermore, spatial models also all predict some acceleration during the initial stages of the conversion process, which
again does not help to explain the observed patters. In fact, the concave shape
of the function at low C has some resemblance to the noninteractive process
(see Figure 6.3b). This observation raises the following possibility: the process
is noninteractive during the very early stages, and then becomes autocatalytic.
For example, initially the proportion of converts in the population increases as
a result of immigration. As the number of converts builds up, the autocatalytic
part of the process rapidly swamps the increase due to immigration. I investigated this scenario with an explicit model, $\dot{C} = (p + rC)(1 - C)$, and found that
as long as $p \ll r$, that is the immigration rate is small, the model predicts precisely the shape observed in the data. An example of the pattern predicted by the
immigration-autocatalytic growth model is given in Figure 6.6b.

To summarize, the analysis of the Bulliet data indicates that the autocatalytic
model fits the empirical patterns overwhelmingly better than the two alternatives, the noninteractive and threshold models. In fact, the autocatalytic model
achieves an unheard-of precision (at least in nonphysical sciences) of 99.98%.
However, this excellent fit is partly due to the specific viewpoint chosen, that
is, fitting temporal trajectories. A more detailed investigation of the relationship
between the state variable (C) and its rate of change as well as its relative rate

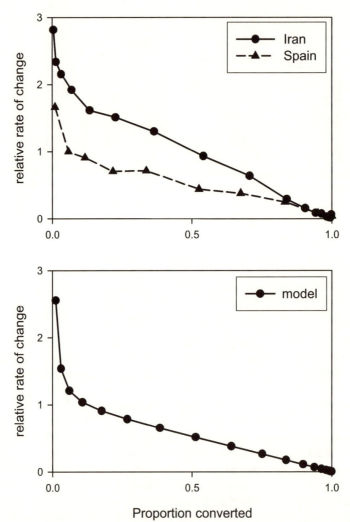

Figure 6.6 (a) Iran and Spain data plotted on a $\dot{C}/C - C$ phase plot. Units of the rate of change $\dot{C}$ are century^{-1}. (b) Relationship between the relative rate of change and proportion converted predicted by the immigration-autocatalytic model.

of change reveals some discrepancies between the predictions of the autocatalytic model and the data. We also found that a somewhat more complex alternative to the simple autocatalytic model, the immigration-autocatalytic process, provides a better empirical fit. It is encouraging that the best-fitting model, even though it was suggested by a post hoc pattern in the data, appears to correspond well with our understanding of what historically happened in Spain after Islamic conquest, when there was indeed a substantial immigration by Muslim Arabs and Berbers. However, we should note that only two replicates are currently available (which is the minimum amount to guard against sampling error). Furthermore, there is the possibility that the observed nonlinearity is a result of some (unknown) bias in the procedure used by Bulliet to estimate conversion dates. Finally, the discrepancy is rather minor, and at best suggests a second-order improvement of the basic autocatalytic model. The simple fact of the matter is that the basic autocatalytic model fits the data awfully well.

6.3.2 The Rise of Christianity

The second case study is more qualitative, simply because we do not have as good data sets documenting the dynamics of conversion to Christianity, compared to the ones developed by Bulliet for conversion to Islam. The material in this section is based on Rodney Stark's *The Rise of Christianity* (1996).

When discussing the rise of Christianity, historians are impressed by how few Christians there were during the first two centuries C.E., and how suddenly their numbers grew—exploded—during the second half of the third century. Most historians of early Christianity concluded that some extraordinary process of mass conversions must have taken place to explain this astonishing expansion (see Stark 1996:14 for quotes). Stark argues forcefully that this argument is based on a misappreciation of the nature of the autocatalytic process. The striking fact about such autocatalytic processes as the exponential or the logistic is that they appear to go through discontinuous stages of growth, while the basic driving mechanism does not change. The driving mechanism is the relative conversion rate (the number of new members per current member that convert in a unit of time). While the relative rate stays constant, the absolute rate (the product of the relative rate and the proportion already converted) increases with time, thus generating an illusion of the process going through qualitatively different stages.

Stark illustrates this phenomenon with an estimated growth curve of Christians up to the middle of the fourth century. He assumes that in 40 C.E. there were about a thousand Christians and that they grew exponentially at the relative rate of 40% per decade. (Stark's use of the exponential model is not really at variance with our model of logistic growth, because the two processes generate essentially the same quantitative predictions for the early stages of growth, and begin to diverge only after the proportion converted exceeds 10–20%.) One thousand people corresponded to 0.0017% of the population of the Roman Empire. By 200 C.E., Stark's projection predicts that there was still less than 1% of the Roman population who converted to Christianity (0.36%, to be precise). Then, the projected growth "suddenly" takes off: 1.9% in 250 C.E., 10.5% in 300 C.E., and 56.5% in 350 C.E. (Stark 1996: Table 1.1). In other words, the startling expansion of Christianity during the period of 250–350 C.E., as compared to an apparent lack of growth during 50–250 C.E. (the "latent period" in epidemiological terms), could have happened without any change in the underlying mechanism of conversion. As long as the early Christians managed to keep their social networks open, they would continue to connect to and convert new members at the same relative rate of change, and the end result would be an eventual explosion of the size of the Christian community.

Stark derived the parameters for the projected conversion curve (the initial number at 40 C.E. and the relative rate of growth) by integrating over rather

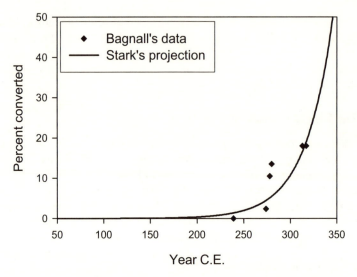

Figure 6.7 Comparison between Stark's projection on the growth of early Christianity in the Roman Empire and Bagnall's data on the proportion of Christians in Egypt.

heterogeneous quantitative and qualitative information from various sources (see Stark 1996:4–12). Several years after he made these estimates, a colleague of Stark attracted his attention to the reconstruction by Roger Bagnall of the growth of Christianity in Egypt. Bagnall examined Egyptian papyri to identify the proportion of persons with identifiably Christian names in various years (Stark 1996: 12–13). Comparing Stark's projected curve to these independent data constitutes a strong test of the theory (in fact, this is a true experimental test, since Stark was unaware of Bagnall's data when he constructed his prediction). Figure 6.7 illustrates the results of this test. The match is quite good, and the coefficient of prediction is a very respectable $R^2_{\text{pred}} = 0.74$. Thus, this test provides a strong quantitative confirmation of the theory.

6.3.3 The Growth of the Mormon Church

The last case study concerns the growth of a modern religion, the Mormons. The data are the total number of members in the Church of the Latter Day Saints from 1840 to 1980, and are tabulated by Stark (1984). In order to fit the logistic model to these data I need to convert them to proportions. Because the Mormon church is a world religion, with branches on all inhabited continents, I expressed the data as the proportion of the world population converted. This procedure probably overestimates the population of potential converts, because the targets of Mormon conversion are those who are not strongly committed to some other religion. However, this caveat does not affect the analysis results, because Mormons are very far from the conversion midpoint, no matter how we define the population at "risk of conversion," and thus the autocatalytic model predicts that they should be growing in an essentially exponential fashion.

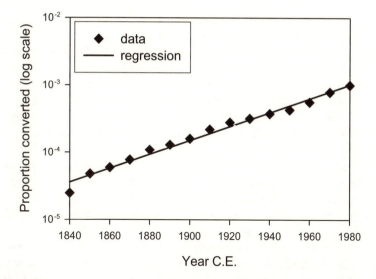

Figure 6.8 Proportion of the world population converted to the Mormon church, 1840–1980. The data are plotted on a logarithmic scale to emphasize the essentially exponential nature of the growth, which characterizes the autocatalytic dynamics at low C.

Fitting the logistic curve to these data indicated that the model explains 98.9% of the variance. Thus, again we obtain a remarkable fit between the theoretical prediction and the observed trajectory (Figure 6.8).

6.4 CONCLUSION: DATA SUPPORT THE AUTOCATALYTIC MODEL

The results of empirical tests are summarized in Table 6.1. The most striking feature of these results is just how well the autocatalytic model fits the data (or predicts, as in the case of Christianity), especially given how simple the model is. It only has two fitted parameters (the initial condition, $C(0)$, and the relative conversion rate, r). The important implication is that not everything in history is

Table 6.1 Summary of empirical tests: the estimated relative conversion rate, $\hat{r}$, and the proportion of variance in the data explained by the autocatalytic model, R^2 (except in the case of Christianity, where R^2 is the proportion *predicted*). The units of r are yr^{-1}.

Case study	$\hat{r}$	R^2
Islam (Iran)	0.028	0.9998
Islam (Spain)	0.015	0.997
Christianity	0.034	0.74
Mormon	0.023	0.989

messy or impossible to predict. Furthermore, a clean test of alternative models is possible. Recollect that we started with three models that were based on different assumptions of how people are converted to a new religion: the noninteractive, the autocatalytic, and the threshold processes. The quantitative tests of all four data sets yield a unanimous result: the autocatalytic model fits the data far better than the two alternatives. This is a heartening conclusion, because according to the current sociological thinking, conversion travels through interpersonal networks (Stark 1996), the mechanism on which the autocatalytic model is based. In other words, a purely data-driven analysis agrees with the theoretical postulates.

If we start dissecting some of the better measured data (e.g., the two cases of conversion to Islam), then we find some systematic deviations between model predictions and data. But this caveat in no way diminishes the accomplishment of the autocatalytic model: it does much better *relative* to alternatives, and progress in science is achieved by successive improvement of theories, by discarding poorly performing alternatives in favor of those that do better. (Actually, in this case, the autocatalytic model does extremely well even in absolute terms, but that is beside the point.) Furthermore, the observed systematic deviations suggest an improved model—initial immigration followed by autocatalytic conversion process—which makes a lot of sense in light of what we know about the history of early Islamic Iran and Spain.

The empirical finding that the autocatalytic process describes the observed conversion dynamics best has important implications for the historical dynamics research program. Logistic growth (unlike, for example, asymptotic growth) has a certain sensitivity to initial conditions built in it. Consider, for example, the growth of Christianity. Let us quantify the temporal scale of conversion by time needed to reach the inflection point on the logistic curve (when 50% of population is converted). Starting with 1000 Christians in 40 C.E. and using Stark's estimate $\hat{r} = 0.034$, the midpoint is reached in 368 C.E. (this is a bit later than Stark's calculation, because Stark used the pure exponential method, while I am employing the logistic model). To contrast the logistic growth with the asymptotic growth, let us assume that the parameter $p = 0.0021$, because with this parameter an asymptotic process starting with 1000 converts in 40 C.E. also hits the midpoint by 368 C.E. The trajectory predicted by the asymptotic model is very insensitive to the initial conditions, how many Christians there were in 40 C.E. (Table 6.2). Whether there are 10 or 100,000 Christians in 40 C.E., the midpoint is still achieved in 368 or 367 C.E. By contrast, every tenfold change in the initial condition changes the logistically predicted midpoint by 69 years (Table 6.2).

Sensitivity to initial conditions makes prediction problematic, especially when initial conditions are hard to measure precisely. In the Christianity case, Stark's estimate of 1000 converts at 40 C.E. could easily be revised by an order of magnitude up or down. Furthermore, the tendency of a nonlinear dynamical system to amplify small variations in initial conditions may cause it to behave chaotically. It is known that, for example, resource-consumer models in which resource grows asymptotically are much more stable than the analogous models in which the resource grows logistically (Turchin 2003). I have already commented on

Table 6.2 Predictions of logistic versus noninteractive models on when 50% of population is converted, depending on the initial condition.

$C(0)$	Noninteractive	Logistic
10	368 C.E.	506 C.E.
100	368 C.E.	437 C.E.
1000	368 C.E.	368 C.E.
10,000	368 C.E.	299 C.E.
100,000	367 C.E.	230 C.E.

the role of logistic growth in the chaotic dynamics of the spatial frontier model (Section 4.2.1).

Finally, in empirical tests I focused on religious conversion, because that is where I could find data. However, religion is just one source of markers for symbolic boundaries between ethnies. The nature of the demarcation markers affects the ease with which they can be crossed. Crossing some boundaries is easy (for example, acquiring appropriate dress), while others are much more difficult or even impossible to cross. For example, if race is one of the defining ethnic characteristics, as in modern Japan, then a European has no chance of being accepted. Language-based boundaries are also difficult for individuals to cross, since the great majority of people, once past puberty, are unable to learn a different language well enough to pass as a native speaker. Furthermore, linguistic assimilation usually does not happen directly from one language to another, but indirectly through a distinct class of bilingual speakers. Thus, ethnic assimilation that involves crossing a linguistic boundary could be even slower than religious conversion. Note that even religious conversion is a surprisingly slow process: in the empirical case studies, reaching the half point of conversion typically required 2–3 centuries.

In the models I considered there were only two classes of individuals: assimilated and not assimilated. Creating extra classes is one way to make models more realistic. For example, linguistic assimilation should probably be modeled by explicitly adding a third variable, the proportion of individuals in the polity who are bilingual speakers. Furthermore, creating multiple classes may be a reasonable approach to modeling the situation when an ethnic boundary involves multiple symbolic dimensions. For example, if assimilation requires both converting to the official religion and learning the language of the core ethnie, we might set up four classes, reflecting all possible combinations of the two religions and two languages. More classes, in principle, could be added to reflect finer divisions, but eventually the model will become so complex as to be unmanageable. An alternative approach is to postulate that there are many continuous dimensions along which two ethnies may differ. Thus, each ethnie is a point in this multidimensional space, or even a cloud of points, if we wish to explicitly model intraethnic variability in individual characteristics. The critical variable, then, becomes the distance separating two ethnies in this multidimensional space. A somewhat similar approach has been used by the creators of the Sugarscape model (Epstein and Axtell 1996), although they modeled cultural traits discretely, as sequences of 1s ("trait present") and 0s ("trait absent").

I discuss these alternative modeling strategies to show that we are not limited to the simple approaches discussed in this chapter. If we find the approach too restrictive, we can use one of the alternatives, although at the expense of complicating the ensuing model.

6.5 SUMMARY

- When a growing empire adds territory inhabited by people who are ethnically different from its core ethnie, it is expected that the initial loyalty of the incorporated ethnie toward the empire will not be high. The subsequent development of the geopolitical power of the empire will depend very much on whether, and if yes how fast, the newly incorporated population (and/or its elites) assimilates to the core ethnie.

- In this chapter I considered three basic sets of assumptions about how people switch their ethnic identity (a process that may involve linguistic assimilation, religious conversion, etc.).

- The noninteractive model posits that each nonassimilated individual has a constant probability of switching ethnic identity (per unit of time). Such an assimilation process results in asymptotic dynamics.

- The autocatalytic model assumes that assimilation occurs as a result of direct interpersonal attachments. The dynamics predicted by the autocatalytic model are the S-shaped logistic curve.

- The threshold model postulates an even more nonlinear mode of conversion: The rate of assimilation is positive if the proportion already assimilated is over a certain threshold. Otherwise, the assimilation rate is negative, leading to the inverse process in which core individuals assimilate to the peripheral identity. The dynamics of the threshold model are metastable.

- Next, I consider spatial extensions of all three models. The noninteractive model is not affected by adding space.

- The spatial autocatalytic model behaves globally in a logistic fashion if the social contact distribution is characterized by a thick tail. What this means in practice is that the assimilation process will not run out of potential subjects, if the already assimilated individuals manage to keep their social networks open, and thus continue reaching out and entering into new and distant social networks. If the contact distribution has a thin tail, then after an initial period of accelerated growth, expansion settles to a linear increase with time. Finally, if there are segments of population poorly connected to the rest, they may remain as unassimilated islands in perpetuity.

- The spatial threshold model suggests that an assimilation process is difficult to get started. A critical mass of assimilated population has to be established in some locality, before the assimilation can start spreading. The spread, if successful, is linear. Gaps in social contacts can lead to a stable coexistence of two or more ethnic identities (this outcome is even easier to achieve than in the autocatalytic model).

- To determine which of the three simple alternative models describes the historical dynamics of identity switching, I investigated several data sets on religious conversion. I contrasted predictions only from nonspatial models, since I lack spatial data. The data concerned conversion to Islam in Iran and Spain, the rise of Christianity in the Roman Empire, and the growth of the Mormon church.

- In all case studies, by far the best model turned out to be the autocatalytic process. The initial acceleration period, predicted by the autocatalytic model, was obvious in all case studies. The autocatalytic model generated predictions of remarkable accuracy (greater than 99% of the variance explained in three out of four cases). The time scale of the conversion process was quite long: 2–3 centuries from the beginning to the midpoint (when half of the population is converted) in the Islam and Christianity cases (the Mormon church is currently quite far from the midpoint).

- More detailed analysis of the two Islamic cases revealed some systematic discrepancies between the predictions of the autocatalytic model and the data patterns. A modification of the autocatalytic model that allowed for immigration of the Muslim populations at a low rate matched this empirical pattern, suggesting this model as a viable contender in future empirical tests.

- An important general implication from this chapter is the demonstration that the formal approach advocated in the book (translating alternative hypotheses into mathematical models, and using data to distinguish between alternative models) can work in realistic historical applications. Furthermore, simple models can yield strikingly accurate results when applied to realistic historical data sets.

Chapter Seven

The Demographic-Structural Theory

7.1 POPULATION DYNAMICS AND STATE BREAKDOWN

Unless prematurely extinguished by an overwhelming external force, empires typically progress through three stages: (1) polity formation and ethnogenesis of the core ethnie, accompanied by initial expansion within an ethnically similar substrate, (2) expansion to peak size, in the process acquiring a multiethnic character, and (3) stagnation, decline, and collapse (perhaps followed by a revival, and another imperial cycle). Mathematical models for the first two phases were advanced in Chapters 4 and 6. In this chapter I aim to investigate the causes of collapse.

A useful starting point is again provided by Ibn Khaldun, who postulated two major causes of state decline: (1) ideological (loss of asabiya) and (2) economic (including demographic and fiscal mechanisms) (Ibn Khaldun 1958:II:118–119). We have already discussed the first mechanism in Chapter 4, so let us concentrate on the second one.

Ibn Khaldun (1958:II:122–123, 135–137) notes that recently established states are moderate in their expenditures and just in their administration. As a result, taxation is light, and little coercion of subjects is needed. Such benevolent rule creates conditions under which people will flourish, and "procreation will be vigorous." General prosperity causes both rulers and people to become accustomed to increased spending ("luxury" in Ibn Khaldun's words). The army and the bureaucracy demand and receive higher pay. Although population numbers build up gradually, eventually (after several generations) the society reaches the limits of its growth. However, habits of luxury continue to increase, and must be paid for, so the state attempts to increase its revenues through heavy taxation, or outright seizure of its subjects' property. Such fiscal policy inevitably leads to the ruin of the economy, and then to famines, pestilence, political unrest, and rebellion.

Such is the argument of Ibn Khaldun in a nutshell. Ibn Khaldun discusses many specific sociological and ecological mechanisms underlying each of the postulated links in his argument (for example, he explicitly connects the spread of epidemics to population density, although the microbial origin of diseases was not known in his days). I refer the reader to Ibn Khaldun's book for further details (as well as innumerable historical accounts of various specific instances of civilization collapse that invoke some variant of this argument).

The hypothesis that excessive population growth has negative effects on social dynamics has been vigorously debated for the last two centuries, ever since the work of Malthus (1798). I cannot review this enormous literature here, but note that theories postulating population growth as a *direct* cause of societal collapse do not appear to be empirically supported. Of much more current interest is the idea that population growth causes social crisis *indirectly*, by affecting social institutions, which in turn affect social stability (Goldstone 1991b). Goldstone refers to his theory of state breakdown as demographic-structural: *demographic* because the underlying driving force is population growth; *structural* because it is not the demographic trend itself that directly causes the state crisis, but its impact on economic, political, and social institutions (Goldstone 1991b:xxvi). I briefly summarize Goldstone's theory below (Goldstone 1991b:24–25).

Population growth in excess of the productivity gains of the land has multifarious effects on social institutions

- First, it leads to persistent price inflation which outstrips the ability of agrarian states to increase tax revenues. Furthermore, increased population leads to expansion of armies and rising real costs. Thus, states have no choice but to seek to expand taxation, despite resistance from the elites and the general populace. Yet attempts to increase revenues cannot offset the spiraling state expenses. Thus, even though the state is rapidly raising taxes, it is still headed for fiscal crisis.
- Second, rapid expansion of population results in an increased number of aspirants for elite positions, which put further fiscal strains on the state. Moreover, increased intraelite competition leads to the formation of rival patronage networks vying for state rewards. As a result, elites become riven by increasing rivalry and factionalism.
- Third, population growth leads to rural misery, urban migration, falling real wages, and increased frequency of food riots and wage protests.
- Another consequence of rapid population growth is the expansion of youth cohorts. This segment of the population is particularly impacted by lack of employment opportunities. Additionally, the youthfulness of the population contributes to its mobilization potential.
- Finally, elite competition and popular discontent fuel ideological conflicts. For example, in early modern Europe, dissident elites and dissatisfied artisans were widely recruited into heterodox religious movements.

As all these trends intensify, the end result is state bankruptcy and consequent loss of military control; elite movements of regional and national rebellion; and a combination of elite-mobilized and popular uprisings that manifest the breakdown of central authority (Goldstone 1991b:25)

One of the strengths of Goldstone's (1991b) analysis is his employment of quantitative data and models in tracing out the mechanistic connections between various economic, social, and political institutions (this is discussed further in Section 7.3.1). However, Goldstone does not develop his theory to the point of an explicit *dynamic* model. In particular, he treats the underlying engine of change, population growth, as an exogenous variable. He suggests that a combination of favorable climate and receding disease may explain the observed doubling of population in most world regions between 1500 and the early 1600s (Goldstone 1991b:25). This choice was, clearly, not made lightly. Goldstone's (1986, 1991a) analysis of population dynamics, prices, and real wages in early modern England led him to conclude that existing endogenous theories are not supported by the data. For example, the Malthusian-Ricardian model assumes that population movements respond to changing prices. However, as Goldstone shows with data, long-term mortality patterns were seemingly independent of real wages.

Perhaps this is the correct approach, and we need to look for specific exogenous factors that explain population dynamics in different periods and regions. However, I do not think that the complete spectrum of endogenous models has been contrasted yet with data. In particular, I would like to explore the possibility that there is a feedback effect of political instability on population dynamics.

How can political stability or instability affect population dynamics? Let us start by assuming a Malthusian-Ricardian model of the interaction between population dynamics and food production. I have in mind something like the logistic model, which has two parameters. The intrinsic rate of population growth is a balance of birth and death rates in the absence of density feedback (that is, for low population densities). The carrying capacity is set by the climate and soil conditions, as well as the current level of agricultural technology (this is made more specific in the next section). Political instability can affect both parameters. Most obviously, when the state is weak or absent, the populace will suffer from elevated mortality due to increased crime, banditry, and internal and external warfare. Furthermore, the times of troubles cause increased migration rate: refugees from war-affected areas, or areas whose productive potential has been destroyed (see below on this). Migration has several effects. First, it can lead to emigration (and we can simply add that to mortality). Second, people on the move cannot afford to have children. Thus, birth rates decline. Third, increased migration leads to epidemics. Increased vagrancy spreads disease by connecting areas that would stay isolated during better times. Additionally, vagabonds and beggars aggregate in towns and cities, increasing their population size. This may tip the density over the epidemiological threshold (the critical density above which a disease spreads). Finally, political instability causes lower reproduction rates, because during uncertain times people choose to marry later and to have fewer children. Incidentally, people's choices about their family sizes may be reflected not only in birth rates, but also in rates of infanticide. Thus, family limitation practices may be disguised as increased child mortality.

Political instability can also affect the carrying capacity. There are many mechanisms by which the state can increase carrying capacity, so I will mention just two of the most common ones. First, the state offers protection. In a stateless society people can live only in natural strongholds, or places that can be made defensible. Examples include hillfort chiefdoms in preconquest Peru (Earle 1997), and the movement of settlements to hilltops in Italy after the collapse of the Roman Empire (Wickham 1981). Fearful of attack, people can cultivate only the small proportion of the productive area that is near fortified settlements. The strong state protects the productive population from external and internal (banditry, civil war) threats, and thus allows the whole cultivable area to be put into production. The second general mechanism is that states often invest in increasing agricultural productivity by constructing irrigation canals and roads, by implementing flood control measures, by clearing land from forests, etc. Again, the end result of these measures is an increase in the number of people that can be gainfully employed growing food, e.g., the carrying capacity.

In summary, political instability can negatively affect both demographic rates and the productive capacity of the society. I will explore both mechanisms in the models developed below. To reiterate, my goal is a theory in which population dynamics is an *endogenous* process: not only is there a link between population growth and state breakdown, but there may be a feedback connection between state breakdown and population growth.

7.2 MATHEMATICAL THEORY

7.2.1 The Basic Demographic-Fiscal Model

Model Development

I begin with the simplest possible model of agrarian state collapse. My purpose is first to expose the most basic logical blocks of the argument, and only then to start adding real-life complexities to it. In this section I will ask the reader to work through the model derivation and analysis with me, because the math is very simple, but at the same time crucial for understanding the main result. In the following sections, math will be banished to the Appendix.

There are two variables in the model, one for the population and the other for the state. $N(t)$ is the population density of subjects at time t. I assume that the state area does not change, so the density is simply the population number divided by the area. Thus, the units of N could be individuals per km^2. $S(t)$ is the current accumulated state resources, which I measure in kilograms (or tons) of grain. The choice of this particular variable is based on the economic nature of the agrarian state, in which food is the main commodity produced.

To start deriving the equations connecting the two structural variables (N and S), I first assume that the per capita rate of surplus production is a declining function of population numbers (this is David Ricardo's law of diminishing returns). There are several socioecological mechanisms that underly this relationship. First, as population grows, the stock of the most fertile land is exhausted, and increasingly more marginal plots are brought into cultivation. Second, increased population growth also means that land is subdivided into smaller parcels. Although each parcel receives more labor, its production rate (kg grain per ha per year) is also subject to the law of diminishing returns.

For the purpose of simplicity, I will approximate the relationship between per capita rate of surplus production, ρ, and population numbers, N, with a linear function

$$\rho(N) = c_1 \left(1 - N/k\right)$$

Here c_1 is some proportionality constant, and k is the population size at which the surplus equals zero. Thus, for $N > k$, the surplus is negative (the population produces less food than is needed to sustain it).

Next I assume that population dynamics are Malthusian:

$$\dot{N} = rN$$

and that the per capita rate of population increase is a linear function of the per capita rate of surplus production, $r = c_2 \rho(N)$. Putting together these two assumptions, we arrive at a logistic model for population growth:

$$\dot{N} = r_0 N (1 - N/k) \tag{7.1}$$

where $r_0 = c_1 c_2$ is the intrinsic rate of population growth, obtained when N is near 0. The parameter k is now seen as the "carrying capacity," or equilibrial population size. When $N < k$, the society generates surplus, and the population grows. If $N > k$, then the society produces less food than is needed for households to sustain and replace themselves, resulting in population decline.

Turning now to the differential equation for state resources, S, we note that S changes as a result of two opposite processes: revenues and expenditures. I will assume that the state collects a fixed proportion of surplus production as taxes. The total rate of surplus production is the product of per capita rate and population numbers. Thus, the taxation rate is $c_3 \rho(N) N$, where c_3 is the proportion of surplus collected as taxes. State expenditures are assumed to be proportional to the population size. The reason for this assumption is that, as population grows, the state must spend more resources on the army to protect and police it, on bureaucracy to collect and administer taxes, and on various public works (public buildings, roads, irrigation canals, etc). Putting together these processes we have the following equation for S:

$$\dot{S} = \rho_0 N (1 - N/k) - \beta N \tag{7.2}$$

where $\rho_0 = c_1 c_3$ is the per capita taxation rate at low population density and β the per capita state expenditure rate.

We are not done yet. Although we have established the dynamic link from N to S, there is no feedback effect (from S to N) in the model. I assume that the strong state has a positive effect on population dynamics; specifically, it increases k, the sustainable population size given the ecological conditions and the current development of agricultural technology, as discussed in the previous section.

Thus, the carrying capacity k is a monotonically increasing function of S. However, k cannot increase without bound. No matter how high S is, at some point all potential land is brought into cultivation, and all potential improvements have been put in place. Thus, there must be some maximum k_{max}, given the historically current level of agricultural technology. Another way of thinking about this mechanism is that the return on capital investment is also subject to a law of diminishing returns. I assume the following specific functional form for $k(S)$:

$$k(S) = k_0 \left(1 + c \frac{S}{s_0 + S} \right) \tag{7.3}$$

The parameter k_0 is the carrying capacity of the stateless society, $c = k_{max} - k_0$ is the maximum possible gain in increasing k given unlimited funds, and s_0

indicates how improvement in k depends on S (when $S = s_0$, $k(S)$ has been improved by $c/2$).

Putting together equations (7.1)–(7.3) we have the complete *demographic-fiscal model* (because it focuses on the fiscal health of the state as the main structural variable). The model has six parameters: ρ_0, β, r, k_0, c, and s_0, but we can reduce this set to four, by scaling $N' = N/k_0$ and $S' = S/\rho_0$. This procedure leaves us with the following parameters: $\beta' = \beta/\rho_0$, r, c, and $s' = s_0/\rho_0$. The scaled equations are

$$\dot{N} = rN\left(1 - \frac{N}{k(S)}\right)$$

$$\dot{S} = N\left(1 - \frac{N}{k(S)}\right) - \beta N \qquad (7.4)$$

$$k(S) = 1 + c\frac{S}{s_0 + S}$$

(where I dropped the primes for better readability). I also impose the condition $S \geq 0$ (that is, the state is not allowed to go into debt).

Model Dynamics

The typical dynamics of the demographic-fiscal model are shown in Figure 7.1a. Starting with the initial value of $S = 0$ and population numbers $N = k_0/2$, the model predicts that initially both N and S will grow. As S increases, so does the carrying capacity $k(S)$, which quickly approaches the upper limit k_{max}. For this reason, the growth of N does not stop at k_0, but continues beyond that critical value. However, at a certain population size N_{crit}, well before N approaches k_{max}, the growth of state resources ceases, and S begins to collapse at an increasing rate, rapidly reaching 0. This means that $k(S)$ also decreases to k_0, and the population size rapidly follows suit.

The mechanics underlying the collapse of S are illustrated in Figure 7.1b. The rate of change of S is determined by the balance of two opposing forces: revenues and expenditures. When N is low, increasing it results in greater revenues (more workers means more taxes). The growth in state expenditures lags behind the revenues, and the state's surplus accumulates. As N increases, however, the growth in revenues ceases, and actually begins to decline. This is a result of diminishing returns on agricultural labor. However, the expenditures continue to mount. At population density $N = N_{crit}$, the revenues and expenditures become (briefly) balanced. Unfortunately, population growth continues toward the carrying capacity, k, and the gap between the state's expenditures and revenues rapidly becomes catastrophic. As a result, the state quickly spends any resources that have been accumulated during better times. When S becomes zero, the state is unable to pay the army, the bureaucrats, and maintain infrastructure: the state collapses.

The equilibrium $N = k_0$ and $S = 0$ is locally stable. This means that, once the state has collapsed, small perturbations in either population size or state resources do not lead away from this equilibrium. In order for another cycle of

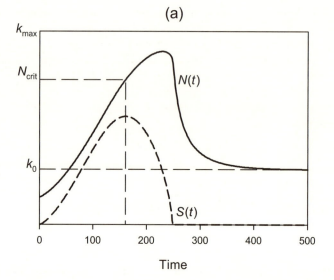

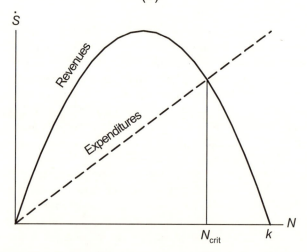

Figure 7.1 (a) Temporal dynamics of the demographic-fiscal model (7.4). (b) The change in state resources ($\dot{S}$) as a balance of revenues versus expenditures. Model parameters: $\beta = 0.25$, $r = 0.02$, $c = 3$, and $s_0 = 10$.

state building-collapse to get going, either N must be decreased below $(1 - \beta)$, or S must be increased above $s_0/[c(\beta^{-1} - 1) - 1]$. Thus, in a deterministic world, once the state collapses, it cannot arise again. In a stochastic world, where a variety of exogenous factors affect both N and S, it is a matter of time before a strong enough perturbation will start the model trajectory going on another state building-collapse cycle. For example, I incorporated stochasticity in the model

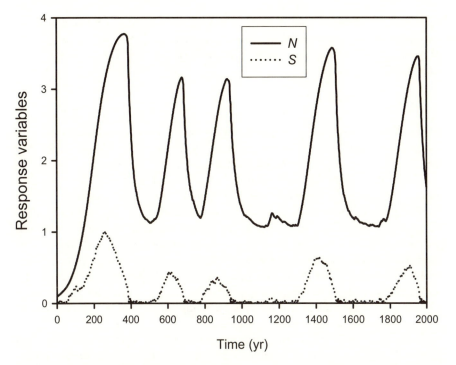

Figure 7.2 (a) Temporal dynamics of the stochastic version of the demographic-fiscal model. Parameters: $\beta = 0.25$, $r = 0.02$, $c = 3$, $s_0 = 10$, and $\sigma = 0.1s_0$.

by adding once a year to S a random Gaussian number with mean 0 and a small standard deviation $\sigma = 0.1s_0$. The dynamics of the stochastic demographic-fiscal model were characterized by recurrent cycles of state building and collapse (Figure 7.2). Note that once the state cycle gets going, its duration is well determined by initial conditions. By contrast, the stateless periods between cycles—*intercycles*—are quite variable in length (because the system must wait until a strong enough perturbation comes about).

A numerical investigation of the influence of parameters on model dynamics indicated that the average length of a political cycle was mainly determined by the value of r, and to a lesser extent by β. The parameter c affects the amplitude of oscillations, since it determines by how much k_{max} is greater than k_0. Parameter s_0 determines whether oscillations occur or not: if it is set too high, then $k(S)$ never increases far enough to get the political cycle going. The parameter β sets the population size at which state revenues fall behind expenses, since $N_{crit} = 1 - \beta$. Finally, the intrinsic per capita rate of population growth, r, affects the temporal extent of the oscillation, since the main determining factor is how long it takes for the population to grow to N_{crit}. A reasonable estimate of r is 0.02 yr^{-1} (or 2% relative increase per year). Note that r is the *intrinsic* rate of growth that obtains when N is near 0. For more typical densities in the vicinity of $N = k/2$, the model predicts per capita growth rates of about 1% per year, which is a typical observation for short-term growth periods in historical populations. For this estimate of r, the model predicts oscillations of 2–3 centuries in duration (Figure 7.2). This is a quantitative prediction of the model that can be tested empirically.

Assessment

Let us now discuss some of the simplifying assumptions about functional forms made during model development. Looking again at Figure 7.1b, it is apparent that the basic argument is quite unaffected by the details of the functional forms governing the relationship between population size and per capita surplus production or per capita state expenditures. For example, if we substitute any nonlinear (but monotonic) function instead of the assumption of linear decline in per capita surplus with population size, then all we will accomplish will be to distort the parabola in some way. The basic shape—increase in the revenues followed by decrease—will be unaffected, because revenues must be 0 both at the end $N = 0$ and the end $N = k$, and there must be a maximum in between. Similarly, the relationship between expenditures and population size can be nonlinear (in fact, it is likely that expenditures will be an accelerating function of N, simply because large populations require more bureaucratic layers to control and tax). Again, however, the expenditures must increase monotonically with N, and thus it is inevitable that at some population size, N_{crit}, the revenue and expenditure curves will cross, with all the consequences for the state's fiscal well-being that were discussed above. The general conclusion seems inescapable: unless the population size can somehow be prevented from crossing the N_{crit} threshold, the state's expenses will inexorably grow beyond its means, and the state will inevitably become insolvent. Once this point is reached, increasing the tax rate or cutting expenses on nonessentials like court luxuries, can at most be a short-term solution. Allowing the state to borrow money (that is, allowing S to become negative until the debt hits some maximum value) similarly only postpones the inevitable.

I believe that this conclusion is of extremely high importance to the dynamics of agrarian polities. The argument based on the model, however, does not imply that all states everywhere inevitably collapse within two to three centuries. But having an explicit model allows us to consider how various features of reality that are left out from the model may affect its basic message.

First, I should stress that the model is applicable only to preindustrial societies. It is conceivable that an industrial or even information-based economy may be able to expand its productive base by innovation and technology implementation, and thus keep ahead of population growth. However, this option is not open to agrarian societies. Traditional societies have a certain stock of technologies that they can utilize to intensify production under increasing population pressure (Boserup 1966, 1981). Eventually, though, the possibilities of further intensification are exhausted (Wood 1998). This is reflected in my assumption that the function $k(S)$ must eventually saturate.

Second, the model ignores factors external to the population–state system. In particular, a population under severe military pressure from outside may be prevented from growing to the equilibrium determined by food production. For example, we can model this situation by adding a density-independent death term, $-\delta N$, to the logistic equation for N [equation (7.1)]. If δ is large enough, then the population equilibrium will be shifted to the left beyond N_{crit}, and the polity will remain indefinitely in the region where revenues exceed expenses. However, such a situation is likely to affect only smallish polities. In large territorial empires, only borderlands should be affected by external military pressure, while the population in the central regions should grow unchecked to the subsistence limits. Conversely, a state may be successful in conquering adjacent areas. If the society pursues an active colonization policy, then population pressure within the empire will be relieved. This mechanism, however, should only postpone the inevitable, since no agrarian empire can expand its territory without limit.

Third, a society may choose to limit its population growth. Voluntary family limitation seems a priori unlikely, because the costs of fewer children are borne by individual families, while the problems associated with overpopulation are spread societywide. In other words, voluntary limit on reproduction has all the earmarks of a collective action problem. However, this may not be an insoluble problem. Furthermore, under certain conditions, family limitation may be a rational strategy for individuals to pursue. This is, therefore, an empirical question, to be determined for any particular society: do its members practice family limitation? Does family limitation result in a population equilibrium below N_{crit}?

Finally, the state may coercively limit population growth. This can be accomplished indirectly, simply by appropriating more than the surplus production. By leaving peasant households with fewer resources than they need to maintain and reproduce themselves, such severe taxation may cause a population decline and, paradoxically, increase the amount of surplus produced (observe how moving N to the left of N_{crit} in Figure 7.1 causes the fiscal surplus to increase). This possibility appears to be the most realistic for historical societies, especially because one does not need to assume that states consciously adopt the strategy of population reduction. All they need to do is to extort a larger proportion of total production from the population, which they have all the incentive to do, if they are anywhere near the N_{crit} point. Furthermore, empirically most agrarian states at most times have been accused of oppressing their productive populations. Therefore, we need to explore this possibility further with a model that is more complex than the one developed here. The main question is what is the mechanism of state coercion? That is, who is doing the coercing in agrarian states? The general answer is the elites. They either directly collect taxes from peasants and then transmit them to the state, or provide the bureaucrats and military officers for the state apparatus that extracts the taxes. In either case, we need to add more structure to the basic model and explicitly consider the dynamics of the state, elites, and commoners.

7.2.2 Adding Class Structure

My next goal is to expand the theory advanced in the previous section by considering how adding class structure affects the theoretical predictions concerning state collapse. To do this, I divide the total population into two socio-economic strata: commoners and elites. The development of this theory relies very much on insights from Jack Goldstone's demographic-structural theory (1991b).

The basic structure of the model is as follows (see Appendix Section A.3 for the derivation and other mathematical details). There are three structural variables: population numbers of commoners (peasants, P), population numbers of elites (E), and the accumulated state resources (S). As in the basic demographic-fiscal model, growth of commoner population results in decreased per capita productivity. Specifically, I assume that production per peasant is a linearly decreasing function of peasant population size. To connect production to population dynamics, I assume that the per capita rate of the commoner population growth is a linear function of the resources available to each producer. If the resources per peasant capita are over a certain threshold, then the peasant population will increase. On the other hand, if too high a proportion is extracted, then the peasant population will decline. In the Appendix I show that if peasants dispose of all resources that they produce, then their population dynamics is described by the logistic equation.

Peasants, however, are not allowed to keep all the food they produce. In the Appendix I derive a model for resource extraction by the elites. The key element of the model is the amount of coercion that the elites are able to bring to bear on the peasants. At low elite numbers, E, the amount of coercion they will be able to generate (and, thus, the proportion of resources that they will be able to extract from the producers) is directly proportional to E. However, as E increases, the nobles cannot extract more resources than what are produced. Thus, although increased elite numbers allow a greater proportion of production to be extracted from the peasants, ability of the elite to extract resources suffers from diminishing returns, so that resources extracted per elite capita decline with increased elite numbers.

The population dynamics of elites is modeled in the same way as that of peasants. If resources per elite capita are high, the elite population grows by reproduction and recruitment from the general populace. If per capita resources are low, then elite population shrinks as a result of reduced reproduction, increased mortality, and downward mobility. It is clear, however, that the threshold amount of resources necessary for an elite household to sustain and reproduce itself is set at a much higher value than the equivalent parameter for commoners.

As in the basic model, the state resources change as a result of revenues and expenditures. On the revenue side, I assume that the extracted resources are divided between the elites (rents) and the state (taxes). However, the portion of the extracted resources that actually ends up in the state's coffers is a dynamic quantity. When the resources extracted from peasants are sufficient to maintain the consumption levels expected by the elites, they will pass along the taxes due to the state. However, as elite numbers increase, and each elite household obtains a diminishing amount of resources for maintenance and reproduction, the elites will divert an increasing proportion of taxes to their needs. Historically, nobles used a variety of practices to appropriate the state's revenues. They petitioned the authorities for tax forgiveness, pleading poverty. Second, they often simply failed to transmit taxes to the state, keeping them for themselves (this option is

available when landowners collect taxes). Third, elite members serving as officials used a variety of corrupt practices to divert state-owed taxes into their own,
and their clan's pockets. The end result in all cases was that, as elites became
impoverished, the state received a decreasing fraction of the product extracted
from the commoners. I model this dynamic by assuming that each elite household keeps the resources they need to maintain themselves and then transmits a
fixed proportion of the surplus to the state.

Next, arguing by analogy with the derivation of the basic model, I assume
that state expenditures grow linearly with elite numbers, because the state has to
provide employment to them as officers, bureaucrats, and priests. This argument
assumes that state expenses associated with increased commoner numbers are
negligible compared to the demands made on the state by elites. (It is certainly
possible to add commoner-related expenditures, but this complicates the model
and does not change the main result.)

Finally, we need to model the effect of S on the population dynamics of P
and E. As discussed in Section 7.1, S can either affect the productive capacity
of the society (as in the basic demographic-fiscal model) or act on demographic
rates. In the Appendix I derive two versions of the model, one for each of these
two cases. The first model is completely analogous to the basic demographic-
fiscal model: high S increases the carrying capacity of the peasant population. In
the second model, I assume that the presence of a strong state imposes peace on
the elites: intraelite competition does not take lethal forms, and elite extinction
rate is low. When the state is absent or weak, however, intense intraelite conflict
leads to increased elite extinction rate.

Both models generate basically the same kinds of dynamics, so I will focus
on the second one, in which S affects elite demography. I will refer to it as the
selfish elite model, because it assumes that elites oppress commoners without
any regard for their well-being, and transmit taxes to the state only if they have
satisfied their own basic requirements.

A numerical investigation of the selfish elite model indicates that it is capable of
three kinds of dynamic behaviors. First, for certain parameters the elites cannot
get themselves established and go extinct. Second, after an initial episode of
state building and collapse, the elites and producers approach an equilibrium and
remain there in perpetuity (Figure 7.3a). (For some parameters, the state never
gets going, and the stateless equilibrium is approached directly.) What happens is
that the growth of the commoner population creates a large resource base, which
allows the elites to rapidly expand their numbers. The state grows in parallel
with this initial elite expansion. However, as elite numbers grow, an increasingly
greater proportion of the extracted product goes just to maintain them at the
minimum level, and the proportion going to the state begins to decrease. At
the same time, the demands of the elites on the state increase, so at some point
expenditures overwhelm revenues. Just as in the basic model, this eventually leads
to state collapse. Meanwhile, the elite demand on peasant-produced resources
becomes so intense that peasants are left with less food than they need to sustain
themselves. As a result of this intense oppression, peasant numbers begin to
decline. After the state collapses, the ensuing period of anarchy is characterized

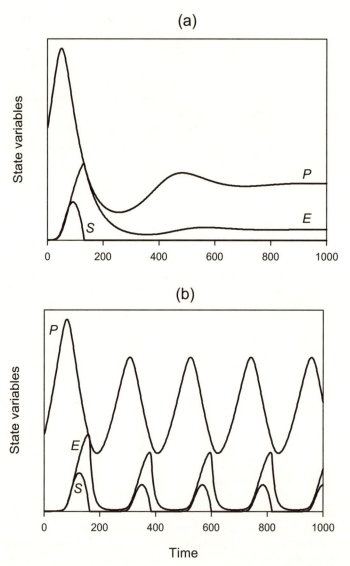

Figure 7.3 Dynamics of the selfish elite model. (a) A stable equilibrium in a stateless society. Parameters are $\beta_1 = \delta_1 = 0.02$, $\rho_0 = 2$, $\beta_2 = 0.5$, $\delta_2 = 0.025$, $\gamma = 10$, $\alpha = 0.2$. (b) Stable limit cycles. Same parameters as in (a) except $\delta_2 = 0.1$.

by intense exploitation of peasants and highly lethal intraelite conflict. As a result, numbers of both commoners and nobility decline, and after some mild oscillations approach an equilibrium.

This kind of dynamics, predicted by the selfish elite model, is analogous to the typical dynamics exhibited by the basic model, except the role of N is now played by E. As in the basic model, although the equilibrium is locally stable, it can be perturbed to go for another state building/state collapse excursion (again, this is analogous to the dynamics of the basic model).

A single state building/collapse episode followed by a stateless equilibrium (in the absence of perturbations) is the dynamics typical for most parameter combinations of the selfish elite model. It is also the typical dynamics of the class-structured model with S affecting the productive capacity of the society. For some parameter values, however, the selfish elite model exhibits a third kind of behavior, in which the system undergoes stable limit cycles of recurrent state building, collapse, a period of anarchy, and then another episode of state building (Figure 7.3b). One way to move the system from the stable stateless equilibrium to recurrent cycles is to increase the elite death rate in the absence of the state. This modification allows elites to die off rapidly and to a low enough point, which creates the conditions for state resources to increase.

One behavior that the selfish elite model does not exhibit is a stable equilibrium between peasants and elites with the state present, $S > 0$. The reason is clear and completely analogous to the mechanism operating in the basic demographic-fiscal model. If E is at an equilibrium, then $\dot{E}$ is necessarily zero (the elites have no surplus to share with the state). Thus, the state gets no revenues, but still must spend on defense, administration, and so on.

One obvious modification of the model that leads to an equilibrium with the state present consists of allowing the state to collect a fixed proportion of the total product extracted from commoners by elites (rather than a fraction of the elite's surplus). With this modification, and for realistic parameter values, P and E approach equilibrium, while S stays positive (actually, S grows with time, but surely the state will find things to spend this surplus on).

This result, however, poses an interesting question. How realistic is it to assume that, during the periods when the elites experience a substantial degree of hardship, they will allow a large proportion of revenue to go to the state? Note that this model assumes that, even when the economic position of the elites is so desperate that their numbers are declining, they will still not attempt to dip into the flow of taxes from peasants to the state treasury. In most agrarian societies the elites were the ones who administered tax collection. It is likely that most elites will feel a greater degree of solidarity with their family and clan, rather than with the whole polity. Thus, I think that this kind of "selfless elite" model is not a particularly realistic description of most historical agrarian states.

7.2.3 Models for Elite Cycles

The models discussed in Section 7.2.2 indicate that the predicted dynamics are primarily determined by the assumptions we make about the elites. This theoretical result supports the argument that the elites play the key role in state breakdown (Goldstone 1991b; see Section 7.1).

In this section I continue the investigation of how elite characteristics affect polity dynamics. I am interested, in particular, in how nomadic elites, or elites originating as nomads, interact with agrarian states. To simplify the matters, I initially assume that the population of commoners does not change with time.

However, after investigating the simple model, I check on how its predictions are affected by the simplifying assumptions (this is the general procedure that I follow in this book).

The Ibn Khaldun Model

The first model that I construct is tailored to the situation in the medieval Maghreb, as conceptualized by Ibn Khaldun (what follows is largely a verbal description of the model, while the equations are banished to the Appendix). The dynamics of the Ibn Khaldunian "world-system" are determined by the interaction between the civilized society and the desert tribes (Section 3.2.1). The civilized region is the site of recurrent state building/collapse episodes. It is inhabited by an indigenous commoner population, who provide the productive basis of the society. The desert is inhabited by stateless tribes, who periodically conquer the civilized region and establish a ruling dynasty there. Desert tribes, thus, supply the elites (nobility) for the civilized state.

In the model I assume that the dynamics of the commoner population are largely disconnected from the elite dynamics. Dynasties come and go, but peasants and merchants continue to grow food, trade, and pay taxes to whichever government is currently in power. Thus, the amount of resources extracted from commoners is a constant, R. During the early years of the dynasty, the extracted resources are divided in two parts: taxes to support the government, γR, and rents to support the elites, $(1 - \gamma)R$. The parameter γ, the proportion of resources going to the state, is assumed to be a constant. The income per noble is therefore $\mu = (1 - \gamma)R/E$, where E is the current number of nobles.

I now introduce two other parameters. Let μ_0 be the per capita income that is necessary to maintain and replace exactly one noble. In other words, when per capita income falls below μ_0, the elite numbers will decline, while if $\mu > \mu_0$, then the elite numbers will increase. The second parameter is μ_{min}, the per capita income that nobles consider to be the minimum that accords with their station. This "minimal acceptable income" is determined socially and can vary between societies. In general, however, $\mu_{min} \geq \mu_0$, since it is unlikely that nobles would consider acceptable an income on which they cannot afford to perpetuate their family line to the next generation. Ibn Khaldun argued that with time former tribesmen forget the rude ways of the desert, and subsequent generations grow accustomed to ever-increasing luxury. Thus, μ_{min} is a variable that starts at some low level (e.g., μ_0) at the beginning of the dynasty and then increases at a certain rate (e.g., δ_μ per year).

As I stated above, elite numbers increase when per capita income μ is greater than μ_0. The rate of elite population growth is proportional to the difference $\mu - \mu_0$, subject to not exceeding the maximum rate of increase, r_{max}. Because the model is tailored to a specific society, in which the elites practiced polygamy, I set $r_{max} = 0.08$ yr^{-1} at four times the intrinsic rate of population increase typical for preindustrial populations. My justification for this assumption is that the legal maximum of wives that a Muslim man could have is four. Of course, in Islamic societies many high-rank individuals would have large numbers of concubines and would usually acknowledge their sons as legitimate heirs. This practice would lead to a much higher rate of population growth. On the other hand, poorer members of the elite might be unable to afford the full complement of legal wives. On balance, I believe that a multiplier of four is a reasonable one to choose as the reference value for Islamic societies (as is usual in theory building, we will need to determine how variation in this and other parameters affect the model predictions).

The next key assumption of the model is that as long as per capita income generated from rents exceeds the minimum acceptable income, $(1 - \gamma)R/E > \mu_{min}$, the state and elites live in harmony. However, if elite numbers grow to the point where their per capita incomes fall below μ_{min}, then nobles become dissatisfied, and will use a variety of usual techniques to divert some of the taxes into their pockets (as discussed in the previous section). The model makes the assumption that at this point $\mu = \mu_{min}$, that is, the elites steal just enough from the state to be able to maintain what they perceive as the minimal standard of living appropriate to their station. If elite numbers grow to the point where $R/E < \mu_{min}$, that is, there is not enough extracted resource to satisfy all the nobles, even if the state gets no taxes, then the model assumes that $\mu = R/E$. In other words, at this point the nobles divide all extracted resource among themselves, and the state gets nothing.

The state fiscal dynamics are modeled as usual, with revenues as described above, and the expenditures proportional to the elite numbers. Thus, the dynamics of S, the accumulated state resources, follows the typical trajectory, in which S grows during the early period of the dynasty, because elite numbers are few and their appetites are modest. At some point, however, the revenues drop to the point where they cannot match expenditures, and S declines and eventually become 0. At this point, the model assumes that the dynasty failed. The state becomes vulnerable to conquest, which (at least in the model) happens immediately, because the desert tribes provide a ready and spatially adjacent source of the next dynasty. A typical trajectory predicted by the model is illustrated in Figure 7.4a.

Note that I chose to frame this model in economic (or fiscal) terms. However, we can easily cast the model in terms of collective solidarity (asabiya). For example, we can reinterpret S as the asabiya of the elites supporting the current dynasty (the conquering tribesmen and their descendants). Then, at the beginning of the dynasty, asabiya is high, and it stays high until elite numbers reach the threshold where per capita income falls below the minimal acceptable level. At that point, intraelite competition intensifies, and the asabiya begins to decline. When asabiya reaches a certain threshold, the dynasty (and the state) collapses, and is replaced by a new tribal group from the desert. The dynamics of such a model are essentially identical to those shown in Figure 7.4a.

A numerical investigation of the effect of parameter values on the dynamics of the Ibn Khaldun model indicates that the main parameters that affect the period of the cycle are the maximum rate of elite population increase (r_{max}) and the rate at which the minimal acceptable income grows with time. Rather rapid cycles of about one century in period, shown in Figure 7.4a, obtain for high values

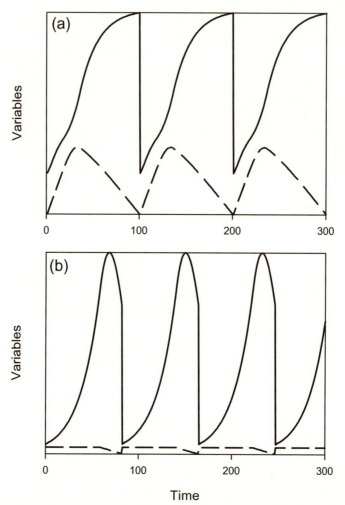

Figure 7.4 (a) Dynamics of the Ibn Khaldun model: elite numbers, E (solid line) and accumulated state surplus S (broken line). (b) Dynamics of the parasitic nomad model: elite numbers (solid line) and elite asabiya S (broken line).

of r_{max} that should be typical for societies where elite polygamy is widespread. By contrast, reducing r_{max} to 0.02 leads to longer cycles, of around 1.5 centuries.

Now that we have some understanding of the dynamics predicted by the Ibn Khaldun model, it would be a good idea to investigate the effects of some of the simplifying assumptions we employed to derive the model. Probably the most drastic simplification was the assumption that we can neglect the commoner dynamics. To check on the validity of this approximation, I developed a more complex Ibn Khaldun model with class structure (see the Appendix for equations). This model predicts essentially the same dynamics for E and S as the simple Ibn Khaldun model (Figure 7.5a). Additionally, it reveals the commoner dynamics

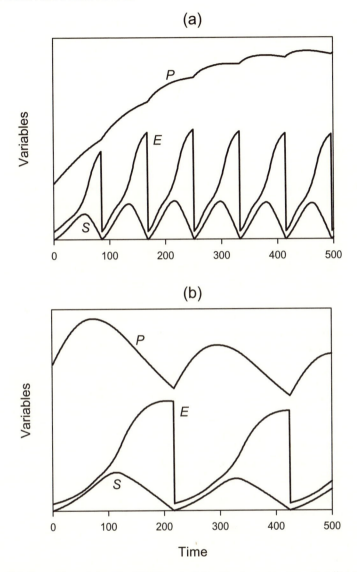

Figure 7.5 Dynamics of the Ibn Khaldun model with class structure. E: elite numbers, S: accumulated state surplus, and P: commoner numbers. (a) Dynamics with high elite reproduction rate and limited extraction ability. (b) Dynamics with low elite reproduction rate and high extraction ability.

during the elite cycle. We see that the growth of the commoner population is slowed by periodic state breakdown, but this effect is slight. Numerical investigation of the model parameters indicates that commoner population declines are more pronounced when we increase the elite extraction ability (by increasing the parameter ϵ, the maximum proportion of commoner production that can be extracted by elites). Additionally, the cycle period is lengthened and the amplitude of commoner oscillation is increased when we decrease the per capita rate of elite reproduction. This happens because longer cycles mean longer periods of very intense exploitation of commoners by elites, resulting in a greater decline of commoner populations by the end of the cycle. A sample trajectory for $\epsilon = 1$ and $r_{max} = 0.02$ is shown in Figure 7.5b.

The Parasitic Nomad Model

The last model that I develop in this section is tailored to the situation on the Inner Asian frontier of China, as conceptualized by Barfield (1989) and further developed by Kradin (2000, 2002). This model is in many ways similar to the Ibn Khaldun model. Again, I focus on the dynamics of nomadic elites (chiefs of various ranks and their kin). Contrary to the Maghrebin situation, however, the nomads of the Inner Asian frontier preferred not to conquer the civilized state, the Chinese Empire, but to extort tribute from it.

Here is the verbal description of the model (the equations are in the Appendix). Let R be the amount of tribute extracted from the Chinese in a particular year (R is a variable whose dependence on other variables in the model will be explained below). Let E be the elite numbers. Thus, the elite per capita income is $\mu = R/E$. The elite population dynamics are modeled exactly as in the Ibn Khaldun model (that is, the elite per capita rate of population change is proportional to $\mu - \mu_0$, where μ_0 is the income level necessary to maintain and replace a member of the elite).

The second structural variable of the model, in addition to E, is S, the asabiya of nomadic elites at the highest organizational level, that of the "imperial confederation." I assume that the asabiya of lower-scale groups is fixed at a high level, typical of nomadic life, so that we do not have to model it explicitly. The process leading to the rise of imperial confederation is conceptualized as follows. Initially, the steppe is divided among numerous "tribes" (nomadic chiefdoms). One particular tribe, through advantageous location, a rise of a charismatic leader, or simply luck, acquires an enhanced ability to extract booty or tribute from the agrarian polity on the other side of the steppe frontier. Using the goods extracted from settled agriculturalists, the tribal chief increases his warrior retinue. This sets in motion a positive feedback dynamic: greater retinue allows the chief to conquer nearby nomadic tribes, incorporate them into the growing steppe army, extract a greater booty/tribute from the agrarian state, attract more warriors, and so on. An imperial steppe confederation is the result. This autocatalytic process runs on until it hits the upper limit of what can be extracted from the agrarian state (remember that the canny nomads do not wish to conquer the agrarian state but just milk it for what the traffic can bear).

Specifically, I assume that the amount of tribute, R, is a nonlinear function of E: first, it rises with E in an accelerating manner, but then approaches an upper asymptote. R is also proportional to the confederation-level asabiya, S. S initially starts at a high level, and as long as the amount of tribute per elite head is abundant, it stays constant ($\dot{S} = 0$). However, if the per capita income, μ, falls below some minimum level deemed appropriate, μ_{min}, intraelite competition is intensified. This has a corrosive effect on the asabiya, and S declines.

Typical dynamics of the parasitic nomad model are shown in Figure 7.4b. The causes underlying the rise of imperial confederations have been explained above. The reason that confederations fail is, in a way, the same dynamic, but running in reverse. When the imperial confederation achieves the maximum extraction rate, its territorial growth stops, but elite numbers continue to grow as a result of the natural population increase of elites. When elite numbers reach the point where $\mu > \mu_{min}$, S begins to decline (Figure 7.4b). Declining S lowers the ability to extract tribute from the agrarian state, which further exacerbates intraelite competition. Eventually, S hits some lower threshold, below which the imperial confederation cannot be held together. The confederation dissolves into a number of warring tribes, and the cycle can begin again. Because the tribe-level asabiya remains high, the preconditions for the rise of another confederation are created immediately upon the collapse of the previous one (thus, the model assumes that the next cycle begins right away).

7.2.4 Models for the Chinese Dynastic Cycle

Historians have long noticed the importance of the dynastic cycle in Chinese history (Meskill 1965). During the early phase of the dynastic cycle, peace and prosperity reign, and population tends to increase. Eventually, however, the dynasty becomes "old and feeble," corruption and public disorder increase, and the dynasty falls. During the ensuing period of anarchy, the population usually declines. Two similar models of the dynastic cycle have been proposed, one by the economist Dan Usher (1989), and the other by the economist Cyrus Chu and the demographer Ronald Lee (Chu and Lee 1994). Because Usher's model is rather complex (having twenty equations), I do not discuss it here, but turn instead to the simpler model of Chu and Lee.

There are three classes in the Chu and Lee model: peasants grow food and pay taxes, bandits steal food and fight peasants and rulers, and self-interested rulers tax farmers and hunt bandits. Food production is increased by extra labor inputs, but this increase is subject to diminishing returns. Peasants have a choice: they can stay peasants and farm, or they can turn into bandits and steal. This occupational decision is based on comparison of the expected utility of bandits and peasants. The utility function is the product of food received and probability of survival. Chu and Lee show that one effect of a larger population is to increase the rate with which peasants turn into bandits. When the number of bandits increases, it has two consequences. First, there are fewer peasants, and thus food production is decreased. This leads to population decrease due to higher child mortality. Additionally, a greater number of bandits means increased risk of death to adults. Second, the growing ranks of bandits improve their survival probability, which causes their population to increase. At some point, the bandit power overwhelms that of the government, and the dynasty collapses.

Assessment

Usher's and Chu and Lee's models are based on a rational choice argument: peasants weigh the utilities of staying peasant or turning into a bandit and then make the appropriate occupational decision. In principle, this is an interesting and potentially powerful approach for building theory and making empirical predictions. Yet, I am troubled by the nature of the utility function that these authors chose: commoner utility is essentially the expected income (in food units) multiplied by their survival probability. My feeling is that this is too much the economist's approach, and that a more sociologically sophisticated approach is needed that would build upon collectively held norms and collectively made decisions.

An even more serious criticism of these two models is that they focus on the popular rebellion as the main mechanism causing the state collapse. Yet, Goldstone (1991b) presents a very convincing argument, buttressed by numerous empirical cases of early modern state breakdown, that popular uprising by itself usually could not bring down the state. Peasants are poorly armed, trained, and organized, and stand almost no chance against the coercive apparatus of the state when backed up by cohesive elites. Goldstone argues that the state collapse is brought about by factional fighting among the elites, which then opens the way for popular rebellion (furthermore, even peasant uprisings are often led by members of the elite). Thus, current theory states that popular discontent is, in a sense, a secondary factor. We should look to elite dynamics for the main mechanism of state breakdown.

Despite the above criticisms, I believe that the models by Usher and by Chu and Lee make an important contribution to building the theory of state breakdown. Note that the underlying force for state breakdown in both models is population growth, which leads to a gradual fall in income per head, until eventually the surplus over bare subsistence is insufficient to provide for the ruling class (Usher 1989). Usher and Chu and Lee did not specify their models to the point where we could determine what type of long-term dynamics they predict. But the basic model that I proposed in Section 7.2.1 does that, and suggests that the dynamics should be characterized by recurrent (if somewhat irregular) state building–state collapse cycles of around 2–3 centuries in length for the likely parameter values.

Furthermore, it would be interesting to see if the rational choice perspective could provide insights about elite dynamics. Thus, it would be instructive to apply the "occupation choice" module not to peasants, but to elites during the period of worsening economical conjuncture, (that is, striving for an official position or turning rebel). This approach, however, would get us well beyond the current goals of the book, so I leave it to future investigations.

7.2.5 Summing up Theoretical Insights

Demographic-structural models discussed in this section suggest two general insights. First, as a result of diminishing returns on labor, population growth in agrarian societies inevitably leads to a gradual fall of per capita income. Eventually, the surplus produced by peasants becomes insufficient for the maintenance of the state. State bankruptcy and collapse can be prevented only if population numbers are kept below the critical threshold at which state expenditures match state revenues.

The second insight is the key role of elites in state dynamics. Elites can limit commoner population growth by leaving commoners with less income than is necessary for bare subsistence. However, there does not seem to be a general mechanism for limiting elite population growth. In some exceptional cases, the state apparatus may be able to function independently of elites, and provide the necessary coercive force to limit elite numbers. In other cases, elites themselves may choose to limit their population growth. In most agrarian societies, however, I expect that elite numbers will increase beyond the sustainable level, leading to state breakdown.

The elite attributes have a strong influence on the period and amplitude of state buildup/breakdown cycles. Two parameters appear to be of main importance: elite reproduction rate and extraction ability. High reproduction rate and low extraction ability lead to fast cycles of the Ibn Khaldun type, with a period of around a century, and mild amplitude of oscillations in commoner numbers. A low reproduction rate, approaching that of commoners, increases the period of the cycles. A higher extraction ability leads to more drastic falloffs of commoner population. Longer cycles also lead to a greater amplitude of commoner population oscillations, because a longer decentralization phase causes commoner numbers to decrease to a lower level. As a result, the dynamics of commoner population in the selfish elite model with low elite reproduction and high extractive ability are similar in their period and amplitude to the population dynamics in the basic demographic-fiscal model.

Note that in all models I assumed that elite recruitment is a result of reproduction. In real societies, of course, elite numbers grow both by reproduction of existing elite families and by upward social mobility from the commoner strata. I investigated the effect of adding this mechanism for elite recruitment to models, and found that it does not affect the qualitative insights from the theory. Essentially, the dynamics depend on how fast elite numbers grow, and it does not matter by what mechanism this growth occurs.

There is a number of ways in which the simple models discussed here can be extended. For example, it would be very interesting to redefine the variables in the Chu and Lee model in terms of the Jack Goldstone theory, with the three structural variables being the numbers of commoners, elites, and dissident elites (or "antielites"). Another interesting direction is to expand the list of variables not only to include the numbers of individuals in any particular stratum, but also to keep track of the average accumulated resources per individual in the stratum. Such a variable would be analogous to the accumulated state resources that enters as an explicit variable in most demographic-structural models. Recently, Malkov and co-authors developed models addressing this issue (Malkov et al. 2000; Malkov and Sergeev 2002).

The final issue that I need to address here is the terminological one. What should we call the dynamics predicted by the suite of demographic-structural models developed here? Models predict very long-term oscillations with periods ranging from one to three centuries, depending on the model structure and parameter values. The dynamics are characterized by two phases: centralization, when political stability is high, and decentralization, when political *instability* is high. The decentralization phase, when the state is weak or absent, can extend for various periods of time and does not necessarily lead to a centralization phase. Thus the oscillations predicted by the models are not necessarily strongly periodic.

Long-term swings or waves on the scale of centuries have been commented on by a number of authors. Cameron (1989) referred to them as the "logistics," Braudel (1988) as the "secular trends," and Fischer (1996) as the "great wave," to give just a few examples. The logistic is a term that I prefer to reserve for the logistic equation, an essential building block of many models considered in this book. The logistic is a first-order model and is not capable of second-order oscillations such as those predicted by demographic-structural models. Thus, calling these cycles "logistics" would cause no end of confusion. "Secular trends" is a much better term, because one meaning of "secular" refers to very long changes occurring on the scale of centuries. However, a "trend" usually refers to a monotonic increase or decrease, while the dynamics predicted by demographic-structural models predict up-and-down swings. For this reason, I propose that we call these dynamics *secular cycles* or *secular waves*. The first term may be used if we want to emphasize the quasiperiodic nature of dynamics, the second if we want to emphasize the irregular up and down pattern (both dynamics are predicted by the models, depending on the structural assumptions). I would further distinguish another category: "elite cycles," in which the general population does not change very much, but most of the action is due to elite interactions.

7.3 EMPIRICAL APPLICATIONS

7.3.1 Periodic Breakdowns of Early Modern States

The demographic-structural theory of Jack Goldstone (1991b) makes detailed and quantitative predictions about interrelations between such variables as population growth, inflation rate, state fiscal distress, intraelite competition, and popular discontent. The theory, thus, can be empirically tested by examining the historical record and determining whether the hypothesized relationships held in different instances of state breakdown. This was the approach followed by Goldstone, who chose four cases studies for a detailed examination: the English and French Revolutions, the Ottoman crisis of the seventeenth century, and the Ming-Qing transition in China (as well as less detailed comparisons to a few other early modern polities). I will focus on the English Revolution of the seventeenth century, because the data base documenting various dynamic variables is the most complete in this case.

The population history of England is known better than for any other region in the world (see Chapter 8). After the fourteenth-century decline and fifteenth-century stability, the population began to grow rapidly. Between 1500 and 1640 C.E. the population more than doubled. The first consequence of this growth was a drastic decline in the land/peasant ratio. For example, whereas prior to 1560, 57% of landholdings were 1 acre or greater in size, after 1620 only 36% were in that category. What was worse, there was a drastic increase of landless peasants (those that had only a cottage with garden): their proportion increased from 11% before 1560 to 40% after 1620 (data from Everitt 1967; Goldstone 1991b: Table 1). These data indicate that by 1650 land was in short supply. Even though land must have been more intensively cultivated (because the labor supply grew), the food production per capita should have declined between 1500 and 1640 due to the law of diminishing returns. A clear indication that this happened was a drastic increase in the price of grain: a rise of 600% from 1500 to 1640. According to Goldstone's (1991b: Table 3) analysis, a simple regression model with a log-transformed population, an index of harvest quality, and time (the dummy variable for technical change) as independent variables explains 99% of the variance in the log-transformed prices.

The second major consequence of population growth was the increasing fiscal strain on the English state. The state finances, strong under Henry VII, deteriorated by the mid-sixteenth century, when ordinary revenues started to lag behind expenses, and finally collapsed in the early seventeenth century (Figure 7.6a). The basic problem was that, while the Crown income kept pace with inflation, the *real* expenses increased with population. First, increased population meant larger armies and fleets. Second, the expanded elite numbers imposed greater patronage costs on the state. Increasingly, from the mid-sixteenth century on, the Crown was forced to sell assets, levy forced loans, and seek parliamentary grants even in peacetime (Goldstone 1991b:93). By the 1630s, Crown lands were largely gone, and the unpaid Crown debt reached the point where the interest on it was greater than the ordinary revenues. Furthermore, prior efforts to secure extraordinary revenues had alienated the elites to the point where they were unlikely to acquiesce to further fiscal demands or entreaties by the Crown.

While the general population doubled between 1500 and 1640, the numbers of the elite expanded even faster. Whereas in 1540 there were 6300 gentry families, in 1600 (only 60 years later) there were 16,500. This number further increased to 18,500 in 1640, then declined to 16,400 in 1688, after the Civil War. In 1760 there were still only 18,000 gentry families—less than at the 1640 peak (Goldstone 1991b:113). The drastic increase of elite numbers affected all strata: between 1540 and 1640 the number of peers increased from 60 to 160, baronets and knights from 500 to 1400, esquires from 800 to 3000, and armigerous gentry from 5000 to 15,000 (Stone 1972:72). The consequence of this rapid expansion (especially during the second half of the sixteenth century) was increased competition for jobs and patronage. Goldstone argues that one way of measuring this competition is by examining the data on university enrollments. University enrollments increased drastically during the second half of the sixteenth century and reached a peak in 1640. By the 1750s, when intraelite competition greatly subsided, the enrollments declined to pre-1600 levels (Figure 7.6b). Another indicator of intraelite competition is the amount of litigation among gentry. Between 1640 and 1750, the number of gentry who appeared in the Courts of Common

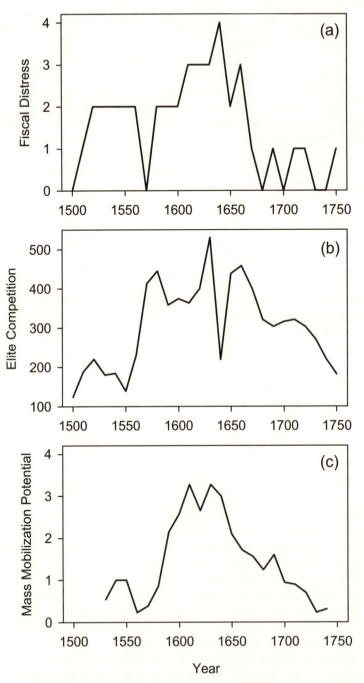

Figure 7.6 (a) State fiscal distress, measured on a scale from 0 (adequate income and credit) to 4 (total bankruptcy) (from Goldstone 1991b: Figure 4). (b) Elite competition measured by enrollments at Oxford University (Stone 1974: Table 1A). (c) Mass mobilization potential (arbitrary scale) (from Goldstone 1991b: Figure 4).

Pleas as plaintiffs or defendants dropped by over 65% (Goldstone 1991b:121; data from Brooks 1989, cited in Goldstone).

The final ingredient in Goldstone's theory of state breakdown is the mass mobilization potential (MMP) of the general populace. Of particular relevance are the urbanized workers and artisans, especially in the capital, because they are located near the centers of power. Goldstone proposed that there are three measurable components in the MMP. First, we can measure the degree of misery affecting the urban masses by the dynamics of real wages (for example, the average laborer wages expressed in the amount of food they can buy). Second, a youthful age structure increases the mobilization potential of the crowd. Third, urban growth concentrates the poor young sons, and thus could play an important multiplier role in further amplifying the popular discontent brought about by increasing poverty. Goldstone proposed the following formula for combining the effects of these three mechanisms in one measure of mass mobilization potential:

$$ \text{MMP}_t = \frac{\overline{W}}{W_t} + \left(\frac{\overline{W}}{W_t} - 1 \right) U_t A_t $$

where W_t is the real wage in decade t and $\overline{W}$ is the average real wage for the period 1500–1750. The lower the current real wage in relation to the long-term average, the greater is the ratio $\overline{W}/W_t$. The second term reflects the interactive effects of urbanization and age structure. U_t was defined by Goldstone as the weighted average of London's growth over the decade and the preceding two decades, and A_t is the proportion of the population 10–29 years old to the population aged over 30 years. Thus, the second term says that U_t and A_t will amplify the effects of W_t if $W_t < \overline{W}$, and otherwise will not have much of an effect on the MMP. The estimated MMP for England during 1530–1750 is plotted in Figure 7.6c.

To summarize, the case of the English Revolution provides a great degree of empirical support for the demographic-structural theory of Goldstone. The three ingredients of the revolution were the state's financial crisis, acute competition and factionalism among the elites, and the existence of a large body of disaffected commoners who could be mobilized by parliamentary leaders against the royalists in London. Measures of all these processes increased during the second half of the sixteenth and the early seventeenth centuries, and peaked around 1640 (Figure 7.6).

7.3.2 The Great Wave

As I noted above, the value of the demographic-structural theory (Goldstone 1991b) lies in its detailed analysis of the interrelations between important social variables mediating the effect of population growth on state stability (or, rather, instability). The enormous amount of quantitative material collected by Goldstone on state breakdown in early modern Europe and Asia provides a solid empirical foundation for his theory. Yet the theory is incomplete: while the effect of population dynamics on state stability is extremely well documented, the feedback effect on population is not. In Goldstone's theory population dynamics is an exogenous variable.

A more complete description of the interactions between population numbers and sociopolitical stability was given in the (verbal) model advanced by the historian David Hackett Fischer (1996). Fischer proposed that during the period of 1200–2000 C.E., western Europe went through four "great waves" of socioeconomic change (Fisher was not the first to notice these waves; I return to this issue in the beginning of Chapter 8). These long-term dynamics were reflected in the history of prices (Figure 7.7), in which periods of price equilibrium (roughly, the Renaissance, the Enlightenment, and the Victorian Era) were interspersed with periods of rapid inflation (the "price revolutions" of the thirteenth, sixteenth, eighteenth, and twentieth centuries). Fischer argues that price movements are correlated with a comprehensive set of societal variables. Periods of price equilibrium were characterized by prolonged prosperity, flowering of the arts, and the spread of optimistic ideologies. Periods following price revolutions were characterized by widespread misery, political disorder, social disruption, and a growing mood of cultural anxiety (Fischer 1996:237).

Fischer's explanation of this wavelike pattern can be summarized as follows (1996:246–251). During the late stage of a price equilibrium, material conditions are improving, social stability is increasing, and cultural expectations are growing brighter. People respond by marrying earlier and having more children; population begins to grow. The aggregate demand grows faster than supply, and prices, especially of food and fuel, begin to rise. Eventually, these developments create conditions for increased poverty; they put a strain on social relationships and intensify class conflicts. Public revenues fall behind expenditures, and the states are reduced to near insolvency. The cultural mood changes; there is a sense of

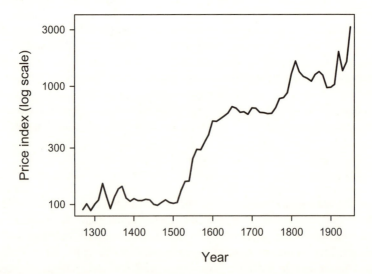

Figure 7.7 Price index of consumables (food, drink, fuel, and clothing) (Phelps-Brown and Hopkins 1956:Appendix B). A decadal average is plotted here.

social pessimism. The changed social environment impacts particularly hard on young people, who find it difficult to get good jobs or start a family. Finally, a triggering event (or, usually, a combination of events) precipitates a major crisis, leading to a protracted period of political disorder, social conflict, economic disruption, demographic contraction, and cultural despair. This general crisis relieves the pressures, so the economic trends run in reverse. Demand falls, prices deflate, and real wages begin to rise (because labor has become scarce). After some lag time, a period of new equilibrium develops, and the cultural mood becomes positive. Population starts to increase, and the cycle begins again.

Fischer collected together an enormous amount of cliometric material: changes in population; prices of food, oxen, and manufactures; import rates of precious metals; real wages, rents, and interest rates; and even crime, bastardy, and alcohol consumption rates. Using this array of quantitative data he then traced out the main stages (price revolution, crisis, and equilibrium) of each of the four great waves that, according to his analysis, occurred in western Europe during the last millennium.

The responses to Fischer's book were largely negative (e.g., Krugman 1997; de Vries 1998; Morgan 1999; Munro 1999). Reviewers criticized Fischer's caricaturization of the conventional theories of inflation, a lack of mathematically convincing models, and his failure to make a distinction between pre- and postindustrial revolution societies. These criticisms are fair. Yet, I think the majority of reviewers would also agree that Fischer managed to identify a very important and broad pattern of European history during the last millennium. (In the Appendix, Fischer briefly points out some similar-looking patterns in the ancient world and East Asia.)

Furthermore, Fischer's account and explanatory model are broadly consistent with the demographic-structural theory. Thus, the Goldstonian waves of early modern state breakdowns (during the seventeenth and nineteenth centuries) correspond to the crisis periods of the Fischerian second and third waves. Also, note that the duration of the three complete waves (3, 3, and 2 centuries, respectively) matches the theoretical predictions of the demographic-fiscal model of Section 7.2.1. Thus, I would argue that the models developed in this chapter may address at least one shortcoming of Fischer's book, its lack of explicit mathematical theory.

7.3.3 After the Black Death

The sudden arrival of the plague pandemic (the Black Death) in the mid-fourteenth century resulted in a massive perturbation of social, economic, and political structures of western Afroeurasian societies. The primary impact of the plague was the removal of one-third to one-half of the population in many communities. Therefore, we can view this perturbation as a "natural experiment" with which to test various theories using population numbers as an important explanatory variable. What is interesting is that different societies followed divergent social trajectories after the impact of the Black Death. The explanation of how the subsequent trajectory depended on the structural characteristics of the society becomes an important goal for comparative historical research. Many of the issues discussed during the Brenner debate (Aston and Philpin 1985) were closely related to this question.

A recent Ph.D. thesis by Stuart Borsch (2001) develops a particularly interesting comparison between post-plague Egypt and England. Both regions lost roughly half of their population, with the initial Black Death and subsequent plague outbreaks combined. In England wages rose, rents and grain prices dropped, unemployment decreased, per capita incomes rose, and the economy fully revived by the year 1500. In contrast, the consequences of depopulation in Egypt were profoundly different. Wages dropped, land rents and grain prices rose, and unemployment levels increased. No economic recovery was anywhere in sight by 1500: agricultural output had declined between 1350 and 1500 by 68%. Thus, one society, England, responded to depopulation in a typical Malthusian-Ricardian manner (however, this response still took more than a century; more on this below), while the other, Egypt, responded in a completely opposite way.

Borsch considers several alternative explanations of these divergent outcomes and focuses on the differences in the landholding systems as the main explanatory factor. From 1250 to 1517 Egypt was ruled by a group of specialized warriors known as Mamluks. Mamluks were "slave-soldiers," Christian or pagan children purchased via Italian intermediaries from the Caucasus. The Mamluk landholding system was very different from the forms it took in western Europe. Rather than forming a loose group of individual landholders closely associated with their estates and the local village communities, Mamluk landholders formed a unified body that would often act together to support their interests in the rural scene. In the postplague period Mamluks used their tremendous collective power in an attempt to maintain the same level of resource extraction from a greatly diminished rural population, resulting in a much higher level of exploitation of individual peasants (this is very similar to the dynamics predicted by the selfish elite model).

In England the elites also attempted to follow this route. The intense exploitation of peasants was one of the main reasons for the repeated peasant uprisings of the late fourteenth and early fifteenth centuries. Yet, as Borsch argues, the struggle between lord and peasant was won not on the battlefield (peasant mobs never had a chance against the heavily armed knights as long as the latter were acting in a cohesive manner), but by peasants voting en masse with their feet. Peasants were willing to abandon the estates if rent or wage conditions were not to their advantage. Eventually, the landlord attempt at collective action broke down and the peasants' demands were slowly but surely met. As rents dropped, rural wages rose, and customary fees and fines were abolished, peasant incomes rose, and the conditions were set for another period of sustained economic and demographic growth.

Potential critics of the Borsch argument may object by pointing to many other divergent aspects of the Egyptian and English societies. To this criticism, Borsch has an excellent response: another comparison, but this time to the situation in Egypt after the Antonine plagues of the late second century. Depopulation was severe, eliminating one-third of the tax-paying population. However, the landholding system of Roman Egypt was more similar to that of medieval England than to that of Mamluk Egypt. As a result Roman Egypt recovered relatively quickly from the devastation caused by the plagues, and in general its social trajectory was similar to that of post–Black Death England.

Assessment

I think that the argument constructed and defended by Borsch is very persuasive. This research is also an excellent example of the strength of the comparative approach in historical sociology. To the case studies of the divergent post–Black Death trajectories in western Europe (England and France) versus central Europe (Prussia, Poland, and Bohemia), discussed during the Brenner debate, Borsch adds two more "data points": Egypt after the Black Death and after the Antonine plagues. It is to be hoped that eventually we will have dozens of such data points with which to do statistics. A formal statistical meta-analysis will go a long way in laying the objections of critics to rest.

However, I would like to add one more element to the Borsch argument, suggested by the demographic-structural models. In particular, recollect that the selfish elite model predicts that the period of population decline is characterized by high elite/peasant ratios and correspondingly high exploitation rates. Eventually, however, the elite numbers decline, as a result of a combination of processes (sliding into the peasant class because of economic difficulties, lower reproduction, and high mortality resulting from civil wars). This is what happened in England by the end of the Wars of the Roses. As elite numbers decline to a low enough level, exploitation of peasants eases off, their per capita consumption rates rise, and the conditions are set for the next secular cycle to begin.

In Egypt, however, Mamluks continued to be recruited from exogenous sources (note that children of Mamluks could not themselves become Mamluks). Thus, while the rural population declined, Mamluk numbers did not, leading to a high elite/peasant ratio *that did not decline with time*. As a result, the Egypt of Mamluks was caught at the equilibrium of low population numbers, high elite/peasant ratio, and intense exploitation of peasants. This vicious equilibrium was apparently stable to internal perturbations and could only be broken by an outside force, in this case, the Ottoman conquest of 1517.

It is interesting that the comparison between the English and French post-plague trajectories provides further evidence for this scenario. Note that economic and demographic growth in England was delayed, perhaps by half a century, in comparison to France (this is discussed later in Section 9.1.2). The recovery of England was probably delayed because "the English nobility was (at least temporarily) able to resolve some of its difficulties at the expense of the French counterpart by means of the convulsions attendant upon the Hundred Years War" (Bois 1985:113). Once the English were expelled from France, they immediately experienced their own period of internal warfare (the Wars of the Roses, 1455–1485). Only after this extensive pruning of the English nobility could the English economy start growing again.

7.4 SUMMARY

- Population growth in agrarian societies leads to a gradual decrease in per capita production, due to diminishing returns on labor inputs into agriculture. The surplus available for the state shrinks and eventually becomes insufficient to provide for the state's needs. Thus, unchecked population growth leads to the fiscal insolvency of the polity.

- State breakdown and ensuing sociopolitical instability have a negative impact on both demographic rates (birth, death, and migration rates) and the productive capacity of the society. As a result, state breakdown is typically followed by periods of population decline.

- A simple mathematical model of the interaction between population dynamics and the fiscal health of the state predicts recurrent episodes of state building and population growth followed by state breakdown and population decline. For the range of plausible parameter values this demographic-fiscal model predicts that state breakdown should occur at somewhat irregular intervals 2–3 centuries apart.

- A more sophisticated model that keeps separate track of the commoner and elite segments of the population predicts similar dynamics (periodic state breakdown). Growth of the commoner population leads to the expansion of elite numbers and, initially, strengthening of the state. However, as elite numbers grow, an increasing proportion of the extracted product is appropriated by the elites for their needs. State revenues decline, while expenditures increase, and eventually the state becomes bankrupt.

- I develop two models focusing on the political dynamics of nomadic elites interacting with agrarian states. The Ibn Khaldun model investigates the situation in which nomads periodically conquer the agrarian state and establish a ruling dynasty there. The parasitic nomad model addresses the situation in which nomads do not conquer the agrarian state, instead imposing a tribute on it. In both cases the models predict faster cycles of polity building and collapse (periods of about a century), compared to cycles generated by the demographic-fiscal model and its class-structured variants.

- I briefly review two economic models advanced to explain the dynastic cycle in Chinese history. The basic logic underlying the explanation offered by these models of the collapse of Chinese Empires is also Malthusian-Ricardian, although they are somewhat more complex than the models I develop.

- The structural-demographic explanation of early modern state breakdown developed by Goldstone (1991b) postulates population growth as the primary cause of state collapse. It is important to emphasize, however, that in this theory (and in the models I develop) population dynamics do not directly cause the state breakdown. Rather, population growth promotes political instability indirectly, by causing the state's fiscal distress, increased elite competition and factionalism, and increased mobilization potential of the general populace. I review one of Goldstone's case studies, the English Revolution, for which a particularly complete cliometric database exists. These data are found to be in very good agreement with the quantitative predictions of the structural-demographic model.

- Finally, I briefly review Fischer's (1996) theory and data dealing with four "great waves" of socioeconomic dynamics in western Europe from the twelfth to the twentieth century. Again, my conclusion is that these ideas and analyses are broadly consistent with the theory developed in this chapter.

- Depending on the structural assumptions and parameter values, the models developed in this chapter can generate a variety of dynamics. Oscillations can be either regular or quite irregular. Average periods are generally long but may range from one to three centuries. Changes in the commoner population may be very drastic or mild (in the case of "elite cycles"). But one general conclusion is that agrarian states are characterized by instability and oscillations on the time scale of centuries. I propose that we call such dynamics *secular cycles* or *waves*.

Chapter Eight

Secular Cycles in Population Numbers

8.1 INTRODUCTION

A major prediction emerging from the demographic-structural theory (Chapter 7) is that population numbers in agrarian societies are expected to go through slow oscillations with a periodicity of approximately two to three centuries.[1] We do not necessarily expect these *secular cycles* to be very regular. What the theory does say, however, is that these dynamics should be of second order. The concept of process order was introduced in Section 2.1.4 and will be further formalized for human population dynamics below. Put in nontechnical language, however, what I mean is that both the increase and decrease phases of population oscillations should occur over periods of multiple human generations.

Secular waves in the socioeconomic and demographic history of western Europe have been described by François Simiand(1932), Wilhelm Abel (1966), Michael Postan (1973), and Emmanuel Le Roy Ladurie (1974) (see also Braudel 1988; Fischer 1996). Recently, Sergey Nefedov (1999, 2002a) presented data suggesting that secular cycles also occur in several macroregions of Asia (China, the Middle East, and India).

Much of the data on population fluctuations with which these authors worked is of a fragmentary nature. Nevertheless, several data series of reasonable length have been compiled and published in recent years. This development presents us with an opportunity to test the predictions of the demographic-structural theory by using the formal methods of time-series analysis in order to estimate empirically the periodicity and process order characterizing long-term fluctuations in population numbers. Performing such an analysis is the main goal of this chapter. I begin by discussing how the process order can be estimated from time-series data on population dynamics. Next, I apply the statistical approach to the available time-series data on historical population dynamics. Finally, I extend the analysis to one case study in which we have data on both population numbers and the dynamics of sociopolitical instability.

8.2 "SCALE" AND "ORDER" IN HUMAN POPULATION DYNAMICS

Population ecologists have recently made great strides in modeling, analyzing, and explaining the population dynamics of nonhuman organisms. I review these

---

[1] Note that in this chapter I will not deal with nomadic societies, or societies dominated by nomadic elites, whose oscillations are predicted to occur on a faster time scale (Section 7.2.3).

developments in my book on *Complex Population Dynamics* (Turchin 2003). Is it possible that we can transfer some of the techniques and insights developed by population ecologists to the study of human population dynamics? Certainly, the set of specific mechanisms that affect human reproduction, mortality, and migration should be very different from those proposed for animals. Many of these mechanisms must be economic and sociological in nature, and it seems highly unlikely that certain ecological models, e.g. a predator-prey model with humans playing the role of prey, would be of use in studying human populations. On the other hand, ecological models such as those dealing with resource-consumer or disease-host interactions may be quite relevant to understanding the dynamics of historic and prehistoric human populations, as long as we do not fall into the trap of biologism, by attempting to explain everything solely in biological terms. What is important to note here is that population dynamicists have developed a set of general approaches to the nonlinear modeling of time-series data coming from population systems. These methods do not assume specific ecological models, that may or may not apply to human populations. Rather, they provide us with tools for quantifying empirical patterns in temporal fluctuations of population numbers.

In Section 2.1.4 I introduced the concept of *process order*. It turns out that this concept is very useful in investigations of population dynamics of nonhuman organisms (Turchin 2003). However, while order is a readily definable property of differential equations (in which context I introduced it in Section 2.1.4), the application of this concept to the analysis of time-series data is not completely straightforward. The important point is that the order that we estimate from data depends on the temporal scale at which population fluctuations are quantified. Thus, a few remarks are warranted on the temporal scale at which various mechanisms affecting population change operate.

Temporal Scale: Years

Let us consider four potential time scales: years, decades, centuries, and millennia. The first of these scales, years, is an important pacesetter for the dynamics of the resource base of human populations, because usually food gathering and production are strongly influenced by seasonal cycles. Additionally, many sources of mortality operate on a yearly (or faster) scale. For example, research on the dynamics of childhood diseases shows that these historically important sources of mortality have their own rhythms: the annual cycle driven by seasonal variation in contact rate (Yorke and London 1973), and a characteristic 2–3 year oscillation associated with the nonlinear nature of population interaction between infants and the pathogen (Schaffer and Kot 1985). Other sources of mortality that should be strongly affected by a seasonal cycle are death as a result of exposure to inclement weather and starvation due to seasonal dearth.

Temporal Scale: Decades and Centuries

The next scale, decades, is the appropriate one for measuring replacement of human populations due to reproduction. The important benchmark here is some measure of generation time. The reproductive age for human females extends from 15 to 45 years of age (Wood 1990). However, the curve of fecundability as a function of age is skewed, so that its mode (maximum fertility rate) is at roughly 20, while its mean (average age of female at birth) is around 25, and in some populations closer to (or even over) 30 years. Certainly, there is a large amount of variation in these measures of generation length for humans, depending on biological (nutrition, mortality schedules) and social (age at marriage) characteristics of the population. It is clear, though, that for most historical human populations generation time should lie in the interval between 20 and 30 years.

General population dynamics theory suggests that population dynamics may have oscillatory components falling within three broad classes: generation, first-order, and second-order cycles (Turchin 2003). *Generation cycles* are characterized by a period of between 20 and 30 years. These cycles are often found in human populations (Keyfitz 1972). They become apparent when population age structure is represented as an age pyramid. For example, the age pyramid for the current U.S.A. population has clear bulges separated by around 30 years, representing baby boomers and children of baby boomers. Generation cycles are even more apparent in the population of present-day Russia, a fact probably explained by two huge perturbations of age structure—World War I/Civil War and World War II—were separated by roughly one generation time, setting a series of ensuing oscillations. Unlike generation cycles in certain insect populations (Godfray and Hassell 1989), however, human generation cycles do not appear to be stable phenomena, and dissipate rather rapidly after a perturbation (Wachter and Lee 1989). Furthermore, generation cycles are usually expressed as oscillations in age structure and have only a weak effect on total numbers.

Unlike generation cycles, which arise as a result of interactions between age classes, *first-order cycles* result from relatively fast density-dependent feedback mechanisms. First-order cycles arise most naturally in discrete population models, and have a typical period of two generations (one generation at high density, the next at low, and so on). The existence of first-order cycles in human populations was hypothesized by Easterlin (1980). Easterlin suggested that, during the twentieth century, U.S. demography was characterized by an alternation of large- and small-cohort generations. A sparse generation enjoys better wages (due to labor shortages) and produces many children. The next generation, however, experiences increased competition and produces few children. This mechanism can theoretically lead to a typical first-order oscillation with an average period of two generations (40–50 years). Although formal models confirm that two-generation cycles can in principle occur, in practice the estimates of parameters are such that they do not place the model in the cyclic regime (Lee 1974; see also Frauental and Swick 1983; Wachter and Lee 1989).

Second-order cycles arise as a result of population size interacting with some other *slow* dynamical variable (see Section 2.1.4). An example of second-order oscillations is the dynamics of the demographic-fiscal model of state breakdown (Figure 7.1). Unlike typical first-order cycles, in which the increase and decrease phases are each one generation long, second-order oscillations are characterized by increase and decrease phases of multiple generations in duration. Thus, the basic trichotomy of generation, first-order, and second-order cycles results in typical periods of one, two, or many generations.

Let us consider what would be an appropriate temporal scale for studying second-order oscillations, were they to exist for human populations. Population theory based on discrete models suggests that second-order cycles are characterized by a minimum period of six generations (Murdoch et al. 2002). Typical periods in such models range from 6 to 12–15 and more generations (Turchin 2003). Bracketing the human generation time by 20 and 30 years suggests that second-order cycles in humans should have periods ranging from 120 to 450 years, with the most likely region of 200–300 years. Of course, this calculation assumes that factor X—the slow dynamical variable, whose interaction with population density drives the oscillations—operates at a temporal scale similar to that characterizing movements of human populations. However, this is probably not a bad assumption, to a first approximation, because if the two interacting variables operate on too different temporal scales then we cannot easily get second-order dynamics (if one variable operates on a time scale much faster than the other, the feedback for the slow variable essentially becomes "fast," and the dynamics become first order). Similar periods are suggested by simple continuous-time models. For example, in the Lotka-Volterra predation model (Section 2.1.3), the period of oscillations is approximately $2\pi/\sqrt{(r\delta)}$, where r is the per capita rate of prey population growth, and δ is the analogous parameter for the predators (it is actually the per capita decline rate of predator population in the absence of prey). Assuming that r and δ are of the same order of magnitude as the intrinsic per capita rate of human population growth, r_0, leads to a (very rough) period estimate of $2\pi/r_0$. Because r_0 of human populations should be around 0.02 yr^{-1} (although in modern times some populations have been known to grow at 4% annual rate, this is probably an overestimate for historical times), the estimate of the oscillation period is 300 years. This estimate is similar to that suggested by the discrete-time theory above. In summary, my expectation is that second-order cycles in human populations, if they exist, should be characterized by periods of 2–3 centuries.

The rough calculations in the above paragraph should be taken only as an indicator of the order of magnitude of period length that might characterize second-order oscillations in human population dynamics. Clearly, periodicity will change depending on the nature of variables, model structure, and parameter values. On the other hand, we do have a theory for population dynamics in agrarian societies (Chapter 7). Models based on the demographic-structural theory predict oscillations with period ranging from one to three centuries, depending on the model structure and parameter values. This theoretical result provides a somewhat firmer basis for the prediction of oscillation periods.

Temporal Scale: Millennia

Finally, I briefly turn to processes operating on much longer—millennial—scales. This is the time scale of evolution of human societies, including their technological and cultural components. The big roadposts are the agricultural and industrial revolutions, respectively around 10,000 and 200 years ago. Currently, the pace of change has become almost frenetic, but prior to the industrial revolution, we can still probably assume some degree of quasistationarity at the scale of each millennium. Thus, according to the estimates of McEvedy and Jones (1978), the typical doubling time of the global human population, prior to the industrial age, was around 1000 years.

Evolutionary change of human societies is certainly something that we have to take into account when analyzing long-term data on human population dynamics (see, for example, Komlos and Nefedov 2002). If our main interest is not in millennial-scale processes, however, we will have to apply detrending to the data. Detrending is particularly appropriate in those cases where we have a clear mechanistic basis for understanding why the carrying capacity has changed historically. Ideally, we would use historical information to estimate how many people a unit of land could maintain, given the contemporary level of technology. Here I will not follow this tack, because it would take me much beyond the scope of this book, and simply employ phenomenological detrending methods.

Implications

The preceding discussion makes it clear that the appropriate temporal scale for studying human dynamics depends greatly on the questions of interest. If we are concerned with the dynamics of measles epidemics, then we should use the scale of months and years. At the other extreme, if we are interested in modeling how the capacity of the Earth to sustain human population evolved as a result of technological and societal change, then our time scale is centuries and millennia. However, if we are interested in first-order processes that regulate human population density, and in mechanisms that may cause second-order cycles, then our temporal scale should be intermediate: decades (the basic time step at which we measure population density) and centuries (the length of time series). More specifically, we need to follow a population for at least 500–600 years, in order to have the minimum sample size, two oscillations (assuming that each oscillation is around 2–3 centuries in length). This is a rough guide, but it suggests that if we have data sampled at yearly intervals, we might just as well subsample the series at 10-year intervals—we are not really throwing out any useful information by doing that. Data series sampled at 20- or 30-year intervals (approximately one human generation) are also acceptable. But any data series that was collected at intervals greater than two generations (50 years) is seriously undersampled. After all, one needs at the minimum four points per cycle to characterize it as such, and one-fourth of a cycle of 200–300 years is 50–75 years.

I searched the literature on historical demography for time-series data of sufficient length (at least 500 years) and sampled at sufficiently frequent intervals (not more than 50 years) for a defined locality (typically corresponding to a modern country or to a province in a country). One problem in obtaining data relevant to our purposes is that historical demographers ask very different kinds of questions. A population dynamicist is primarily interested in relative changes of density with time, and knowing the absolute scale is not as important. By contrast, historical demographers typically attempt to estimate the absolute density at a particular point in time. Another problem is that a large amount of guesswork is often involved in reconstructing the historical dynamics of human populations. Historical demography is a very controversial subject, and hugely different estimates of population numbers can be proffered by different authorities. One possible way of getting around the subjective element is the methods of archaeology, and I will discuss some archaeological data sets below.

8.3 LONG-TERM EMPIRICAL PATTERNS

8.3.1 Reconstructions of Historical Populations

I begin with what I consider the best data set, the population history of England and Wales between 1080 and 2000 C.E. (Figure 8.1). This data set involves the least amount of guesswork, compared to the rest (with the exception of the archaeological data). For the period of 1800–2000, we can use the results of regular censuses. The period of 1540–1800 is almost as solid, because it is based on the excellent work by Wrigley, Schofield, and co-workers, who used the technique of population reconstruction based on parish records documenting births and deaths during this period (Wrigley and Schofield 1981; Wrigley et al. 1997). The earliest period, from 1080 to 1540 C.E. (taken from Wrigley 1969), is the one where the subjective element is the strongest. Still, the population dynamics of medieval England are known as well as those for any other country. At the beginning of

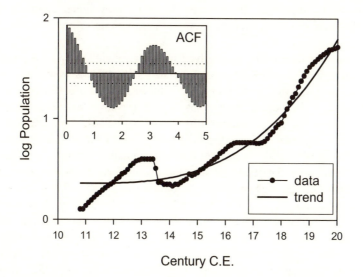

Figure 8.1 Population of England and Wales, 1080–2000 C.E. Population numbers, in millions, sampled every 10 years, are plotted on a log scale. Trend: fitted curve $Y = a + bX^\theta$, where $Y = \log N(t)$ and X is time scaled to the interval 0–1. ACF: the autocorrelation function of the detrended data. All time units (including ACF lags) are in centuries.

the period, the population record is anchored in the Domesday Book census. The timing of the population collapse associated with the Black Death is also solidly dated. The uncertainty primarily concerns the height of the pre–Black Death peak and the depth of the postplague collapse (Hatcher 1996).

Two features are readily apparent on Figure 8.1. The first is the increasing trend. The trend is nonlinear and greatly accelerates around 1800. The mechanism underlying this trend is probably uncontroversial (the Industrial Revolution), and does not concern us here. To quantitatively characterize the trend, I fitted a power relationship to the data in Figure 8.1. The second feature of the data is the oscillation around the general trend. In order to be able to characterize the oscillatory component, I detrended the series by subtracting the fitted power curve from the data.

The detrended data were subjected to time-series analysis. First, we calculate the autocorrelation function (shown as the inset in Figure 8.1), which has a clear oscillatory tendency, reaching the first peak at 3.1 centuries. The next step is to apply some standard tools from the population dynamicist's kit (time-series techniques for the analysis of population data are described in Turchin 2003: Chapter 7). The basic idea of the analysis, developed by Box and Jenkins (for a readable introduction, see Chatfield 1989), is to regress the current population density, N_t, on lagged population densities $N_{t-\tau}$, $N_{t-2\tau}$, etc. where τ is the time lag. I used the approach known as nonlinear time-series modeling (NLTSM), which approximates the relationship between current and lagged densities using a modified polynomial scheme (for details of the implementation, see Turchin 2003). There are two structural parameters that also need to be estimated from the data: the number of lagged densities, d, and the polynomial degree, q. We are primarily interested in d, because it provides us with an estimate of the process order.

One question that has to be resolved in order for the analysis to proceed is, what value of the time lag, τ, is appropriate? The series is sampled at 10-year intervals, but this was done simply for convenience. Above, I argued that the generation time for human populations should lie somewhere in the interval of 20–30 years. To be safe, therefore, I used both lag values, $\tau = 2$ and 3 decades, and checked how this choice affects the results (and I repeat this procedure below, in the analysis of the long-term data on population dynamics in China). As Table 8.1 indicates, the results of the analysis with either choice of τ are congruent. Both choices suggest a high signal/noise ratio ($R^2 = 0.7$–0.8) and rather unstable dynamics (Λ near 0). The evidence that the dynamical process is of second order (or higher) is very strong. It is noteworthy that, although different choices of τ result in different estimates of d, when we express the maximum process order in physical units (τd), we obtain the same value, 60 years. To summarize, the analysis of this data series suggests a second-order, oscillatory population process, with a strong deterministic component, but rather low amplitude (at least, by the standards of nonhuman population dynamics; see Turchin 2003). These results appear to be robust with respect to various choices that we need to make in the process of the analysis. For example, I reanalyzed the data

Table 8.1 Summary of nonlinear time-series modeling analysis of the English and Chinese population data. Quantities: number of data points n, time lag τ (in decades), measure of amplitude (standard deviation of log-transformed data) S, dominant period T (also in decades), autocorrelation at the dominant period ACF[T] (** = ACF is significantly different from 0 at lag = T; * = same at lag = $T/2$), estimated process order d, polynomial degree q, the coefficient of determination of the best model R^2, and the estimated dominant Lyapunov exponent Λ.

Location	n	τ	S	T	ACF[T]	d	q	R^2	Λ
England	93	2	0.11	31	0.60**	3	2	0.72	−0.04
England	93	3	0.11	31	0.60**	2	2	0.77	0.02
China 1	64	2	0.15	23	0.21*	2	2	0.63	0.08
China 1	64	3	0.15	23	0.21*	2	2	0.32	0.08
China 2	64	2	0.10	31	0.40**	2	1	0.54	−0.40
China 2	64	3	0.10	31	0.40**	3	2	0.15	−0.20
China 3	64	2	0.05	13	0.04*	2	1	0.64	−0.26
China 3	64	3	0.05	13	0.04*	2	1	0.16	−0.42

Data: England (including Wales): 1080–2000 C.E., China 1: 200 B.C.E.–430 C.E., China 2: 440–1070 C.E., China 3: 1080–1710 C.E. (all series detrended). Note that all series are sampled at 10-year intervals; therefore, all periods (T) and time lags (τ) are indicated in the same time units, decades.

using a quadratic detrend instead of the power function; I also analyzed separately the 1500–2000 C.E. segment, where the amount of guesswork in obtaining the numbers was minimal. In all cases, the general results were unchanged.

The implications of this analysis are startling, but before making any far reaching conclusions, we need to check on these results by looking at other data sets. The first obvious place to look to is other western European countries during the last millennium. I am unaware of any data sets similar in quality and length to the one constructed by Wrigley and co-workers, but a useful overview, albeit of lesser quality, is provided by the population atlas of McEvedy and Jones. This in many ways excellent compilation of long-term population dynamics, organized by country, suffers, in my opinion, from one failing: the tendency of the authors to underemphasize the degree of fluctuation. To give an example where we can obtain an independent check, McEvedy and Jones suggest that population numbers in England increased throughout the seventeenth century (although at a declining rate): 4.25, 5, and 5.75 million in 1600, 1650, and 1700 C.E., respectively. Yet the population reconstruction by Wrigley and co-workers, which became available after the publication of the McEvedy and Jones atlas, suggests that all population increase occurred during the first half (from 5.05 to 5.83 million), and in fact population slightly decreased by the early eighteenth century (to 5.73 million in 1710). Nevertheless, there is a virtue in the conservatism of McEvedy and Jones:

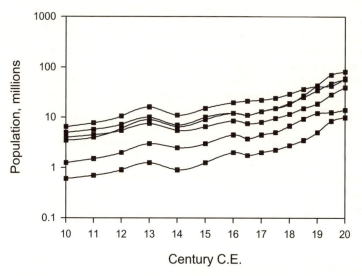

Figure 8.2 Population of several European countries, 1000–2000 C.E. The countries are (in order of population magnitude at 1000 C.E., from larger to smaller) France, Italy, Spain, Germany, Czechoslovakia, Portugal. Data from McEvedy and Jones, supplemented by U.S. Census Bureau for year 2000.

where they indicate sharp changes in population numbers, it is likely that the historical evidence for such events is quite strong.

In Figure 8.2 I reproduce the population trajectories suggested by McEvedy and Jones for the four largest western European countries, as well as for two smaller ones, located to the southwest, and east, respectively, of the big four. Although the data are not detailed enough for formal analysis, we see that the general pattern exhibited by England is also present in other European countries: an increasing millennial trend, and three secular cycles around the trend, with population growth slowing down or reversing in the fourteenth, seventeenth, and late twentieth centuries. Only France does not exhibit a seventeenth-century decline, which is a result of the McEvedy and Jones conservatism referred to above (as we shall see in the next chapter, where I look at more detailed French population data). Additionally, the averaging of the dynamics of southern and northern France serves to further mask the degree of change. It is well documented, for example, that the population of southern France declined during the period of 1680–1750 (Le Roy Ladurie 1974), while northern France lost population earlier (for example, see Reinhard et al. 1968: Figure 13). Currently (2000 C.E.), all European countries exhibit a deficit of births over deaths, and in half of them, where immigration does not compensate this deficit, population is actually declining (U.S. Census Bureau data).

I now turn to the opposite end of Eurasia, and consider the population dynamics in China. The picture for China is complex. On one hand, the central authority in China (when it existed) conducted detailed censuses for tax purposes. On the other hand, corrupt or lazy officials often falsified or fabricated population data

(Ho 1959). Conversion coefficients between the number of taxable households and the actual population are often unknown, and, what is worse, these coefficients probably changed from dynasty to dynasty. The area controlled by the state also continually changed. Finally, it is often difficult to determine whether the number of taxable households declined during the times of trouble as a result of demographic change (death and emigration), or as a result of the state's failure to control and enumerate the subject population. Thus, there is a certain degree of controversy among the experts (Ho 1959; Durand 1960; Song et al. 1985). However, the controversy primarily concerns the absolute population levels, and there is a substantial degree of agreement on the *relative* changes in population density (which are, of course, of primary interest for our purposes). The Chinese population, essentially, expanded during periods of political stability and declined (sometimes precipitously) during periods of unrest. As a result, population movements closely mirror the "dynastic cycle" in China (Ho 1959; Reinhard et al. 1968).

The most detailed trajectory of population dynamics in China was published by Chao and Hsieh (1988). These authors give estimates of Chinese population numbers at irregular time intervals. In order to make the data suitable for time series analysis, I interpolated Chao and Hsieh data using an exponential kernel with bandwidth of 10 years and then subsampled the resulting smoothed trajectory at 10-year intervals. The trajectory is clearly nonstationary and has at least two abrupt steplike changes: (1) until the eleventh century, the population peaked in the vicinity of 50 million; (2) from the twelfth to the beginning of the eighteenth century, population peaks doubled to around 100 million, (3) beginning in the eighteenth century the population started growing at a very rapid pace, reaching 400 million during the nineteenth and more than 1 billion during the twentieth century. The mechanism underlying the shift from period 1 to period 2 is known. Prior to the eleventh century, the center of gravity of the Chinese state was situated in the north, with the south lightly settled. Under the Sung dynasty the south matched and then overtook the north (for example, see Reinhard et al. 1968: Figures 14 and 115).

Dropping the third period as least amenable to detrending, I focused on the period from 200 B.C.E. to 1710 C.E., which gives us 192 points (sampled at decadal intervals). If we divide this series into three equal-sized pieces, then the second division neatly separates the 50 million peak period from that characterized by 100 million peaks (see Figure 8.3). The splitting of the series into 6.4-century-long pieces seems appropriate, because each piece should be long enough for several oscillations (= "data points").

The results of analyzing these three series, using both delay choices (two and three decades), are presented in Table 8.1. The analysis detects a somewhat lower signal/noise ratio and more negative Lyapunov exponents in the Chinese series compared to the England data (the difference is especially clear when $\tau = 3$ is used). This is probably due, at least in part, to the greater measurement error, but there also seems to be a genuine difference between western European and Chinese dynamics, in that Chinese oscillations are much more variable in period.

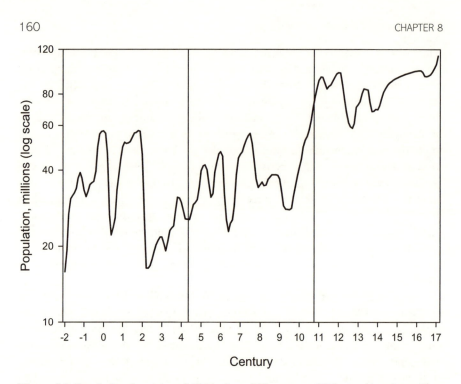

Figure 8.3 Population dynamics of China from 200 B.C.E. to 1710 C.E. (data from Chao and Hsieh 1988). Vertical lines indicate where data were split.

Additionally, the nature of the periodicity is complex, with several oscillations appearing to be superimposed on each other. Thus, in the second and third pieces, there appear to be two coexisting oscillations: a short one with the period of 1.3–1.5 centuries, and a longer one with a period of 3–4 centuries. Given such variability in periodicity estimates among the three series, we should take these results with a grain of salt: the evidence for periodicity in the Chinese data is not strong. By contrast, the evidence for second-order dynamics is completely consistent across replicate series and time-delay choices (Table 8.1). To conclude, although the results of this analysis should be interpreted cautiously, given the uncertainty associated with estimates of Chinese population numbers, it provides important confirmatory evidence to the detection of second-order oscillations in western European data.

Population reconstructions for other areas are not as good as those for western Europe and China and thus not suitable for formal time-series analysis. One example is the very interesting data presented by Whitmore and co-workers (Whitmore et al. 1993) on population dynamics in Mesopotamia, Egypt, Yucatan, and the central Mexican plateau. These data show that the typical state of human populations is not stasis or slow growth, but oscillations—periods of growth interspersed with periods of decline (sometimes very sharp). Unfortunately, the data are not sampled frequently enough to be useful for time-series analysis. Interestingly, Whitmore and co-workers suggest that the "pace" of human dynamics has greatly increased with history, so that oscillations (or "waves," as they call them) in the distant past were slow, taking many millennia to complete their course, while oscillations in the more recent past are only a few centuries in period. My problem with this generalization is that it could easily arise as an artifact of our incomplete knowledge of history. Since early history is much less known than more recent history, it is quite possible that we "missed" many more instances of population decline in the distant compared to the proximate past. Such a systematic bias could produce the same pattern of apparently accelerating oscillations. A possible example is the case of Maya population history. The first archaeologists who studied the ruins of the Maya civilization did not even suspect that at some point in their history Maya societies sustained highly dense populations. The original picture was that of ceremonial centers embedded in a matrix of rainforest cultivated by swidden agriculturalists. Later archaeological work showed beyond any degree of reasonable doubt that at their peak (or, more likely, peaks) Mayan societies cultivated large areas very intensively. Accordingly, early reconstructions proposed a long period—more than 1000 years—of very slow increase, followed by a rapid (1 century) collapse. Even more recent evidence shows that there were repeated cycles of centralization followed by state collapse in the uplands of Guatemala and Peten (Culbert and Rice 1990). Thus, it is becoming clear that Mayan population history was quite complex, although we will have to wait for more archaeological data and better methods before we have a data series suitable for analysis by the methods discussed in this book.

8.3.2 Archaeological Data

The methods of archaeology offer great promise for resolving many current controversies about the dynamics of historic (and prehistoric) populations. A general problem with archaeological sources of population estimates is that they are indirect. They rely on a physical record left by humans: most often, on the number of houses or settlements that were occupied at a certain period in time. Human density can also be estimated by the amount of food they grew, using, for example, pollen cores. The problem in all these cases is to translate the quantitative measures of human activities in the archaeological record into the number of people. For example, if we have an estimate of how many structures were present at some point in time, we need to also know how many people, on average, inhabited each structure. I note that this is not an insurmountable problem. In fact, in population ecology researchers often rely on indices of population density that may even be nonlinearly related to density itself (an example is the data on the famous 10-year cycle in lynx fur returns). Furthermore, our primary interest is in *relative* population fluctuations, which are easier to document than absolute population densities.

The great advantage of archaeological methods is that they offer a potentially more objective way of reconstructing population history. These approaches clearly can have biases and require a lot of thought in real-life applications (Dewar 1991; Curet 1998), but generally the amount of subjectivity and guesswork is reduced.

As I stated in Section 8.2, to be useful for our purposes, a population history must be sampled at no longer than 50-year intervals. Thus, most population estimates published in the archaeological literature are not yet suitable for analysis. An example of a data set that comes close is a very interesting reconstruction of the population history of the Deh Luran Plain in the Middle East (Dewar in Neeley and Wright 1994:211), which shows at least three huge oscillations in density (ten-fold peak/trough ratios). However, the sampling interval is around 200–300 years, which is much too sparse for formal analysis.

There are, however, several examples in which the sampling rate is starting to approach the one we need. The first example relates to the question of the population history of the Roman Empire, which has been hotly debated for decades (Scheidel 2001). The issue is what role depopulation may have played in the collapse of the Roman Empire. The problem is that the first evidence of depopulation shows up as early as the later decades of the Republic (Brunt 1971). A remarkable data set, recently published by Lewit (1991) throws a new light on this problem (Figure 8.4). It turns out that there were two episodes of settlement abandonment in the Roman Empire: during the third and fifth centuries. The third-century decline (and the fourth-century revival) must have involved quite substantial changes in population numbers, since change in the proportion of settlements occupied underestimates the amplitude of population change. These data are discussed further in Section 9.1.

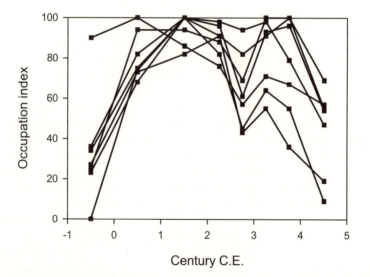

Figure 8.4 Relative proportion of excavated settlements occupied during each period in seven western areas of Roman Empire (Britain, Belgica, Northern and Southern Gaul, Italy, and Northern and Southern Spain). (Data from Lewit 1991)

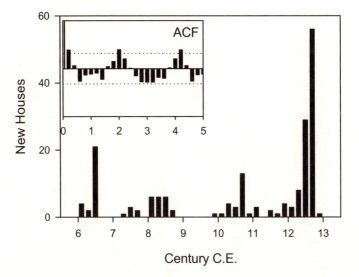

Figure 8.5 New houses built on Wetherill Mesa. ACF: the autocorrelation function of the square-root transformed data (lag units in centuries).

Another example of site occupancy data, this time from the New World, was published by Hally (1996) for platform mounds in Georgia during 1000–1600 C.E., suggesting three oscillations in the northwestern part of the area, but only two oscillations in the southeast. Lack of space prevents me from providing more examples of this kind. However, one last data set (Varien 1999), also from the New World, needs to be mentioned because of its uniquely fine temporal resolution. The data come from Mesa Verde (Colorado) where, as a result of the dry climate, logs used in house construction can be preserved for centuries (and, incidentally, used over and over in building houses). Using dendrochronological methods, archaeologists can precisely date the time when the logs were cut. The distribution of times when logs found at one site, Wetherill Mesa, were cut is shown in Figure 8.5. These data show that there were four spurts of house-building activity on Wetherill Mesa, occurring during the seventh, ninth, eleventh, and thirteenth centuries, suggesting that these centuries were periods of rapid population growth. Following periods of building activity were typically periods of no building at all (around the years 700, 900, and after 1300; only during the twelfth-century did low levels of building activity persist between the eleventh- and thirteenth-century peaks). Unfortunately, we cannot analyze these data using the standard NLTSM approach, because the structure of the process generating them is very different from regular population processes (in effect, we have some information on what happens during the population increase periods, but data on population declines are completely censored from the data set). However, we can calculate the ACF, after transforming the data, to ameliorate the skewness (see the inset in Figure 8.5). The ACF clearly reveals a two-century cycle in the data.

8.4 POPULATION DYNAMICS AND POLITICAL INSTABILITY

While the finding of secular oscillations in human population data is in basic agreement with the demographic-structural model, it is possible that other sociodemographic processes could produce the same empirical pattern. It would be much more satisfying to test the predictions of the demographic-structural theory directly, by examining whether the relationship between population fluctuations and political instability in the historical record conforms to the pattern predicted by theory. One very interesting paper that addresses this issue is that of Cyrus Chu and Ronald Lee (1994), which I already discussed in the context of models of the dynastic cycle in China. These authors analyzed the population time series for China developed by Chao and Hsieh (1988) and two dummy variables for peasant rebellion and incidence of war. The dummy variables take the value 1 if rebellion (or war) is present, otherwise they are set to 0. An additional predictor variable used by Chu and Lee was the temperature time series.

Chu and Lee fitted a series of models to the data, starting with simpler ones and then increasing the number of explanatory variables. They found that the model that included the effect of temperature and warfare, but not peasant rebellions, explained a small proportion of the variance in the population data ($R^2 = 0.021$). By contrast, the R^2 of the model that also included rebellions was about five times as high, 0.116. The coefficient characterizing the effect of rebellion on population change was highly significant. There was also a statistically significant effect of population density on the incidence of rebellion.

One of the reasons for a small R^2 characterizing the effect of rebellion on population change is the nature of the data used by Chu and Lee. Because they only had a dummy characterization of revolt, they did not know the scale of the uprising, and consequently their analysis did not distinguish between small and large uprisings (Chu and Lee 1994:367). Apparently, Chu and Lee were not aware of the data set on the incidence of internal war in China constructed by J. S. Lee (1931). This index gives us a graduated scale for measuring political instability in China. Plotting the population and internal war data on the same graph, we observe that there appears to be some sort of dynamic relationship (Figure 8.6; focusing on the relatively stationary period from 200 B.C.E. to 1070 C.E.).

To formally investigate the interactive effects of population dynamics and political instability on each other, I used an extension of the nonlinear time-series analysis of the Chinese data in Section 8.3.1. We found there that the process order of Chinese population dynamics, when measured on the generational time scale, was definitely 2 (or higher). I now would like to test the hypothesis that political instability is the endogenous variable that drives the second-order oscillations. If this hypothesis is correct, then we should detect a strong influence of political instability on the per capita rate of population change.

I fitted a series of models to the per capita rate of population change, defined as $r_t \equiv \ln(N_t/N_{t-\tau})$, characterized by the same general form

$$r_t = f(N_{t-\tau}, W_{t-\tau}) + \epsilon_t, \tag{8.1}$$

where W_t is the index of political instability. J. S. Lee's incidence of internal warfare was reported at five-year intervals, while the population data come on

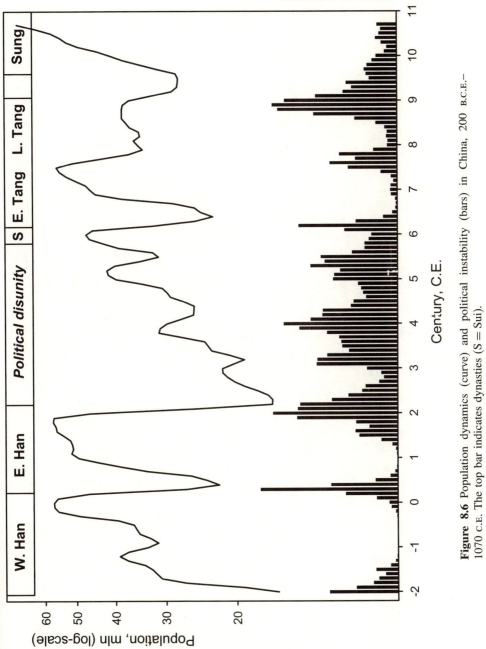

Figure 8.6 Population dynamics (curve) and political instability (bars) in China, 200 B.C.E.–1070 C.E. The top bar indicates dynasties (S = Sui).

Table 8.2 Coefficients of determination in models fitted to population rate of change and political instability index.

	Period		
Response variable	200 B.C.E.–430 C.E.	440–1070 C.E.	1080–1710 C.E.
	$\tau = 20$		
Population	0.59	0.57	0.59
Instability	0.82	0.62	0.37
	$\tau = 30$		
Population	0.67	0.67	0.61
Instability	0.66	0.36	0.11

a decadal scale. To bring both sets of data to a common temporal resolution, I smoothed Lee's index using an exponential kernel regression with bandwidth $h = 10$ years, and resampled the resulting curve at 10-year intervals, giving me the variable W_t ($t = -200, -190, \ldots, 1700, 1710$ C.E.). In other words, I treated the internal warfare data in the same way as population data (see Section 8.3.1).

Because the functional form of $f(\cdot)$ in equation (8.1) is not known, I approximated it using the response surface methodology (RSM) of Box and Draper (1987). RSM is a modified polynomial approximation scheme, in which the predictor variables (in this case, $N_{t-\tau}$ and $W_{t-\tau}$) are subjected to the Box-Cox transformation. There was strong evidence for curvilinear effects (see below), and thus I used second-degree polynomials to approximate $f(\cdot)$. For the analysis I broke the whole time series from –200 to 1710 C.E. into three equal-length pieces of 64 data points each (this is the identical procedure to that used in Section 8.3.1). It reduces the influence of nonstationarity, and also allows us to check on whether the relationship between population dynamics and political instability changes with period. Finally, to make sure that a specific choice of the base lag τ does not unduly affect the results, I performed all analyses for two choices, $\tau = 20$ and 30 years.

There was a highly significant effect of political instability on population dynamics in all three periods and for both choices of τ (Table 8.2). The density dependence and political instability jointly explained around 60% of the variance in r_t. The direction of the effect was as expected from theory (Figure 8.7).

Population density had a negative effect on the population rate of change, reflecting the basic density-dependent pattern of population dynamics. Political instability also had a negative effect on population increase. Interestingly, the effects of density and instability were synergistic, as indicated by a statistically significant interaction term. We can see this effect in Figure 8.7: the population decline was particularly pronounced if *both* population density and political instability were high.

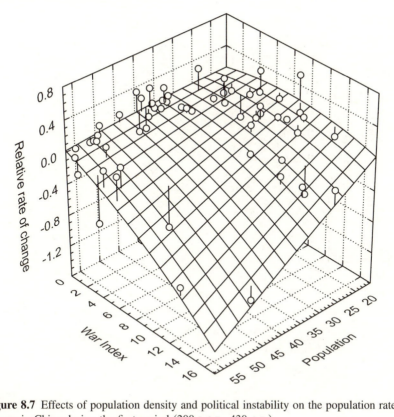

Figure 8.7 Effects of population density and political instability on the population rate of change in China during the first period (200 B.C.E.–430 C.E.).

A similar analysis was performed on political instability as response variable (I log-transformed W_t in order to make the data more normally distributed). The proportion of variance explained by the model declined from the earliest to the latest period (Table 8.2). The population density at time $t - \tau$ had a positive effect on instability at time t (Figure 8.8). The past value of instability ($W_{t-\tau}$) also had a positive effect on the present instability (W_t) (Figure 8.8).

In summary, the analysis of Chinese data provides strong empirical confirmation of the endogenous version of the demographic-structural model. Both links, from population to instability and back, are substantiated in the data. The coefficients of determination are high, generally over 50% (except in the case of the N on W effect during the third period).

8.5 SUMMARY

- I searched the literature to locate any data set on relative population fluctuations that was at least 5 centuries long, and sampled at intervals of 50 years or better. I identified a number of such data sets from Europe, China,

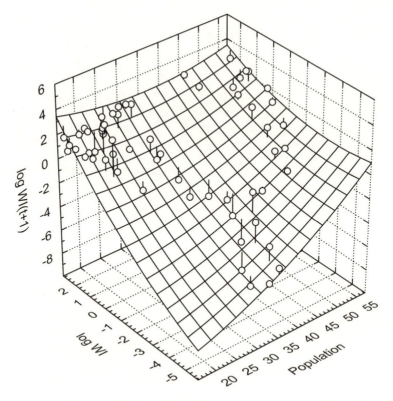

Figure 8.8 The effect of population density and previous political instability on the current instability in China during the first period (200 B.C.E.–430 C.E.).

and North America. Some data were historical reconstructions of population dynamics, others relied on archaeological data.

- Standard approaches to nonlinear time-series analysis suggest that in the best historical data sets the evidence for second-order regulation (England, China) and periodicity (England, Mesa Verde) is quite strong. A general pattern, common to all the data sets, is oscillations—periods of population growth, followed by decline—characterized by a variable degree of periodicity. Population declines tend to occur at intervals of 2–3 centuries.

- The observed patterns are consistent with predictions of the demographic-structural theory (Section 7.2), which also predicts somewhat irregular oscillations with an average period of 2–3 centuries. This result, therefore, constitutes an empirical confirmation of the demographic-structural theory. However, informal calculations suggest that most second-order processes involving population size as one of the main variables should lead to oscillations of roughly the same period. Thus, the possibility that some other theory may explain these patterns as well remains open.

- A direct test of the demographic-structural model, addressing the caveat above, was performed by jointly analyzing the data on population numbers and the incidence of internal warfare (an index of political instability). The regression results suggest that both the influence of density on instability, and the reverse connection, are statistically highly significant. Time-series models fitted to the data generally resolve a high proportion of the variance. Thus, at least in one case, China from 200 B.C.E. to 1710 C.E., we have direct and quantitative evidence for the demographic-structural theory.

Chapter Nine

Case Studies

One of the main themes of this book is the need for an objective, rigorous approach to testing various theories explaining historical dynamics. Following this approach, I discussed several such theories, including geopolitical, ethnodynamic, and demographic-structural ones. All theories were subjected to one or more empirical tests, which they passed with various degrees of success. So it seems that each theory, when examined separately, has some empirical justification. However, it is not yet clear how we should combine the various models together to explain the holistic phenomenon of historical dynamics. We need to generate ideas, and this requires a less rigorous attitude than that involved in testing the hypotheses based on the ideas. Accordingly, in this penultimate chapter, I shift gears and use a very different approach from the one used before. My goal is to look at some specific case studies and discuss how specific mechanisms may be operating in each particular case, how different mechanisms may interact with each other, and what sorts of more rigorous hypotheses we may attempt to develop for future research.

I chose to focus on two polities: France and Russia in the *longue durée* (from the origins to 1900 C.E.). These two cases are a sample from the universe of successful European territorial empires (in particular, both were members of the Great Powers club during the eighteenth and nineteenth centuries). Both polities are situated on the northern European plain, although France is at its extreme western end, while Russia occupies the opposite northeastern quadrant. The two countries, however, followed very different social, political, and economic trajectories. Thus, any similarities that may emerge from the comparison have a good potential as generalizations.

My discussion of historical dynamics in the two case studies is organized as follows. First, I focus on the dynamics of asabiya and the associated issues of frontiers and ethnogenesis. Second, I trace out the secular cycles involving linked demographic, social, and political processes.

9.1 FRANCE

9.1.1 The Frontier Origins

On the Roman Frontier

The western end of the northern European plain during the first two millennia C.E. was successively incorporated into three polities: the Roman Empire, the Frankish

Empire, and the Kingdom (later Republic) of France. After the Roman conquest and until the beginning of the third century, the Roman frontier ran through what is now Benelux and Western Germany (the cultural regions of NED, WGE, and SGE; see Figure 5.1 and Appendix B). Northern and eastern France (NFR and EFR) were lightly affected by the frontier. The situation changed during the calamitous third century, when the Roman Empire experienced a prolonged period of state collapse and internal warfare. During this time of trouble, the Roman frontier became completely porous to Germanic invaders, who repeatedly devastated the Roman Gaul. Three groups, Franci, Burgundi, and Alamanni, coalesced on or moved near the Roman border and penetrated into formerly Roman territory to a greater or lesser degree (Geary 1988; Wolfram 1997). As a result, the NFR and EFR regions themselves became part of the Roman frontier.

After the respite of the relatively stable fourth century (which, however, was characterized by continued southward penetration by the Franks), the "barbarian" advance resumed. The Franks expanded to incorporate most of NFR into their empire, the Burgundi invaded deep into Roman Gaul and established their kingdom in EFR, while the Alamanni pushed south into Rhaetia (which is outside our area of interest). During the fourth and fifth centuries the intensity of the frontier passing though NFR and EFR was greatly enhanced by the religious fault line: whereas Roman Gauls were Christians, Franks and Alamanni were pagans (the Franks converted around 500 C.E., and the Alamanni during the seventh century).

On the March of Frankish Empire

After the Franks established their empire, NFR remained on the frontier, albeit of a different polity. During the fifth century the peninsula of Brittany was colonized by Celtic people from the British Isles who established their own polity, independent of the Merovingian Franks. As a result, the area between the lower Seine and Loire became the march of Brittany. The intensity of the frontier, however, decreased because both Bretons and Franks (after 496 C.E.) were Christian, although there were significant religious differences between their two brands of Christianity. The Carolingians subjugated the Bretons for a brief period of time, but were unable to convert their military superiority into lasting political control (Galliou and Jones 1991). Although the civilizational difference between Bretons and Franks was not very great, nevertheless, during the ninth century the intensity of warfare between the two ethnies was very high (Dunbabin 1985:66). As a result of continuous raiding and counter-raiding, a whole swath of territory running between the lower Seine and the lower Loire became depopulated to a significant degree. This was precisely the area into which the Norman invaders managed to wedge themselves (Searle 1988).

Vikings first settled in the areas around the mouths of the Loire and the Seine. The Loire settlement was ultimately unsuccessful, but the Seine one expanded by degrees. During the ninth and tenth centuries, the area between Rouen and Paris and north of the Loire again became a very intense metaethnic fault line, combining religious, linguistic, and military pressure components. Only after the

Normans assimilated (both religiously and linguistically) to the Latin Christian metaethnie did the intensity of the frontier decline.

To summarize, from the third to the tenth century, NFR was the site of a major frontier, first part of the Roman *limes* and then as a Frankish march. The intensity of this frontier waxed and waned between high and medium levels, as various Germanic invaders assimilated to the Romance language and Christian religion, but the frontier conditions were essentially continuous. According to the metaethnic frontier theory, it was precisely this ethnic cauldron where the French experienced their ethnogenesis and France was born. Before discussing this process, however, I briefly review the events in the neighboring region of NED.

Ethnogenesis of Franks

NED (modern Benelux plus a piece of Germany west of the Rhine) became a frontier earlier, during the first century, and also ceased to be a frontier before NFR, in the late eighth century (after the Carolingians conquered and converted the Frisians and Saxons). Thus, ethnogenesis in NED preceded that in NFR. Prior to the Roman conquest of Gaul the region was inhabited by a variety of small tribes lacking any cultural means for scaling up collective solidarity. After the Roman frontier was established in the first century B.C.E., the selective pressure for such cultural mechanisms became very intense (Miller 1993). The Roman Empire during the Principate exerted an enormous amount of military pressure on the region (the limes ran right through the middle of NED). Conversely, during the troubled third century and the Dominate, the "push" exerted by the Empire became an equally irresistible "pull." As I discussed before, the pull factor provides a strong selection pressure for scaling-up structures, since in order to acquire really significant loot, large raiding parties need to be organized, capable of taking whole cities (which during the Dominate began acquiring fortifications). Additionally, the religious gradient across the frontier became very steep after 300 C.E.: the Empire became Christian, while the Franks practiced a rather aggressive form of paganism, which acted as an important unifying force in the Frankish ethnogenesis (Miller 1993). Another factor was the political mechanism evolved by the Franks: the "long-haired kings" (Scherman 1987). Prior to 300 C.E., western Germans did not have the institution of kingship (unlike eastern Germanic tribes like the Goths). The amalgamation of various tribes (Chamavi, Chattuari, Bructeri, Amsivarii, Salii, and others) into a single Frankish ethnie (Geary 1988:78) is precisely what the metaethnic frontier theory predicts. In sum, Frankish ethnogenesis fits the frontier model very well.

The French Ethnogenesis

When most of NFR became incorporated into the Merovingian Empire, its ethnic composition was very diverse. On the Gallic substrate (which itself was ethnically very heterogeneous, but that is another story), two other groups were superimposed. First, there were the colonists from the rest of the Roman Empire—legionnaires, who served and then settled on the frontier, plus their dependents and descendants (Geary 1988:15). Second, there were Franks moving from the north. Frankish farmers were probably the dominant ethnic element north of the Seine and a substantial influence down to the Loire. The reason that this region experienced such heavy colonization during the third to fifth centuries is probably because of the drastic population decline which occurred during the second half of the third century, when the proportion of archaeological sites occupied was only 45% of the second-century peak (Lewit 1991). After a brief rise during the fourth century, the population of north Gaul collapsed even lower, so that only 9% of dwellings were occupied after 400 C.E. (Lewit 1991). Such drastic depopulation of a countryside is one of the typical characteristics of a high-intensity metaethnic frontier.

During the fifth century the western part of NFR was colonized by Bretons (Musset 1975:112). The final substantial ethnic infusion occurred during the ninth and tenth centuries, when various Germanic peoples from Scandinavia established the Duchy of Normandy (Searle 1988). These diverse ethnic groups were relatively rapidly assimilated to a common religion (Christianity) and language (vulgar Latin evolving into northern French—*langue d'oïl*). The process was particularly rapid for Normans, who accomplished it within two centuries. Linguistic assimilation of the Franks was probably a more drawn-out process, with islands of Frankish language, the precursor of modern Dutch, persisting into the eleventh century. Assimilation of the Bretons took the longest time (the majority of Bretons switched to French only in the nineteenth century).

The relative rapidity with which Germanic intruders (Franks and Normans) assimilated to the region's common culture raises a set of interesting questions. Why did Normans assimilate so rapidly (in the course of two centuries), while Bretons required more than a millennium? As was discussed in Chapter 6, current sociological thinking suggests that the rapidity of assimilation depends on the nature of social networks. Were there significant gaps between the Breton network and the rest of the population in NFR? Did the Normans rapidly establish dense connections with the Frankish network? A related observation is that the linguistic assimilation of southern France was quite slow. Although the region was conquered by the French in the thirteenth century, three centuries later only large cities were French speaking, while the majority of inhabitants spoke Occitan (*langue d'oc*). The midpoint was crossed only after three more centuries elapsed, during the late 1800s. Incidentally, the multiethnic nature of France during most of its existence is the reason I refer to it as an empire. Even by 1868, essentially at the end of the period of interest, French was the native language of only one-third of the inhabitants of France. Another third spoke it as a second language, and the rest could not speak it at all (Weber 1976).

By the eleventh century, NFR (with the exception of Brittany) appears to have been ruled by what was, despite its disparate origins as Roman-era landowners, Frankish counts, or descendants of Vikings, a fairly homogeneous elite, at least if we focus on linguistic and religious characteristics. However, the region was not politically unified. Instead, multiple foci of territorial power simultaneously formed and consolidated, starting in the middle of the ninth century, when the Neustrian march was created by Charles the Bald, and intensifying in the late tenth century (Dunbabin 1985; Bates 1995). The most dynamic polities were organized around the Dukes of Normandy and the Counts of Anjou and Paris (the latter secured for himself the French Crown in 987, although at the time it was largely of symbolic value). Other, less aggressive incipient polities were organized by the Counts of Blois (who acquired Champaign) and the Dukes of Bretagne. This intense episode of polity building is very reminiscent of the dynamics of the spatial frontier model. If this analogy is valid, then the conquest of England by the Normans in late eleventh century can be interpreted as an example of the reflux effect. In fact, the dynamics of England for the next three centuries should probably be interpreted as an offshoot of NFR. As is well known, after the Norman conquest, the native English elites were "destroyed as a class," and replaced with members of Duke William's host, who mostly originated from northern France and the Low Countries. There was another infusion of north French when England passed to the Angevin dynasty of Plantagenets in the mid-twelfth century. The process of mutual assimilation of French-speaking elites and English-speaking lower strata took no less than the following two centuries, and can probably be thought complete only after the Plantagenet-Tudor transition.

A Digression on the Role of Nonelite Asabiya

A contrast between the ultimate fate of Norman England and a polity having similar origins, Norman Sicily, is instructive. Both were created at approximately the same time and had a similar initial sociopolitical trajectory. Thus, both polities were cited as examples of precocious state building in twelfth-century Europe. Both were unusually centralized for their times and had solid fiscal bases. The trajectories of these two states, however, radically diverged after the twelfth century. The Kingdom of Sicily (which occupied the whole SIT region) rapidly declined, and went through a sequence of owners: German Emperors, Angevins, Aragonese, Castilians, and finally Piedmontese. In short it was an object rather than a subject of international politics. By contrast, England, following a period of relative insignificance after its expulsion from the continent in the mid-fifteenth century, eventually achieved the status of a Great Power, and even a hegemonic one during parts of the eighteenth and nineteenth centuries. This comparison, limited as it is to a single pair of data points, suggests the importance of the asabiya of the lower stratum of the society. SIT was an imperial core for at least half a millennium after the Roman frontiers moved away in the first century B.C.E. The theory suggests that this region should have a thoroughly depressed asabiya. By contrast, SBR was the locus of an intense frontier from the fifth through the eleventh centuries. It is clear that on the eve of the Norman conquest the English were already well on the way to building a coherent and aggressively expanding state. This observation leads to the hypothesis that while a polity's dynamics in the short run may depend more on the asabiya of its elites, the long-term success or failure must depend very much on the asabiya of the general populace. At this point, this proposition is just a hypothesis, but it is clear that we can construct a test by considering the universe of polities, where there was a significant ethnic difference between the elites and general population, and examining how the estimated asabiya of the population affected the durability of the polity.

Dynamics of Frontier Intensity in NFR and Size of the French Polity

In Figure 9.1 I plot the frontier intensity in NFR and the territorial extent of the French polity. The curve starts in 987 C.E., when Hugo Capet was elected King of France. Around 1000 C.E., the Capetians controlled a small area of northern France around Paris and Orléans. Initial expansion was slow, and by 1200 C.E. the royal domain was still less than 0.1 Mm^2 in size. For comparison, the Angevin domain at that time encompassed 0.4 Mm^2. Then, during the first half of the thirteenth century the territory expanded rapidly to over 0.3 Mm^2, and stabilized at that level. Most of this growth spurt occurred at the expense of the Angevins, and as a result of Albigensian Crusades. Thereafter, growth continued to 1900 C.E., but with some oscillations that will be discussed in the next section.

What is striking about this trajectory is how slow—long term—the processes are. NFR was affected by frontier conditions for around eight centuries. After the tenth century, the frontier rapidly declined and then disappeared. Yet the first substantial spurt of growth occurred only during the thirteenth century. The French polity continued to expand for another six centuries and began showing signs of declining asabiya only recently (the string of military defeats from Germany in 1870, 1914, and 1940; loss of the overseas empire). These observations suggest that the temporal scale on which asabiya waxes and wanes is very long. In fact, the dynamics of asabiya appear to be substantially slower than the

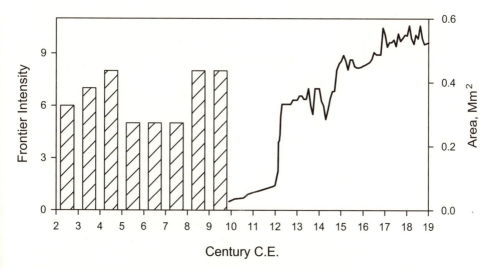

Figure 9.1 Frontier intensity in NFR and the area of French polity (excluding overseas possessions).

kinetics of linguistic or religious assimilation or the secular cycles resulting from demographic-structural processes.

9.1.2 Secular Waves

The Principate Wave

If the archaeological data presented by Lewit (1991) and discussed in Chapter 8 really reflect population oscillations, then Roman Gaul must have gone through two oscillations, separated by a period of population decline during the troubled third century. The character of the cycle ending with the third-century decline (let us call it "the Principate wave," since that is what the Roman Empire during this period is often called) is quite clear. Most of Gaul (apart from the Roman Province in the south) was added to the Empire in the first century B.C.E. During the first century C.E., the frontier moved north and east, and Gaul began an extended period of peace and prosperity. As a result, the population grew (Figure 9.2).

From the first century B.C.E. to the second century C.E., the site occupation index increased by a factor of 3, so the actual population increase was probably even greater, because it is reasonable to suppose that settlement size also increased. This pattern of population growth was mirrored in the rest of the Empire (at least, in all the western provinces). According to the demographic-structural theory, such unchecked population growth should have inevitably led to state insolvency and eventual breakdown. This is precisely what happened. During the second century C.E., the Roman Empire experienced a great wave of inflation (Fischer, 1996: Figure 5.03). The state collapse followed, and during most of the third century, the empire lacked central authority. The proximate reasons for population decline were multifarious: famine, disease (the Antonine plagues),

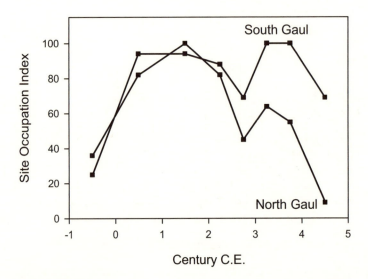

Figure 9.2 Population history of Roman Gaul. (data from Lewit 1991)

internecine fighting that affected most of the territory, and barbarian invasions. Additionally, during this period Romans practiced various reproduction control practices (mainly infanticide; see quotes in Stark 1996). Ultimately, however, it can be argued that all these causes of increased mortality and decreased fertility are connected to a high level of sociopolitical instability. Thus, Lewit shows that the depth of population decline in a province was correlated with the level of warfare it experienced during the calamitous third century.

The Dominate-Merovingian Wave

It is interesting to observe that the population trajectories of the north and south Gaul, which moved in parallel up to the third century, diverged thereafter (Figure 9.2). The site occupation index in the north declined to a lower level and enjoyed only a moderate increase after order was restored at the end of the third century. It then declined to a much lower level during the fifth century. The probable reason is that during the Dominate period northern Gaul became part of the Roman frontier and, as was discussed above, frontier conditions are not conducive to high population densities. The more intense the frontier, the sparser the population in the region, and apparently the frontier in northern Gaul was very intense.

As was discussed in the previous section, northern Gaul was a frontier between the old empire and challenger ethnies: mainly the Franks, but also the Alamanni and Burgundi. The Frankish chiefdom established a foothold just north of the Roman border during the third century, slowly penetrated south into northern Gaul during the fourth century, and came into its own—*Regnum Francorum*—during the fifth century. After its peak during the first half of the sixth century, it fragmented. By 600 C.E. there were four independent polities (Neustria, Austrasia, Burgundy, and Aquitaine), which continued to fragment to even smaller pieces during the seventh century. According to Slicher van Bath (1964:78), the low point of the post-Roman population probably came between 543 and 600 C.E. (see also Russell 1985). In other words, the population decline of the sixth century was accompanied by increased political instability, precisely as predicted by the demographic-structural theory. Again, there is no single factor that can be pointed to as the cause of population decline. Certainly both diseases (the plagues of Justinian) and warfare played a very important role. One interesting feature of this secular wave was the correlation in population declines between widely separated regions, belonging to separate polities, e.g., Gaul and Anatolia.

The Carolingian Wave

After about a century of political turmoil, the secular trend again reversed itself, from decentralization to centralization. By 700 C.E. a rejuvenated Frankish polity was expanding again, reaching its peak in 800 under Charlemagne. There was a population upswing during the Carolingian era (starting during the seventh century), followed by a downturn after 900 (Reinhard et al. 1968, Duby 1974). Several contemporaries describe the heartland of Charlemagne's empire (in NED) during the ninth century as full of people, or bursting at the seams with too many people. However, large areas of the empire were still available for assarting. Thus, the population peak of the ninth century, in absolute numbers, was nowhere near as great as the peak of 1300. But locally, in those areas that were cleared of forests, population density appears to have been high.

During the ninth century the Carolingian Empire fragmented. The east Frankish Kingdom was taken over by Saxons and eventually reorganized into the Holy Roman Empire, but that is outside the geographic region of current interest. The west Frankish Kingdom of Charles the Bald fragmented into duchies and counties. In the south, counts lost control over viscounts and castellans, resulting in an extreme dispersal of power in such areas as the Massif Central (Zimmerman 1995). Clearly, this was another secular trend inversion, and it was again correlated with population change. The population decline and political fragmentation were accompanied by increased incidence of internal warfare and external invasions, of which the most significant for northern France was the Viking incursion.

The Capetian Wave

The period of political fragmentation following the collapse of the Carolingians was particularly long. As I discussed in the previous section, three particularly aggressive challenger polities/protoethnies arose on the Frankish march in NFR: Normans, Angevins, and Capetians. Although their origins were highly mixed, by the eleventh century the ethnic boundaries separating the Norman, Angevin, and Capetian elites were quite blurred (Bates 1995), and there was a considerable degree of intermariage and movement across them. Thus, it was very likely that one polity would incorporate the others, and forge first the elites and then the general populace into a single ethnie. This is what happened, although things were complicated by the Norman conquest of England. During the twelfth century it looked as if the successful polity would be the Angevins, but eventually the Capetians triumphed.

However, the reason for the anomalously long stretch of time between the population peaks of 800 and 1300 C.E. is now apparent—the tenth through twelfth centuries were an intercycle period. The centralization phase of the secular cycle could not get going until there was a unified polity of substantial size. As matters stood, France acquired a strong monarchy only by about 1200 C.E. Population growth began prior to this event and continued strongly throughout the thirteenth century. By 1300 C.E., France (as well as most of western Europe) was crammed with people. During the first half of the fourteenth century, population growth completely ceased, and signs of decline became visible, even before the 1348 epidemic of bubonic plague. This was the time of frequent subsistence crises and an onset of internal warfare. The Hundred Years War is portrayed in textbooks as a dynastic conflict between French and English kings. In reality, this war was a period of great political instability *within* France (Salmon 1976; Braudel 1988). The main conflict was that between the great seigneurs of France, the dukes, and the counts, of whom the King of England was just one.

The Valois Wave

The qualitative population dynamics during the fourteenth and fifteenth centuries are well understood, even if we may lack precise quantitative estimates (Dupâquier et al. 1988a). The French population (similarly to that in other western European polities) began declining after 1300 C.E., then experienced a precipitous drop in the Black Death epidemic of 1348, followed by further losses as epidemics recurred and fighting in the Hundred Years War intensified. Overall population numbers declined by about one-half (Dupâquier et al. 1988b:149). After that, for about a century population numbers fluctuated at a low level, and started to increase only during the second half of the fifteenth century. The nature of population dynamics can be seen in one particular example, Normandy (Bois 1984:76). Rural population numbers fluctuated back and forth, with three declines (in the mid-fourteenth and the early and mid-fifteenth centuries), interspersed by periods of partial recovery. The absolute minimum was achieved around 1460, after which the population finally entered an era of sustained increase.

The prolonged "stagnation" of population (actually, fluctuations at a low level) during the 1350–1450 period presents a serious challenge to most standard demographic theories. Certainly, the crude version of the Malthusian-Ricardian theory predicts that populations should have started growing by the end of the fourteenth century, not a century later (Brenner 1985). After all, land was plentiful, and large amounts of surplus could again be generated (and they apparently were produced, judging by the practically universal decline of grain prices, roughly by a factor of two from 1300 to 1400 C.E.). The effect of the plague similarly declined and reached a minimum (at least, as judged by the number of localities affected; see Biraben 1975:120). In fact, the incidence of plague started a slow increase after 1400 to another peak during the seventeenth century. Thus, some other factor, acting with a long delay (a second-order mechanism, in the terminology adopted here), was responsible for preventing population increase.

As I argued in Chapter 7, the underlying cause of secular waves in human population numbers is the interaction between population and political stability. According to the demographic-structural theory, then, it was ultimately political instability that prevented immediate population increase once the demographic pressure was relieved. The situation in France during 1350–1450 appears to support this prediction. The Hundred Years War was a period of almost continuous political unrest, although there were two particularly bad periods, c. 1360 and the 1420s. Certain regional studies provide further evidence for the connection between political instability and population dynamics. For example, the population of Normandy began increasing after the worst crises of the 1360s and 1370s were over. However, this increase was not long lived and was succeeded by another period of depopulation during the 1420s and 1430s. This is perhaps not surprising, given that Normandy was a primary battlefield between the English and French during these periods.

The two particularly acute periods of French state collapse are reflected in the territorial trajectory (Figure 9.1), which reached local minima in 1370 and 1430. The latter nadir was a time of particularly desperate straits for the kingdom, when even the capital was lost to the Anglo-Burgundian forces. However, the secular trend was about to reverse itself, and while the current situation looked grim, France was actually on the brink of another period of territorial expansion (Figure 9.1).

The reason for this turnaround is suggested by the selfish elite model. Recollect that this model predicts that, in order for the state to be viable, it needs to keep a relatively low ratio of elites to commoners. The model, thus, makes a prediction that a centralization trend could not get going until the number of French nobles declined below a certain threshold. This is a prediction that may be tested with data. Qualitatively this proposal seems likely, given the enormous numbers of French nobles dispossessed during this period (Wright 1998). Additionally, the massive slaughter of "the flower of French nobility" at Crécy and Agincourt must have made a noticeable impact on their numbers. Thus, Dupâquier et al. (1988a:342) estimate that about 40% of the French nobility was lost at each battle.

The years 1430–1510 C.E. were a period of rapid and continuous expansion for the French state (Figure 9.1). First, by 1453 the English were expelled almost completely from the continent (retaining only a tiny area around Calais). By 1480, France took over half of the Burgundian inheritance. Finally, in 1494 the French embarked on their most ambitious venture, the attempt to dominate Italy. This adventure lead to the Valois-Habsburg wars of the sixteenth century and ultimately ended with the expulsion of the French from the Appenine Peninsula. One possible explanation is that France overextended itself geopolitically; this seems very likely, but needs to be tested in a thorough and quantitative fashion. For example, it would be very interesting to see how much it cost France to deliver armies to Rome or Naples, compared to the same task for Spain. The French had to travel overland, through mountain passes in the Alps. The Spanish, by contrast, shipped troops by sea, and it looks as if they had a geopolitical advantage. But this is just a qualitative argument, and a more quantitative approach is needed. Note that the model of logistical loads is one theory that I have not been able to test directly (so far).

Whether because of logistical constraints, or for some other reason, the territorial expansion of France ceased by the mid-sixteenth century. The sixteenth century was also a period of sustained population growth in France, which was, as usual, reflected in the movement of food prices (Figure 9.3). Between 1460 and 1560 the population of France doubled (Dupâquier et al. 1988b), reaching 20 million, and then stagnated at that level to the end of the century (in fact, this level was not exceeded until the middle years of Louis XIV; Salmon 1976:32). The elite numbers increased even faster. Thus, the total number of noble families in the *élection* of Bayeux increased from 211 in 1463 to 559 in 1598 (Wood 1980). At the other end of France, in Montpellier, the number of officeholders almost quadrupled from 112 in 1500 to 442 in 1600 (Greengrass 1985:122). Thus, the demographic-structural machinery became engaged again, leading to increased fiscal distress, elite competition, political instability, and eventually state collapse.

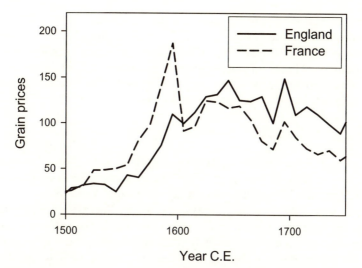

Figure 9.3 Movement of grain prices in France and England from 1500 to 1750 C.E. (Data from Abel 1966)

The Bourbon Wave

The period of political instability in France was about a century long, roughly 1560–1660 C.E. There were two episodes of state collapse: the peak of the religious wars (around 1590) and the Fronde (around 1650). The first one resulted in a dynastic change from Valois to Bourbon. The authorities lost control of the capital both times, and internal warfare was extremely bloody, particularly in northern France.

The period between the religious wars and the Fronde was relatively stable, with the exception of Louis XIII's minority. According to Dupâquier et al. (1988b:152), there were three periods of population decline: 1580–1597, 1626–1631, and 1660–1663. These population crises were quite serious, especially the first and the last. The first crisis may have resulted in a population loss as high as 20% or more (Benedict 1985:96). During the last, certain provinces in the north and east probably lost close to a half of their inhabitants (Dupâquier et al. 1988b:152).

The end of the time of troubles, by mid-1660s, led to another bout of territorial expansion (Figure 9.1). Thus, we see that the French state experienced three major episodes of expansion: thirteenth century, fifteenth century, and the period of 1660–1710. In other words, the secular cycle had a direct effect on the ability of the state to expand. Note also that each successive wave of expansion was shorter and gained less territory. This trend can reflect either a declining asabiya or logistical constraints (or both).

The Bourbon cycle concluded with the French Revolution. The events leading to it are well known, and have been discussed by Goldstone from the point of view of the demographic-structural theory, so I will not review them here. I only note that the period of political instability extended from 1789 to 1848, and that during this time France experienced the Great Revolution, Bourbon restoration, a revolution in 1830, another one in 1848, and, finally, the establishment of the Second Empire. After that France embarked on another imperialistic expansionary period (although this time it did not do very well), but this quickly takes us beyond our self-imposed boundary of 1900 C.E.

A Digression on Synchrony

One interesting aspect of the Bourbon wave was that France's period of instability was shifted in time with respect to the rest of western Europe. Thus, central Europe's period of instability was during the Thirty Years War (1618–1648). England's was 1640 to 1690 (English Revolution, Stuart Restoration, and the Glorious Revolution). Spain's crisis years were during the 1640s: rebellions in Portugal, Catalonia, and southern Italy (although we should not forget about the Dutch revolt of the second half of the sixteenth century). Only Russia seems to be on the same trajectory as France (as will be seen in the next section).

This quick comparison raises a number of interesting issues. First, why did early modern state breakdown tend to occur in waves (Goldstone 1991b)? The crisis of the seventeenth century and the age of revolutions during the nineteenth century affected Europe, the Middle East (Ottoman Turkey), and East Asia (China). Second, although there was a rough synchrony between different polities, it was not by any means perfect, as the fine structure of the "seventeenth-century crisis" shows. Additionally, although Russia was in synchrony with France during the seventeenth-century crisis, it subsequently shifted out of phase, since it experienced revolutions and state collapse in the early twentieth century, not in the mid-nineteenth as was the case for central and western Europe.

We can look for explanations in purely exogenous factors, such as climate fluctuations (Galloway 1986; Goldstone 1991b). Thus, it is possible that the plague pandemic of the fourteenth century (itself a consequence of the Mongolian superempire) "reset" a number of polities to the same starting conditions. Another possibility is some "contagion" leading to positive spatial autocorrelations. For example, almost synchronous uprisings in Portugal, Catalonia, and Sicily could happen because the revolt in one region could encourage others to do the same. Similarly, it is known that the wave of European revolutions in 1848 fed on news from other parts of the continent. The third possibility is suggested by the dynamical systems theory.

If two oscillatory systems are driven by the same mechanism, causing them to cycle with the same period, then they may oscillate in synchrony by chance alone, simply because they happened to get started at approximately the same time (Turchin and Hall 2003). If that is the case, then differences in phase will tend to be perpetuated in time. For example, it happened that France came out of the fourteenth-century crisis before England. Whereas France was already on the ascendant by 1450, England had yet to experience the last bout of its own state collapse, the Wars of the Roses (1455–1485). This may have delayed the English demographic-structural cycle by roughly half a century, compared to France.

Thus, we would expect that the next period of England's state breakdown should begin after that of France. This is what apparently happened: France was in a full-blown crisis by 1590, while England's turn came only in 1640. Of course, there is another possible explanation for this shift in phase. The demographic-structural theory predicts only how pressures for crisis evolve. The actual beginning of the crisis needs a triggering event, which may come sooner or later. For example, in agrarian monarchies, the triggering event is often a disputed succession. Thus, two polities under identical amounts of pressure may go into crisis 10 years apart, depending on when their respective monarchs die. In the early modern French and English cases, however, it seems that there was a genuine difference in pressure for crisis. Food prices are a particularly good indicator of fiscal pressure, and note how food prices in France started increasing prior to those for England (Figure 9.3). French prices reached a peak in 1590 (and a second one during 1620–1640). In contrast, in England food prices reached a peak only in 1640. These data, thus, suggest that France and England were genuinely shifted in phase. Note that during the next episode of political instability, it was France again that led the way with the French Revolution. By contrast, England's period of political crisis was acute (but did not cause state breakdown; Goldstone 1991b) during the 1830s.

The considerations discussed above are suggestive, but no more than that. However, it is clear that meaningful empirical tests can be devised to distinguish between the three different explanations of apparent synchrony (as well as persistent phase shifts). Furthermore, in reality all three kinds of mechanisms (exogenous, endogenous, and spatial autocorrelations) may contribute to the observed pattern of synchrony (Turchin and Hall 2003). For example, an exogenous force may interact with the inherent tendency of the dynamical system to oscillate with a certain period to produce synchronous oscillations in different polities. One possibility, a strong exogenous shock delivered to all systems at the same time (the Black Death pandemic), was already mentioned above. Another, more subtle, mechanism is when slight changes in climate affect the carrying capacity of populations. Numerical exercises show that correlated changes in carrying capacity, even when quite small (e.g., 10–20%), may synchronize the dynamics of two polities driven by the selfish elite model.

Fine Structure of Decentralization Phases

Another interesting pattern apparent in the French case is that decentralization phases are not uniformly awful, but have their own rhythms. Thus, the Hundred Years War had two periods of particularly acute crisis (c.1360 and the 1420s), separated roughly by half a century. During the next decentralization phase, there were again two peaks of political instability, in the 1590s and c.1650. The most acute crisis of the French Revolution was around 1790, after which the internal situation was reasonably stable under Napoleon and the Bourbons. After this respite, another period of instability followed with the revolutions of 1830 and 1848. It is hard to say whether this is just a coincidence, or whether some regular pattern is involved. If real, one possible explanation of such oscillations may be that after a prolonged period of instability, e.g., a decade, people begin to yearn for stability. Even if the basic conditions that brought about the crisis in the first place have not been resolved, people may acquiesce in any political arrangement that restores order. Thus, the generation that grew up during the time of trouble is likely to support order at any cost, even if the regime is perceived as lacking in legitimacy. The next generation, however, does not have direct experience with turmoil and therefore is easier to persuade to support an overturning of the existing order. Such a dynamic should result in two-generation cycles of 40–60 years in duration. Furthermore, it is possible that some mechanism similar to that described by Richard Easterlin (1980) may be operating. Heightened sociopolitical instability depresses birth rates, resulting in a smaller cohort and, consequently, less competition among the next generation. The next generation, therefore, does well economically, has a lower mobilization potential, but also produces a large number of babies. Such a mechanism should lead to an alternation of small/docile versus large/belligerent generations. The two possible explanations, discussed above, are not alternatives, but can work together. Additionally, there could be some interesting implications here for the connection between Kondratieff waves and warfare (Goldstein 1988), and some recent literature from the world-systems research program (Modelski and Thompson 1996).

9.1.3 Summary

Counting the centuries of sociopolitical instability and population decline (which are more easily detected in the historical record), we observe the following sequence for Gaul-France: III–VI–IX–XIV–XVII–XIX, or six oscillations during the 2000-year period. All oscillations but one are of 2–3 centuries in duration. The only exception is the X–XIV period, which as I argued above is an intercycle. Thus, the periods of the secular waves conform well with those predicted by the demographic-structural theory. Additionally, although we lack quantitative data, such as J. S. Lee developed for China, we have traced the qualitative dynamics in this region, and they appear to be in line with the theoretical predictions.

9.2 RUSSIA

9.2.1 The Frontier Origins

On the Great Steppe Frontier of Europe

The importance of the steppe frontier in Russian history has been pointed out by numerous historians (Presniakov 1918; McNeill 1964; Kargalov 1974; Wieszynnski 1976; Armstrong 1982; LeDonne 1997; Khodarkovsky 2002). In 1992, a whole issue of *Russian History* was devoted to this topic (see Hellie 1992 and following articles).

The great grasslands dominate the interior of the Eurasian continent. The Eurasian steppe runs practically uninterrupted from Khingan Mountains in the east (on the northern border of China) to the Carpathians in the west, and beyond the Carpathians to the Hungarian plain. Within eastern Europe the grassland-woodland transition runs in the northeast-southwest direction, roughly through the following cultural regions (see Figure 5.1): KAZ, SRU, UKR, and ZAP. In addition, the Eurasian steppe curls around the Black Sea into MOL and VLH, and there is an extension into central Europe (HUN, the Hungarian plains). Finally, the Anatolian Plateau (ANT) can also be considered as an extension, although this area belongs to the dry steppe variety.

From at least the times of Cimmerians (the beginning of the first millennium B.C.E., Riazanovsky 2000) and until the eighteenth century the grasslands were dominated by nomadic pastoralists. The woodlands were inhabited by settled agriculturalists since the fourth millennium B.C.E. (Riazanovsky 2000:13). Thus, the forest-steppe transition zone was the locus of a metaethnic frontier throughout almost all of its history (and a large chunk of prehistory). Note, however, that the steppe frontier was not stationary but tended to sway back and forth (more on this below). Furthermore, its intensity tended to wax and wane. Although very little is known about the period when the steppe was dominated by the Indo-European nomads (Cimmerians, Scythians, and Sarmatians), the cultural difference between the agriculturalists and pastoralists may not have been too great. Thus, many religious terms in the modern Russian are of Iranian origin, suggesting that there were some common elements in the religion of east Slavs and Iranian-speaking nomads (Scythians and Sarmatians). Beginning from the late third century C.E., the Iranian nomads were replaced on the steppe by repeated waves of Turkic and Mongolian peoples. It is likely that the cultural distance across the frontier increased as a result of this development. But the greatest intensity was achieved by the frontier when two world religions, Christianity and Islam, extended their sway over eastern Europe. Settled agriculturalists tended to embrace Christianity, while nomads converted to Islam.

The socioethnic complexity of the southern part of the steppe frontier was further enhanced after the seventh century B.C.E. as a result of Greek colonization of the northern shore of the Black Sea (Olbia, Chersonesus, Tanais, Pantikapaeum, and Phanagoria; see Riazanovsky, 2000:14). This colonization led to the establishment of the Bosporan kingdom, which eventually passed to the Romans and then to the Byzantines. As a result of these developments, the Pontic Steppe was squeezed between two very different frontiers: the southern frontier between civilized (in the sense of being urban) empires and the steppe (MOL, ZAP, AZV), and the northern frontier between the steppe and the settled agriculturalists of the woodlands (MOL, ZAP, UKR). The metaethnic frontier theory predicts that this area should have been the locus of intense ethnopolitogenesis.

This is precisely what happened (a quick overview is given in Riazanovsky 2000:13–16). The first strong polity was established by the Scythians, who ruled the Pontic Steppe from the seventh to the third century B.C.E. The Scythians were defeated and replaced by the Sarmatians (also known as Alans). The Sarmatians ruled the area until roughly 200 C.E., when they were defeated by the Goths. The Gothic period is dated from 200 to 370 C.E., when Huns—probably a Prototurkic people with large Mongol and Ugrian contingents—arrived on the scene. The Hun invasion represented a watershed of sorts, since it and all later nomadic waves were non-Indo-European speaking peoples (Ugrians, Turks, and Mongols).

After the defeat of the Ostrogoths and Visigoths by the Huns, the Pontic Steppe ceased to be the locus of strong polities. Successive waves of invaders originating in central Asia passed through the Pontic Steppe and established their polities west or south of it. The center of the short-lived Hun polity was in Pannonia (HUN region). Avars (whose invasion is dated to 558 C.E.) and Magyars of the ninth century followed in the Huns' steps. Bulgars, by contrast, pressed south to the northeastern Balkans, where they established the empire of the Danubian Bulgars in the seventh century. At about the same time, another nomadic empire, Khazaria, was established to the east, with its center in the Volga Delta. Thus, until about 900 C.E., the Pontic Steppe was a contested ground between strong polities to the west (Avars, then Magyars), south (Bulgars), east (Khazars), and eventually north (Principality of Kiev, from the ninth century).

The Kievan Prelude

The origins of the Principality of Kiev are not completely understood and are still the subject of some debate among historians. What is clear is that by the ninth century, the UKR region was inhabited by Slavs, whenever and however they got there (authorities still disagree on this issue). The Slavs of the forest-steppe transition zone had partly assimilated Iranian, Baltic, and Finno-Ugric people (Novoseltsev 2001). The grasslands were inhabited by nomadic pastoralists, of very complex ethnic origins, as indicated in the quick historical summary above.

From the seventh century, the eastern Pontic Steppe was dominated by Khazaria. Khazaria was the first large state in the history of eastern Europe, and it exerted a defining influence on the ethno- and politogenesis in this region (Novoseltsev 2001). The Khazarian ethnie formed during the sixth and seventh centuries probably as a result of an amalgamation of Prototurkic, Ugrian, and Iranian elements (Novoseltsev 2001). The core region of the Khazar state was located in Daghestan (northeastern Caucasus), which at the time was situated on the northern frontier of the Sassanian Empire. The final triggering event leading to the crystallization of the Khazarian polity was the invasion of Khazaria by the Arabs, after the latter conquered the Sassanian Empire in the middle of the seventh century. The Arabs, from their bases in Derbent and on the main passes of the Caucasus Mountains, exerted a significant amount of geopolitical pressure on Khazaria, eventually even taking the Khazar capital city of Samandar in 737 (Novoseltsev 2001). In what appears as a classical reflux effect (Section 4.2.2), the main thrust of the Khazarian expansion was directed northward (see the map in Farrington 2002:83). By the middle of the eighth century, the Khazars ruled the Crimea, the lower Don, and the lower and middle Volga areas. According to the Russian chronicles, at some point in time, the Polanian Slavs were also subjugated, while other east Slavic groups payed tribute to the Khazars (Novoseltsev 2001). Thus, by the ninth century, the Slavs inhabiting the UKR region found themselves on an imperial frontier of an aggressive and ethnically alien empire.

The last element of the ethnic melting pot in the UKR region was the Scandinavian traders and raiders, referred to as the Varangians in Russian chronicles. Working from the Baltic Sea, the Scandinavians established a network of settlements along such important trade routes as the Volkhov, Volga, and Dnieper Rivers. With time, some of these settlements, most notably Novgorod and Kiev, changed in nature from trading posts to the nuclei of territorial chiefdoms, and eventually states.

The most powerful of these incipient polities was the Principality of Kiev, or the Rus Kaganate (as it was referred to in the Arabian sources). The Rus Kaganate was a federation of elite warriors living on trade and booty and drawing tribute from the Slavic, Baltic, and Finnish agricultural peoples of the forest and forest-steppe land (Hosking 2001:33). At this stage in its development, the Kievan polity was a rather typical complex chiefdom, with the Great Prince in Kiev as the paramount chief, and princes of various East Slavic tribes as subordinate chiefs. The cohesive forces holding this polity together were rather standard for a frontier "barbarian" tribal confederation: defense and predation.

Settled agriculturalists living on Europe's steppe frontier had always had to deal with raiding by the nomads. During the eighth and ninth centuries, as stated above, many east Slavic tribes had to pay tribute to Khazaria. After 900, however, the intensity of raiding pressure on east Slavs intensified, because a new steppe polity, the Pechenegs (or Patzinaks), broke through the area controlled by the Khazars (Novoseltsev 2001) and established itself in the Pontic Steppe (Hosking 2001:34). As I pointed out above, there were no large-scale nomadic polities based in this area (ZAP and AZV) during the previous five centuries. It is probably not by chance alone that the Principality of Kiev coalesced practically at the same time as the Pecheneg Confederation. The mechanism underlying the rise of the Pechenegs was probably similar to that described by Barfield (1989) for the interaction between agrarian societies of China and nomadic empires of central Asia, and modeled in Section 7.2.3. This hypothetical dynamic can be quickly sketched as follows. Varangians based in Kiev using their military superiority impose tribute on the surrounding Slavic tribes, perhaps offering them increased protection from the competing predators of the steppe. Steppe dwellers now have to increase the size of their war parties in order to overcome the stronger defenses of the agriculturalists. Additionally, a concentration of both staple and prestige goods in Kiev and eventually other towns presents a greater incentive for scaling up the political organization on the steppe. As a result, pressure from the steppe significantly increases. This provides extra centralizing incentives for agriculturalists, and the positive feedback loop causes both polities, the agrarian and the nomadic, to centralize until the process is stopped by ecological and logistic constraints.

Mutual defense was not the only force generating scaled-up asabiya in the Kievan Rus. Varangians, the warrior elite of this polity, were notable predators themselves. The richest target was Constantinople, and a number of raids were directed against the Byzantine Empire, including the campaigns of Oleg and Igor in the tenth century. Furthermore, under Prince Sviatoslav (the second half of the tenth century) the Rus sacked the capital of the Volga Bulgars, delivered a death blow to Khazaria, and captured the capital of the Danube Bulgarians. Both the necessity of gathering the large forces needed to overcome these powerful polities and the enhanced reputation resulting from the success must have been powerful sources of collective solidarity for the Rus warrior elites.

It would be interesting to speculate why the Kievan state coalesced in the UKR (and not in the SRU or ZAP) region. History books stress the importance of trade (see, for example, Kliuchevskii 1911 on the importance of waterways). This hypothesis is supported by the current anthropological theory that emphasizes the importance of prestige goods in the evolution of chiefdoms (Earle 1997). Eastern Europe of the second half of the first millennium had two main trading routes, one associated with the Dnieper and the other with the Volga. It is interesting to note that the loci where the Dnieper and Volga trading routes intersect the woodlands-steppe transitional region were both centers of intense political development at about the same time (Kiev in UKR and Great Bulgar in KAZ). Similarly, the next great trade artery is the Danube, which is precisely where the Danubian Bulgars established their state.

An important event for the metaethnic landscape of eastern Europe was the arrival of world religions toward the end of the first millennium. The first was Judaism, which was adopted as the state religion in Khazaria. However, Judaism had very little impact on the area after the fall of Khazaria in the tenth century. The Volga Bulgars were Muslim, and were instrumental in converting Mongols to Islam during the thirteenth and fourteenth centuries. Eventually, all nomads in eastern Europe became Muslim (apart from a later intrusion of the Buddhist Kalmyks). By contrast, the Slavs and other agricultural people converted to Orthodox Christianity. Thus, the religious frontier that emerged during the early second millennium coincided with the economic frontier dividing agriculturalists from pastoralists. This development resulted in a significant deepening of the metaethnic fault line running through eastern Europe.

Russian Ethnogenesis

The locus of Russian ethnogenesis was northeastern Rus, also known as Vladimir-Suzdal Rus. Right away I should state that by "locus" I do not mean a precisely delineated area. Thus, Moscow itself, the Volga-Oka mesopotamia, the northeastern Rus, and the rest of the formerly Kievan lands, as well as the Golden Horde to the east, all contributed to the process of Russian ethnogenesis, but the importance of these contributions varied, generally decreasing with greater distance from Moscow.

Vladimir-Suzdal Rus was a northeastern frontier of the Principality of Kiev (note that I use "Rus" to refer to the pre-Mongolian period, and "Russia" to the period after Mongolian conquest; because the core regions of Rus and Russia were distinct, "northeastern Rus" became "central Russia"). On the eve of the Mongolian conquest, it was inhabited by people who were some kind of mixture of Baltic, Finnish, and Slavic tribes. Some Russian historians (e.g., Kliuchevskii 1911) argued that northeastern Rus was populated as a result of massive colonization by the Slavs. Others (Paszkiewicz 1983) thought that the Great Russians were simply a slavicized Merya (a Finnish tribe that inhabited the Volga-Oka mesopotamia). Whatever the details, it is clear that the population of northeastern Rus during the first few centuries of the second millennium was increasingly assimilated to the Slavic language and Orthodox Christian religion. At the same time it was subjected to one of the most intense and prolonged metaethnic frontiers in European history.

In the eleventh century, the northeastern frontier of the Kievan Rus had a rather mild quality. It was a frontier between Slavic-speaking Christians and largely Finnish-speaking pagans. Additionally, Kievan Rus had an increasingly urban culture and, as population densities grew, more intense agriculture than indigenous peoples. On the other hand, it is likely that the process of Christianization of Slavs was gradual (see Chapter 6). Meanwhile, non-Slavic people were increasingly converted to Christianity.

During the twelfth and especially the thirteenth century, the steppe frontier advanced north. This occurred partly as a result of decentralization processes within the Kievan polity (see below), and partly because of the arrival of new nomadic hordes from central Asia: first the Cumans (Polovtsy) in the mid-eleventh century, then Mongols two hundred years later. In the twelfth century the core of the Kievan state was both the site of internecine warfare between various Ryurikid factions, and the subject of increasing raiding pressure from the Cumans. As population density declined and many settlements were abandoned, nomad raiders had to press further north in quest of booty and slaves. In the thirteenth century, both the Cumans and East Slavic principalities were decisively defeated by the Mongols. Although northeastern Rus became part of the Golden Horde, it did not lead to a cessation of pressure from the steppe. First, the Mongols did not rule Russia directly, instead relying on local rulers to deliver tribute. This relationship required periodic punitive expeditions to remind both the elites and the population of the alternative to paying taxes. There were a number of urban risings in Russia against the Mongols during the late thirteenth and fourteenth centuries. People objected particularly to the enslaving of householders who could not pay their dues (Hosking 2001:55). Second, no steppe ruler could completely control all his followers, and there was a certain amount of raiding, which intensified when the central authority in the Golden Horde weakened in the middle of the fourteenth century.

By the middle of the fifteenth century, the Golden Horde had undergone a final dissolution. Three strong polities arose on its former periphery: the Principality of Moscow and the Khanates of Kazan and Crimea. Russian lands came under an extremely intense raiding pressure from the Kazan and Crimean Tatars. The prime motivation of nomadic raiders was obtaining slaves. By some estimates, 150,000 to 200,000 Russians were captured in the first half of the seventeenth century (Khodarkovsky 2002:22)

I rate the intensity of the metaethnic frontier in CRU during the thirteenth to the sixteenth centuries as 9, the maximum possible value. The religious divide between Christianity and Islam gets a rating of 3, the linguistic difference is 2, the economic way of life is 2, and the intensity of warfare is 2. The last index reflects the essentially genocidal quality of the steppe frontier during this period. The large swath of the forest-steppe transitional zone was depopulated due to the combined effects of mortality and slave taking resulting from raids, and emigration of the remaining population to more protected regions. Thus, the former core of the Kievan state was completely abandoned by agriculturalists. Most of the Principality of Ryazan was also abandoned, including the old capital (the new capital had to be moved northwest to Pereyaslavl-Ryazansky). The remaining population was hanging on precariously in the northwestern corner of the principality.

The steppe frontier was not the only metaethnic fault line running through Russia in the first half of the second millennium. Another source of geopolitical pressure on the lands of east Slavs was the Lithuanian state, which arose in the thirteenth century and rapidly grew during the fourteenth century, conquering most of the former Kievan Rus, except the northwestern (Novgorod and Pskov) and northeastern (Vladimir-Suzdal) lands. Interestingly, the expansion of this empire, the largest in Europe of the fifteenth century, did not result in establishing an intense metaethnic fault line. The initially pagan Lithuanian elites were very rapidly assimilated to the culture of Kievan Rus. The Lithuanian army, administration, legal system, and finance were organized on the Russian pattern, and Russian became the official language of the new state (Riazanovsky 2000:134). Even when the Lithuanian/west Russian nobles began converting to Catholicism, as a part of Polonization resulting from the Poland-Lithuania dynastic union of 1385, no sharp ethnic boundaries arose. Up to the twentieth century, Slavic dialects between Moscow and Warsaw formed a seamless linguistic matrix. There was no sharp religious fault line, because Polonization affected primarily the upper strata (and even them incompletely, since many nobles stayed Orthodox). Thus, the "civilizational fault line" (*sensu* Huntington 1996) between the Catholic and Orthodox worlds was rather blurred in this part of Eastern Europe.

A rather different situation developed to the north. During the thirteenth century, the east Baltic region became one of the crusading frontiers of Latin Christendom (Shaskolsky 1978; Bartlett 1993; Murray 2001). The Danes invaded Estonia, the German crusading knights intruded in Livonia, and the Swedes conquered southern Finland. These Germanic-speaking Catholic peoples began exerting a significant amount of pressure on the northwestern Russian city-republics of Pskov and Novgorod. In my view, the Baltic frontier qualifies as a major metaethnic fault line for at least two reasons.

First, there is the ideological dimension—a crusade was declared against the enemies of Latin Christians, pagans as well as "schismatics." This development suggests that by the 1240s the western and eastern brands of Christianity had diverged far enough to be considered separate metaethnies. It is interesting that it was during the thirteenth century that the metaethnonym *Nemtsy* arose in Russian (Lind 2001). *Nemtsy* designated all non-Slavic peoples of western Europe. During the thirteenth century old ethnic terms for Danes and Swedes (*Don'* and *Svei*) completely disappeared from the Russian language. When the need to distinguish between various ethnic groups of *Nemtsy* arose around 1500 C.E., new terms had to be created (*Datchane, Shvedy*), while *Nemtsy* became reserved for the Germans.

The second reason is the intensity of conflict, which at times acquired ethnocidal and even genocidal character. The impact of Baltic Crusades on native peoples such as the Prussians is well known. But even as late as the sixteenth century, during the Livonian War, the fighting on the frontier was so intense that the entire Novgorodian region was largely depopulated.

To summarize, after the Kievan Rus imploded, its northern borderlands became "contested grounds," squeezed between two metaethnic frontiers. The most intense metaethnic fault line resulted from a northward shift of the steppe frontier. The pressure from the steppe resulted in a depopulation of the UKR and SRU regions, while the CRU and KAZ regions saw the formation of multiple centers of power during the fifteenth century (Tver, Moscow, and Kazan). The second metaethnic frontier, of somewhat lower intensity (I rate it as 6), arose in the northwest. When the Muscovite state conquered Novgorod (and Tver) by the end of the fifteenth century, it came under the influence of both frontiers. The subsequent history of Russia is very much the story of how these frontiers were moved away from the Volga-Oka heartland. Russia was a frontier state until at least the eighteenth century. The steppe frontier was closed down only with the conquest of the Crimean Khanate in the late eighteenth century. The acquisition of Poland and Finland around the same time, as well as the entry of Russia into the system of European Great Powers also changed the quality of the Baltic frontier, but these developments occurred toward the end of the period of interest, so I will not pursue it here.

9.2.2 Secular Waves

The Kievan Wave

Although the population of Kievan Rus grew rapidly during the eleventh century, from around 3.5 million in 1000 C.E. (McEvedy and Jones 1978) to 7–8 million in the twelfth century (Riazanovsky 2000:48), it is unlikely that the peasant/land ratio was anywhere near the Malthusian subsistence limits. A much greater threat to the political stability of the Kievan state came from the growth of the elites, particularly from "the ever-increasing princely family with its numerous branches" as Riazanovsky (2000:49) characterized them.

The Kievan state reached its zenith during the reign of Iaroslav the Wise (1019–1054). The reigns of Iaroslav's successors introduced a long period of decline, characterized by increasing intraelite conflict and eventually state collapse. Of the 170 years following Iaroslav's death, 80 witnessed civil war (Pogodin, cited in Riazanovsky 2000). However, the decentralization phase of the secular cycle had two periods of particularly intense internal conflict with a period of relative stability in between (we have already noticed this pattern in the French case). The period of stability was the reigns of Vladimir Monomakh and two of his sons (1113–1139). The second period of civil war in the mid-twelfth century led to the final collapse of the Kievan state. In 1169 Andrei Bogoliubskii sacked Kiev and transferred the capital to Vladimir in northeastern Rus. Kiev was sacked again in 1203 and suffered complete destruction in 1240 at the hands of the Mongols (Riazanovsky 2000).

The Golden Horde Intercycle

By the year 1200 the core of the Kievan state had undergone a complete disintegration. The southern half of Kievan Rus was the arena for a three-way struggle between branches of Ryurik's clan: the Rostislavichi of Smolensk, the Olgovichi of Chernigov, and Roman Mstislavich of Volynia (Fennell 1983). Two relatively stable polities, Novgorod and Vladimir, were preeminent in the north. The spatial pattern of an imploded core, surrounded by rising marcher states, is a typical feature of the postimperial landscape (Chapter 4). The endogenous evolution of Kievan Rus, however, was forcibly interrupted by an intrusion from central Asia. For about two hundred years, from the mid-thirteenth to the mid-fifteenth century, Rus (and especially its northeastern part) became the periphery of the Mongolian Empire (or the Golden Horde, after the empire was divided among the descendants of Chinggis Khan). As a result of this change of status, the political dynamics of northeastern Rus, or central Russia (CRU), as I will refer to it from now on, were determined by exogenous forces, originating from an imperial steppe confederation. For this reason, I refer to these two hundred years as an "intercycle" period. I should note, however, that recently Sergey Nefedov (2002b) persuasively argued that the Mongolian period can be considered as a complete secular cycle in its own right, especially in the Novgorodian land, where the Mongolian influence was weak.

The demographic-structural models of Chapter 7 suggest that agrarian states with monogamous elites tend to have longer secular cycles compared to nomadic confederations with polygamous elites. Because central Russia became a periphery of a steppe polity, it was affected by a distinctly different "rhythm of history," than what was typical either before or after the period of Mongol domination. The following summary of events on the Eurasian steppe and environs is from Grousset (1970).

The huge territory conquered by the Mongols during the first half of the thirteenth century contained four large "cultural areas" inhabited by settled people: China, Transoxania, Persia (including Mesopotamia), and eastern Europe. From the middle of the thirteenth century, these four areas were ruled by four separate Chinggisid dynasties: (1) Kublai and his successors (the Yuan dynasty) in China; (2) Jagataids in Turkestan (which included Transoxania); (3) Hulagu and his successors (Il-Khans) in Persia; and (4) Juchids (Batu and his successors) in the Kipchak Steppe (the Golden Horde). According to the theory advanced in Chapter 7, these four polities should be subject to the Ibn Khaldun cycles of around a century in period. This is indeed what happened.

In China, the civil war between the successors of Kublai broke out in 1328. The 1350s saw numerous revolts led by native leaders, and in 1368 one of these leaders expelled the Mongols and established the Ming dynasty.

Turkestan was unified until 1333–1334, when a nomad-led insurrection broke out against the Jagataid regime in eastern Turkestan. By 1350 the power in Transoxania passed into the hands of local Turkic nobles. After a period of turmoil, a new dynasty was established by Timur. Timur unified Transoxania in 1379 and conquered Iran during the 1390s. The Timurid dynasty also lasted about a century. In 1469 Persia was lost to the White Sheep Horde, while Transoxania splintered between warring branches of Timur's descendants.

The Persia of Il-Khans underwent dissolution in 1335. After a period of civil war it was conquered by Timur (see above). When the Timurids lost Persia in 1469, another turbulent period followed, and eventually, by 1500, Persia was unified by a native dynasty (Safavids).

A similar course of events occurred in the Kipchak Steppe. The Juchids' rule ended in 1359, when the Kipchak Steppe fell into anarchy. After a period of civil war, the Golden Horde underwent a revival under Timur Qutlugh, who expelled Tokhtamysh in 1391 (with Timur's help). In 1399 Timur Qutlugh won a signal victory over the Lithuanians and consolidated his dominion over Russia, although a series of punitive expeditions were required during the early fifteenth century to keep the tribute flowing. In the middle of the fifteenth century, however, the revived Golden Horde began disintegrating again. The first piece to secede was the Crimean Khanate in 1430. The Khanates of Kazan and Astrakhan followed (in 1445 and 1466, respectively).

The Moscow polity went through its own period of civil war during the second quarter of the fifteenth century, which, curiously, coincided with the civil war on the steppe that lead to the final splintering of the Golden Horde. As soon as the civil war ended, Muscovy became de facto an independent state (de jure independence had to wait until 1480).

To summarize, all Chinggisid dynasties went through typical Ibn Khaldun cycles of about a century in period. In China, a native dynasty expelled the Mongols after one cycle, while in Russia and Iran the steppe dynasties went through two cycles before giving way to native rulers. Incidentally, the central Eurasian steppes continued to undergo Ibn Khaldun cycles, until their conquest and division between the Russian and the Chinese empires.

The Muscovy Wave

After the end of the succession wars in 1450, Muscovy embarked on a century-long period of practically uninterrupted expansion. By the early sixteenth century the "gathering of Russian lands" resulted in the Muscovite state's absorption of virtually all the lands of Kievan Rus that were not part of Lithuania. During the 1550s Russia conquered Kazan. Once the barrier of this moderately strong state was removed, the Khanates of Astrakhan and Siberia quickly fell, and rapid eastward expansion into the stateless territory of north Asia became possible (this is an example of the "breakthrough effect," discussed in Section 4.2.2).

By the 1570s, however, the Muscovite expansion ran out of steam. The prolonged Livonian war (1558–1583) actually resulted in a loss of territory. Historians have proposed many explanations of Russia's defeat by Poland-Lithuania and Sweden, but I suggest that the root cause was the inversion of the secular trend.

Indeed, evidence supports a demographic-structural interpretation of the sixteenth-century crisis of the Muscovite state that culminated in the Time of

Troubles (1598–1613) (Dunning 1998). The population of Russia grew rapidly, possibly doubling, during the sixteenth century, with most increase occurring during the first half of the century. The numbers of the aristocracy (members of the Boyar Duma) and the lower class of service nobility increased even faster than the general population. The price of grain increased by a factor of 4–5, while for many Russians taxes rose sevenfold (adjusted for inflation). During the 1570s, the decline of the Russian economy reached catastrophic proportions, leading to a massive flight of peasants and urban taxpayers. Population declined both in the central region of the Muscovite state and on its northwestern frontier (the Novgorodian lands, which were also badly affected by fighting during the Livonian war). The result was a huge loss of revenue, both for the state and for the service nobility (Dunning 1998).

Political instability affected Russia in two waves. The first period of heightened instability was the *Oprichnina* years of 1565–1572 (Riazanovsky 2000:149–151). The peculiarity of this period was that it was a coup d'état lead by the monarch himself, using one part of the elite (*oprichniki*) against the rest. The reign of Fedor (1584–1598) was an interlude relatively free of internal conflict, during which Russia prosecuted a successful war against Sweden, recovering the lands previously ceded to Sweden by the peace treaty of 1583 (Riazanovsky 2000). However, Fedor's death without a natural successor introduced the second period of instability, the Time of Troubles. During this period, four Tsars ruled Russia in rapid succession: Boris and Fedor Godunovs, False Dmitry, and Vasily Shuisky, followed by the interregnum of 1610–1613. There were several popular uprisings led by dissident elites, foreign interventions of Poland, Sweden, and the Crimean Tatars. In short, this was a typical state collapse, proceeding according to the demographic-structural scenario. Note that the peaks of the two periods of instability, 1570 and 1610, are forty years, or roughly two generations, apart.

The Romanov Wave

In 1613 Michael Romanov was crowned as Tzar, beginning the 300-year reign of the Romanov dynasty. However, the period of instability was not yet completely over. Although Russia did not experience a full-blown state collapse, the fiscal health of the state remained shaky throughout Michael's and his successor's reigns. It also took a while to recover social stability. In fact, various riots and uprisings occurred until the early years of Peter the Great's reign.

Nevertheless, gradually, from the middle of the seventeenth century on, the centralizing tendency and associated territorial expansion began to reassert itself, beginning with Poland ceding the left-bank Ukraine to Russia in 1667. What followed was one of the longest and most successful periods of territorial expansion known in history. During the eighteenth century Russia either toppled its seventeenth-century adversaries from Great Power status (Sweden, Turkey), or outright conquered them (Crimean Khanate, Poland). The status of a Great Power was followed by a brief period of European or perhaps even Eurasian hegemony during 1815–1850. Of course, this hegemony was not due only to the internal strength of the Russian Empire (forged on the anvil of the steppe frontier with

a hammer of Baltic crusades, if I may be forgiven a poetic metaphor). Much of
the explanation is also due to Russia getting out of phase with the secular cycles
of other Eurasian empires, as a result of the anomalously long period of expansion. Note that the "crisis of the seventeenth century" was Eurasia-wide, affecting
western Europe, Russia, the Ottoman Empire, and China (although not Persia or
India). During the first half of the nineteenth century, both China and Turkey were
well into their respective decentralization phases (which turned out to be the last
one for the Ottoman Empire). More importantly, western Europe was experienc-
ing its Age of Revolutions (1789-1848), which allowed Russia to play the role
of the "gendarme of Europe" (e.g., the suppressing of the Hungarian revolution
of 1849). Even England, while avoiding a full-blown state collapse, experienced
significant sociopolitical instability during the 1830s (Goldstone 1991b). Thus,
it was the *relative* strength of the Russian empire that explains its geopolitical
preponderance during the first half of the nineteenth century.

The explanations underlying the Russian expansion of 1650–1850, I suggest,
are twofold. First, Russia originated from a maximally intense metaethnic frontier,
which, according to the theory, should produce a very high level of asabiya.
Second, at the beginning of the expansionary period Russia acquired huge areas
of "black-earth lands" that were lightly populated but quite suitable to agriculture.
Colonization of these lands allowed peasant numbers to grow from around 10
million in 1600 to more than 100 million in 1900. This enormous expansion of
the productive stratum allowed the Russian society to find employment for all
the elites. Because Russia was a strictly monogamous society, the elites grew no
faster than commoners. Nobility constituted only 1–2% of the population in the
Russian Empire (Mironov 2000), significantly reducing the potential for intraelite
competition.

However, no growth can go on forever. During the nineteenth century the population of European Russia tripled from 36 to 100 million (McEvedy and Jones
1978). Peasant/land ratios declined, food prices increased, and food shortages
became common. Although the numbers of nobility stayed at around 2% of the
population, new kinds of aspiring elites (*raznochintsy*, intelligentsia) were on the
rise. Thus, by the second half of the nineteenth century the demographic-structural
machinery has caught up with the previously "runaway" growth of the Russian
empire.

The inversion of the secular trend, combined with logistical strains, started to
exert a negative influence on the geopolitical prospects of the Russian empire
around the middle of the nineteenth century. The defeat in the Crimean war was
a temporary setback, but the abandonment of the Treaty of San Stefano (1878)
under the pressure of the other Great Powers was a significant check on the expansion at the expense of the Ottoman Empire. The dynamic underlying this shift
in relative geopolitical power was, first, the onset of the decentralization phase
in Russia. Second, the other powers had just concluded their own decentralization phases and had entered on the expansionary imperialistic ones. Thus, Russia
could continue to expand only in regions that were out of reach of European
powers, such as central Asia. The clearest illustration of the effect of weaken-
ing internal structure on geopolitical expansion is the Russo-Japanese war. Even

though Russia had a very disadvantageous logistics situation, and lost its expeditionary naval force in the battle of Tsushima, it managed to mass enough troops for a decisive push into Manchuria. However, the revolution of 1905–1907 caused the government to abandon the plan of land-based attack against the Japanese, because it needed the troops to quell the uprising.

The dynamics of political instability in Romanov Russia followed the by now familiar two-generation pattern, or, in the Russian case, the "fathers-and-sons" pattern (with apologies to Turgenev). The first period of unrest occurred during the reign of Alexander II. The 1860s and 1870s saw peasant riots and a terror campaign by revolutionaries, ending with the assassination of the tsar in 1881. The following reign of Alexander III was, by contrast, a time of stability. The next instability period culminated in the revolutions of 1905–1907 and 1917, although there was a large contributing effect of geopolitical stress brought about by war, especially in the case of World War I and the 1917 revolution.

9.2.3 Summary

Despite Russia and France being very different countries, each with its own geography and culture, a number of common themes emerge when we look at their history through the lenses of the metaethnic frontier and demographic-structural theories. First, both regions experienced two ethnogenetic events: the Franks and the French, the Rus and the Russians. All four ethnies arose on metaethnic frontiers. All states went through secular cycles, and there was an intercycle period between the Frankish Empire and France and between the Kievan Rus and Russia. Finally, the decentralization phases of secular cycles are almost invariably characterized by the fathers-and-sons fine structure, in which instability occurs in waves about two generations apart.

Chapter Ten

Conclusion

10.1 OVERVIEW OF MAIN DEVELOPMENTS

In Chapter 1 I outlined a research program for investigating historical dynamics. The main features of the proposed approach are (1) translation of verbal theories into mathematical models, (2) derivation of quantitative predictions from two or more alternative theories/models, and (3) empirical tests to determine which of the rival theories predicts data best. This general approach worked very well in the natural sciences, but can it be applied to social and historical questions? I believe it can, and I attempted to show how a consistent application of the approach can yield nontrivial advances in the understanding of territorial dynamics of agrarian polities.

10.1.1 Asabiya and Metaethnic Frontiers

Perhaps the most novel development that I discuss in the book is the theory of asabiya, the capacity of a group for collective action (Chapter 3). I advanced the hypothesis that asabiya increases on metaethnic frontiers and declines in the core regions of large polities. I explored this hypothesis with a simple analytical model and a more complex spatial simulation, and determined under what conditions we should observe repeated cycles of imperial rise and demise (Chapter 4). I then developed an empirical apparatus for testing the theory. This turns out to be a nontrivial task (and very much work in progress), but such difficulties are probably to be expected when new concepts are advanced and raw empirical facts need to be translated into *normalized data* (Rozov 2000:25). Applying this apparatus to the history of Europe during the first and second millennia (Chapter 5), I found that the predictions of the theory are borne out by the data. The match between theory and data is not perfect, but that is as expected, since all scientific theories are at best approximations of reality. Furthermore, an alternative theory, based on the geopolitical marchland advantage, does a much worse job of predicting where large polities ("empires") originate; in fact, it "guesses" right no more frequently than would be expected by chance alone.

I submit that the results of this worked example, which starts with a verbal formulation of theory and pushes it all the way through to an empirical test, are an indication that the general approach can work in historical applications and yield nontrivial insights. Note that the value of this exercise does not depend on whether the metaethnic frontier theory continues to be corroborated or is ultimately rejected in favor of some better alternative. The important point is that, by passing the test successfully, the theory now establishes a standard that needs to be bettered, so rejection of it in favor of a better alternative would necessarily lead to further advances. Whatever the ultimate explanation, there is a striking association between metaethnic frontiers ("civilizational fault lines") and the subsequent development of aggressive empires from such regions.

As I argued throughout the book, exclusionary religions such as Christianity and Islam play a key role in many metaethnic frontiers. Yet my theory treats the appearance of world religions in a particular place as an exogenous event. As the anonymous reviewer of a previous book draft pointed out, "the theoretical question is left open: under what conditions do world religions appear, and where do they spread, relative to existing geopolitical configurations?" This is an excellent question, and I wish I could answer it. However, at this point in time I do not have any credible hypotheses about how we could endogenize the spread of world religions, so I must leave this issue for future research.

10.1.2 Ethnic Assimilation

I continued to apply the same approach to two other theories. The first one, the kinetics of religious and linguistic assimilation (which I dubbed "ethnokinetics"), had been largely developed in a verbal fashion and is still relatively unmathematized. Thus, I was forced to start at the ground level, by considering which of the basic modes of growth provides a reasonable starting point for modeling ethnic assimilation. Empirical tests with three case studies (conversion to Islam, the rise of Christianity, and growth of the Mormon church) uniformly indicate that the autocatalytic model does much better than the noninteractive and threshold alternatives. Incidentally, fitting the autocatalytic model to the temporal trajectory of proportion converted yields, in one case, a remarkable R^2 of 0.9998. This is not a result of overfitting, because the model is very simple, with just two free parameters, and the data set is quite large, being based on many hundreds of biographies. In other words, high degrees of precision are not limited to physical applications. However, I need to reemphasize the point made in the previous section: it is not the absolute value of R^2 that matters, but the process by which we arrive at successively better theories. The Islamic conversion example, in fact, illustrates this idea very nicely, because a more detailed investigation of the observed patterns yielded evidence of a systematic deviation between model predictions and data, which allowed us to advance an alternative model that explained this pattern (and without adding more parameters).

Despite this encouraging beginning, the study of ethnokinetics is just beginning. Of key importance are two issues. First, how to characterize the social space within a polity: where are connections between people dense and where are there gaps (fortunately, social networks appear to be a topic of much current interest in sociology, so hopefully we can profit from this literature). This is important, because assimilation spread can be inhibited by gaps in networks. It is even possible that two alternative stable states become established on each side of the gap, as perhaps happened in Iran, where a certain minority never converted to Islam, staying Zoroastrian. The second issue is quantitative estimates of coefficients, such as r, the relative assimilation rate. Thus, the estimated r for Iran was almost twice as large as that for Spain (Table 6.1). Why did the Iranians convert at twice the rate of the Spanish? Furthermore, cases exist where the assimilation process reversed its direction (for example, Germanization of the Czechs in the Habsburg Empire in the eighteenth versus the late nineteenth century). In short, we need a theory that can make predictions about the numerical values of coefficients.

10.1.3 Demographic-Structural Theory

The last theory for which I attempted to travel all the way from verbal beginnings to empirical tests is the demographic-structural theory (Chapter 7). This theory has already been well developed and tested by Goldstone and others, which greatly simplified my treatment of it. However, the Goldstonian version of the theory treats population dynamics as an exogenous variable, while I wished to examine the hypothesis that it is actually dynamically linked to state breakdown. I hypothesized that political instability has a negative effect on population growth. Translating this hypothesis into models, I found that somewhat irregular cycles of 2–3 centuries in duration are predicted for agrarian polities. Irregularity arises (in the simple model) as a result of variable periods of time passing from state collapse to the beginning of the next demographic-structural cycle.

The empirical survey of available long-term data on population dynamics suggests that oscillations of 2–3 centuries in period are the rule rather than an exception (Chapter 8). Furthermore, building on previous work by Chu and Lee, I analyzed a data set containing estimates of both population dynamics and political instability in China from –200 to 1710. The results of this analysis suggest very strongly that population and instability are endogenously linked to each other. Qualitative surveys, one by Fischer for the whole of western Europe, and my more focused one on France and Russia, also support this view (further support for the theory comes from recent work by Sergey Nefedov).

The theory also predicts faster cycles for nomadic imperial confederations, with periods of about a century. Although the nomadic polities are not a primary focus in this book, a brief excursion into the post–Chinggis Khan history of Central Asia (Section 9.2.2) provided some supporting evidence for such dynamics.

10.1.4 Geopolitics

One theory that I was unable to subject to a thorough empirical test is the theory of geopolitics (Chapter 2). However, it was still possible to make a lot of progress just on the strength of translating the verbal theory into mathematical models. Thus, we found that the mechanisms postulated, for example, by the Collins version of the theory—geopolitical resources, logistical loads, and marchland advantage—led to *first-order dynamics*. In other words, the theory cannot explain prolonged declines that characterize many historical empires. This purely theoretical development illustrates one of the strengths of mathematical, as opposed to verbal, models. What may look reasonable when the problem is stated verbally does not necessarily have the proposed dynamical consequences when we formalize the description in the language of dynamical systems. Nonlinearities and lags affecting historical (and physical, and biological) systems require a specialized mathematical apparatus for connecting assumptions to predictions.

One empirical application of the geopolitical theory, although limited, was my test of the effect of positional advantage of a region on the maximum polity size originating from it. I found no statistical association between the two variables, suggesting that marchland position confers no fixed geopolitical advantage. This is not to say, however, that marchland position may not confer a temporary advantage. In fact, there are many convincing examples of states losing wars that they fought on two fronts, such as Germany in the two world wars. However, this idea remains to be rigorously tested. We need to go beyond anecdotal approaches: after all, Prussia during the Seven Years War was also fighting on multiple fronts, yet it triumphed. The empirical development of geopolitics is another area where further research is needed. An objective test that would address all military interactions within a defined area and period of time would be most satisfying, because it would avoid any conscious or unconscious selection of cases. However, developing a set of worked examples would be a very useful first step in this direction, like the example I suggested in Chapter 9 on the sixteenth-century struggle for Italy between France and Spain.

10.2 COMBINING DIFFERENT MECHANISMS INTO AN INTEGRATED WHOLE

Although it can be argued that useful advances have been made in all theories (apart from, perhaps, geopolitics) separately, it is not completely clear how to develop an approach that would integrate them. Tracing how different mechanisms may have interacted in specific polities (Chapter 9), however, suggests some hypotheses that can be developed in future work. Here I describe my current thinking about this problem (with the caveat that this is hypothesis building, so all of the following is subject to change in the light of new models and data).

One of the most useful aspects of the dynamical-systems approach is that it forces us to worry explicitly about the temporal scale on which a certain mechanism is operating. The initial discussion of temporal scales can be found in Section 8.2, and here I can refine it in the light of empirical developments that occurred after that section. One "natural" time scale of high relevance to historical dynamics is the human generation time (20–30 years). This is the scale at which population increases and declines, political elites are renewed, and culture is transmitted and modified. A much smaller scale of years is where "ecological" mechanisms operate: the agricultural cycle, outbreaks of disease, etc. The scale at which asabiya, ethnokinetic, and demographic-structural mechanisms operate is much longer than years, or even generations. The secular wave has the best defined period: it is around 2–3 centuries (in agrarian empires), or an order of magnitude longer than the human generation. Such a large, tenfold, difference means that generation cycles will be nested within demographic-structural cycles, and the two will not interact strongly (at least, this is the working hypothesis, which should be tested). Thus, any disequilibria in the age structure, such as baby booms, should proceed largely independently of the longer secular cycles. Another type of shorter-period dynamics is the two-generation cycles with period of about 40–60 years. Possible examples include Kondratieff's waves, Easterlin's cycles, the long waves of Goldstein (1988), and the fathers-and-sons oscillations during decentralization phases, noticed in Chapter 9. It is interesting to note, in this respect, that long price time series, such as the one shown in Figure 7.7, apparently have two dominant periods: around 300 years, corresponding to the secular oscillation, and around 50 years, perhaps reflecting some bigenerational cycle. The two cycles appear to be simply superimposed on each other (although the 50-year cycle may have a greater amplitude during the period of political instability). Even shorter cycles, such as the 11-year sunspot oscillation may be superimposed on top of the longer ones. So it may be appropriate to think about historical dynamics as a set of cycles of different periods nested within each other.

Now let us consider longer-term dynamics, and in particular the relationship between secular waves and the pace of an assimilation process or asabiya change. Using the estimated rate parameters for religious conversion (Table 6.1), I estimate that the time needed for passing from 10% to 90% of the population converted is between 150 and 300 years. In other words, assimilation appears to occur on roughly the same temporal scale as the secular cycle.

By contrast, the dynamics of asabiya occur on a much longer scale (in fact, discovering just how slow this process is was one of the most interesting empirical findings of Chapter 5). Looking at large territorial empires of greater than 0.5 Mm^2 at the peak (the "Great Powers"), we observe that the duration of metaethnic frontiers in their regions of origin was from three to ten centuries. Thus, one secular wave is the *minimum* period of asabiya incubation, and usually two or three such periods have to pass before a new aggressive polity/ethnie is born. The temporal extents of successful empires are similarly long. In fact, we can measure the longevity of an empire in how many secular cycles it has survived. This is a particularly appropriate scale, because the final collapse of empires typically occurs during one of the demographic-structural crises.

Measured in this way, a "typical" empire is good for two or three secular cycles. The Roman polity, for example, survived three: the Republic, the Principate, and the Dominate. France, as we saw in Section 9.1, went through three cycles prior to 1900 c.e. (Capetian, Valois, and Bourbon), and is now in the fourth one. The Frankish Empire went through two cycles (Merovingian and Carolingian), although an argument can be made that there was a third cycle—the Ottonian and Salian emperors of the medieval German Empire who were direct successors of the Carolingians (thus, the Rhine valley was the geographical core of both the Carolingian and Holy Roman Empires; see Barraclough 1998:118). Russia went through two cycles prior to 1900: the Muscovite and the Imperial (or Romanov) waves. China had a succession of empires, with a typical duration of two secular cycles: East and West Han, then a long period of fragmentation (an intercycle); Early and Late Tang, another intercycle; Sung and Southern Sung, followed by a period of alien rule (Mongols, or the Yuan dynasty); and finally Ming and Qing (although the latter can be considered as another alien dynasty). I can go on, but it looks as if examples of imperial duration of one or four secular cycles are rare. One example of a short-lived empire is the Principality of Kiev, which managed to survive for only one cycle (from the tenth to the twelfth century, with the coup de grace delivered by the Mongols in 1240).

Thus, the interaction between the demographic-structural and asabiya mechanisms is likely to be limited to periods of instability, at least to the first order of approximation. Therefore, I advance the hypothesis that large successful empires are destroyed by a combination of asabiya decline and the decentralization phase of the secular cycle. When asabiya is still high, an empire will reconstitute itself after a time of troubles. If asabiya has declined too far, then the period of instability will spell the end of the empire.

Because ethnokinetic and demographic processes occur on roughly the same time scale, these mechanisms may interact in more intricate and unpredictable ways. The basic problem is that the phase of the secular cycle may affect the magnitude and even the sign of the assimilation rate. During the centralization phase, when the elite/general population ratio is favorable, the imperial core elites are likely to be open to the entry of peripheral aspirants. Such a situation is highly conducive to strong pressures for assimilation. By contrast, during the decentralization phase, imperial elites close their ranks against newcomers aspiring to better their position, who then have no choice but to build alternative power networks, and challenge the established order. These "counternetworks" are likely to be based on peripheral identities. The specific symbolic markers used to differentiate the core elites from the dissidents may be based on religious, linguistic, or regional differences. Thus, social conditions during the decentralization phase may actually favor "reverse assimilation," in which members of a core ethnie living in a peripheral region are under pressure to assimilate to the peripheral identity. At this point, this is just a hypothesis, but certainly capable of being tested empirically.

Furthermore, there is a feedback effect from assimilation dynamics to demographic-structural mechanisms (Chapter 6). If the process of assimilation has largely run its course, then those particular markers (religious or linguistic) will probably not serve as a basis for elite fractures. Otherwise, under the pressures of the decentralization phase, the elites will fracture right down the ethnic lines, potentially with disastrous consequences to the empire.

Another conjecture is that during the time of troubles we should expect a "narrowing down" of the asabiya profile. That is, whereas during good times the members of the elite may identify themselves primarily with the empirewide ethnie, when times are bad, they may fall back on their regional (subethnic) identity.

Finally, there is the possibility that bigenerational cycles interact with the secular ones. In Section 9.1.2 I briefly touched on the pattern of two-generation cycles in political instability that seem to succeed each other during the decentralization phases. There may be a connection here to the Kondratieff waves, which are of the same duration (40–60 years). For example, Joshua Goldstein (1988) argued that the Kondratieff waves have an effect on war dynamics in Europe. This is another avenue clearly worth pursuing.

10.3 BROADENING THE FOCUS OF INVESTIGATION

At the beginning of this book, I deliberately narrowed down the focus of the research program to the dynamics of agrarian polities. I believe such a focus is appropriate, especially during the beginning of an investigation. Here is the time, however, to discuss what was left out.

One important class of societies that I discuss in a very inadequate manner is the nomadic pastoralists. Addressing these societies should be the first order of business, particularly because nomadic polities were so important in the history of Eurasian empires.

Another class, which I completely left out, is the *thalassocratic* polities such as classical Athens, medieval Venice, or early modern Holland. Thus, my focus has been entirely on land-based rather than sea-based power, *tellurocracies* rather than thalassocracies. Again, this choice was deliberate. The basic resources of tellurocracies are land and people (thus my emphasis on territorial and population dynamics). I believe this makes tellurocracies particularly amenable to analysis with rather simple models. Note that I tried to avoid any monetary issues (at least in models). Also, the economic submodel in the demographic-structural theory is quite simple, focusing entirely on food production. Such an oversimplified approach will clearly not do for thalassocracies.

My focus on land power has led me to largely ignore the voluminous literature on hegemonic cycles (Modelski and Thompson 1996), even though I find this literature extremely fascinating. Another excellent field of research that I touched upon lightly is world-systems theory (Wallerstein 1974; Chase-Dunn and Hall 1997). The reason is my focus on the polity as the main subject of analysis. This focus leads to a certain bias, which I readily acknowledge: a tendency to look for endogenous causes of the rise and fall of empires. At this point, I can only state that I wholeheartedly agree with the idea that we need to understand how systems of interacting polities work. This is also clearly the next order of business.

Finally, there is the issue of what the theories and results discussed in the book mean for modernity. Generally, I tried very hard not to cross the self-imposed temporal limit of 1900, for reasons explained in Section 1.2.2. It was not, however, my intention to imply that the insights from models and data for agrarian societies are completely irrelevant to modern societies. Clearly, we cannot directly apply some models, for example, those in Chapter 7, to western industrialized states because population growth in these societies does not lead to starvation. On the other hand, some of the ideas developed for the dynamics of elites in agrarian states may yield fruitful hypotheses about modern polities (see, for example, the discussion in Goldstone 2002). For example, modern societies may be susceptible to elite overproduction. A recent article in the *Economist* (November 14, 2002) reported that the proportion of Britons between 18 and 21 years old going to college has more than *doubled* during the 1990s (from 15 to 33%). Is British society approaching a crisis? This is the kind of hypothesis that can be addressed in future research.

Other theories may also be of relevance to current affairs. Judging by the burgeoning literature on social capital, the ability of groups and whole societies for concerted and effective action is of great interest to sociologists and political scientists. Geopolitical arguments were used to successfully predict the demise of the Soviet Union (Collins 1995). And the dynamics of assimilation or, conversely, ethnic fissioning and mobilization are the key elements of current international politics (Moynihan 1993). All these directions are extremely interesting and should eventually be followed. Still, I continue to argue for a conservative approach of first honing the theories and analytical approaches on the historical material, and applying them to contemporary issues only once we are reasonably sure of how well our approaches work.

10.4 TOWARD THEORETICAL CLIODYNAMICS?

If the combined modeling/empirical approach to investigating history, advocated in this book, has the potential to become a fruitful research program, then it would be a good idea to come up with a better name for it than "historical dynamics." I propose to call it *cliodynamics*, by analogy with cliometrics. The term cliometrics was originally used for the new economic history in a rather derogatory sense (Williamson 1991), but now cliometrics is an accepted and mature direction within history. If we understand cliometrics in the general sense (that is, a focus on any quantitative data in history, not just economic ones), then it is an extremely valuable complementary discipline to the historical dynamics research program. Cliodynamics needs cliometrics for the raw empirical inputs. But I would argue that cliometrics needs something like cliodynamics as a source of theories and hypotheses to guide the empirical research.

Appendix A

Mathematical Appendix

A.1 TRANSLATING THE HANNEMAN MODEL INTO DIFFERENTIAL EQUATIONS

If we start with the equations on p. 18 of Hanneman et al. (1995), replace discrete time derivatives with continuous derivatives, and change the delayed effect of war success on prestige into instantaneous, then we have the following system:

$$C = (L_0 - L)S$$
$$W = \delta_p C$$
$$\dot{S} = W$$
$$\dot{L} = W$$

where C (C_t in the Hanneman et al. notation) is the level of conflict initiated by the focal state at time t, L (L_t, also PR_t) is the legitimacy level, W (WS_t) is the current degree of war success, and S (CS_t) is the accumulated record of past successes and failures. The parameter L_0 (LG in the Hanneman et al. notation) is the legitimacy goal, and δ_p ($= (E - EP)/(P + EP)$) is the power differential between the focal state and its adversaries. Substituting the relationships for C and W into the differential equation for L, we have

$$\dot{L} = \delta_p(L_0 - L)S \tag{A.1}$$

Since $\dot{S} = \dot{L}$, $S = L - d$, where $d = L(0) - S(0)$ is the initial difference between accumulated success and legitimacy. Substituting this relationship into equation (A.1), we have

$$\dot{L} = \delta_p(L_0 - L)(L - d) \tag{A.2}$$

This is essentially the logistic model (it would be precisely logistic if $d = 0$), and its dynamics appear to match the behavior of the Hanneman et al. simulation (1995:21–24).

Let us now investigate the consequences of the Hanneman et al. assumptions for territorial dynamics, using some components from Section 2.2.1. First, recall that the rate of territorial change is directly proportional to war success; thus $\dot{A} = gW$. Since $\dot{L} = W$, $\dot{L} = \dot{A}/g$. Integrating this equation, we obtain $L = q + A/g$ (q is the integration constant). Substituting this relationship in equation (A.2), we have

$$\dot{A} = g\delta_P(L_0 - q - A/g)(q + A/g - d) \tag{A.3}$$

We are not done yet, because the power differential δ_P is a function of A: $\delta_p = cA\exp[-\sqrt{A}/h] - a$ (Section 2.2.1). Employing this relationship, we have the final result:

$$\dot{A} = g\big(cA\exp[-\sqrt{A}/h] - a\big)(L_0 - q - A/g)(q + A/g - d) \qquad \text{(A.4)}$$

Although this equation looks quite complex, note that its form is $\dot{A} = f(A)$. The complexity of $f(A)$, however, does not matter. The major conclusion from this exercise is that the legitimacy-conflict model is described by a *single-dimensional ordinary differential equation*. This model can have multiple equilibria, and depending on the initial values of $A(0)$ and $L(0)$ (which affect the integration constant q), the trajectory will be attracted to one or another of the stable ones. But this model is incapable of predicting boom/bust dynamics.

A.2 THE SPATIAL SIMULATION OF THE FRONTIER HYPOTHESIS

The simulation takes place in a spatial "arena" consisting of 21×21 cells. Each cell represents a small regional polity or a province within a larger territorial empire (thus the spatial resolution is quite coarse). The simulation, therefore, assumes that there are two spatial levels (single-cell regions and multicell empires). To start things off, a single empire occupying several cells (for example, a 4×4 square area) is placed somewhere within the simulation arena. Each cell has two numbers associated with it: the imperial index (indicating which empire it belongs to) and its value of asabiya. At the start of the simulation, cells belonging to the first empire are indexed by 1, while the rest have an index of 0 (corresponding to the nonimperial hinterland).

The asabiya value of a cell represents the average degree of collective solidarity felt by the population inhabiting the region for the supraregional empire within which they may find themselves. (If the imperial index of a cell is 0, then the asabiya refers to itself as a regional polity.) Asabiya dynamics are determined by the position of the cell with respect to the imperial boundaries. If a cell is next to an imperial boundary (that is, one of its neighbors has a different imperial index from its own), then the asabiya of the cell increases according to the following rule:

$$S_{x,y,t+1} = S_{x,y,t} + r_0 S_{x,y,t}(1 - S_{x,y,t}) \qquad \text{(A.5)}$$

This equation is simply a discrete version of logistic growth, $\dot{S} = r_0 S(1-S)$. The subscripts x and y index the spatial position of the cell within the arena, and t is time. This formulation imposes an upper limit on asabiya, $S = 1$ (the same as in the nonspatial model of Section 4.2.1). The asabiya of a cell that is not on a boundary decays exponentially at the rate δ:

$$S_{x,y,t+1} = S_{x,y,t} - \delta S_{x,y,t} \qquad \text{(A.6)}$$

Note that the neighborhood of a cell is defined as the four cells sharing a linear boundary with it (this excludes the four diagonal cells that only touch corners with the focal cell). Furthermore, cells within the nonimperial hinterland are considered to be on a boundary only when they are adjacent to an empire.

Territorial empires are characterized by two numbers: the number of regions they control, $A_{i,t}$, and the average asabiya,

$$\bar{S}_{i,t} = \frac{1}{A_{i,t}} \sum_{\{x,y\}\in i} S_{x,y,t} \tag{A.7}$$

Here i is the imperial index.

At every time step each cell considers an attack on its four neighbors. The attack does not take place if the neighbor belongs to the same empire (but non-imperial hinterland cells can attack each other). The success of the attack depends on the relative powers of the attacker cell and the defending cell, P_{att} and P_{def}, respectively. The power of a cell x,y at time t is calculated as follows:

$$P_{x,y,t} = A_{i,t}\bar{S}_{i,t}\exp[-d_{i,x,y}/h] \tag{A.8}$$

where $\bar{S}_{i,t}$ is the average asabiya of the empire i to which the cell belongs, $d_{i,x,y}$ is the distance between the imperial center and the cell, and h is the parameter determining how fast the power declines with increasing distance. The *imperial center* is simply the center of gravity of the empire. Thus, the x coordinate of the imperial center is calculated by averaging the x coordinates of all cells belonging to the empire, and the y coordinate is calculated analogously. Note that equation (A.8) is analogous to the equation for $\dot{A}$ in the nonspatial asabiya-territory model [see equation (4.5)], with the only difference that here the effects of logistical constraints are modeled with a negative exponential form, while in equation (4.5) I used a linear approximation of the negative exponential.

In order to determine the success of an attack, the powers of the attacker and defender are compared. If

$$P_{att} - P_{def} > \Delta_P \tag{A.9}$$

then the attack is successful, the defending cell is taken over, and its imperial index is changed to that of the attacking empire. The asabiya value of the con-quered cell is reset as the average of its asabiya prior to attack and the asabiya of the conquering cell. If the attack is unsuccessful, then nothing happens. The parameter Δ_P is the minimal power differential necessary for a successful attack.

Finally, I included in the simulation the possibility of imperial collapse if the average asabiya of the empire becomes too low. At the end of each time step the average asabiyas of all empires are checked. If $\bar{S}_{i,t} < S_{crit}$ then the empire is dissolved, and all cells belonging to it are classified as nonimperial hinterland (indexed with 0).

Some technical points. The order in which cells become potential attackers (during a time step) is random and changes at every time step. This procedure guards against any systematic directional biases that would be imposed by a fixed order of choosing the attacker. Similarly, the order in which the four neighbors are considered for potential attack is also randomized at each step. These two randomizations are the only way stochasticity affects the model dynamics; otherwise, all effects are deterministic. The boundary conditions in the simulation are of the reflecting kind. Cells on the edge of the arena are not called to attack neighbors, and at the end of each time period, their asabiyas and imperial indices are set equal to those of the nearest nonedge cell.

The model is quite simple and has only five parameters that determine its behavior. The reference set of parameters which served as a starting point for exploring the dynamics was as follows: $r_0 = 0.2$, $\delta = 0.1$, $h = 2$, $\Delta_P = 0.1$, and $S_{crit} = 0.003$.

A.3 DEMOGRAPHIC-STRUCTURAL MODELS WITH CLASS STRUCTURE

Modeling Extraction

I begin by considering the interaction between commoners and elites. The structural variables are the size of the producer (peasants, commoners) population, P, and the size of the exploiter (elites, nobility) population, E. Let us assume that the production per producer is a linear function of producer population size: $\rho = \rho_0(1 - gP)$. The parameter ρ_0 measures the maximum rate of food production by each producer, and g quantifies how the per capita production declines with increasing producer numbers. To connect production to population dynamics, I assume that the per capita rate of producer population growth, r_P, is a linear function of the resources available to each producer, ρ_P:

$$r_P = \beta_1 \rho_P - \delta_1 \tag{A.10}$$

This equation implies that if $\rho_P > \delta_1/\beta_1$ then the producer population will grow; otherwise, it will decline. The parameter β_1 can be thought of as a coefficient translating surplus production into babies, while δ_1 is also the rate at which peasants die off when they have no food.

If producers dispose of all resources that they produce (that is, $\rho_P = \rho$), then their population dynamics are described by the following equation:

$$\dot{P} = r_P P = (\beta_1 \rho - \delta_1)P = [\beta_1 \rho_0(1 - gP) - \delta_1]P$$

It is easy to see that this equation is the logistic model with the intrinsic rate of producer population growth $r_0 = \rho_0(\beta_1 - \delta_1)$ and producer carrying capacity $k = \rho_0(\beta_1 - \delta_1)/g$. In other words, so far we are following in the tracks of the basic model, although now our focus is on the *total* production, rather than the surplus.

In the presence of exploiters, however, producers will not be able to keep all the food they produce. We now need to derive a model for resource extraction by exploiters. The key element of this model is the amount of coercion that the exploiters are able to bring to bear on the producers. I assume that at low exploiter numbers, the amount of coercion they will be able to generate (and, thus, the proportion of resources that they will be able to extract from producers) is directly proportional to exploiter numbers: aE. However, as E increases, the exploiters cannot extract more resource than is produced. Accordingly, I assume that the proportion of resource extracted by the exploiters is governed by the hyperbolic function $aE/(1+aE)$. Incidentally, this function can also be derived more mechanistically by considering how the exploiters control the territory on which the producers live. The parameter a, then, becomes the maximum size of the area that can be controlled by one exploiter. Note that this formula assumes that in the limit, as exploiter numbers increase, the proportion of product extracted approaches unity. To have a slightly more general model, let us set the proportion extracted to $\epsilon aE/(1+aE)$, where the new parameter ϵ is the maximum proportion of product extracted from producers.

The total extraction rate is the proportion extracted multiplied by the total production rate (which is itself, in turn, the product of per capita production rate and the number of producers:

$$\frac{\epsilon aE}{1+aE}\rho_0(1-gP)P$$

The remainder that is left to producers is

$$\left(1-\frac{\epsilon aE}{1+aE}\right)\rho_0(1-gP)P = \frac{1+(1-\epsilon)aE}{1+aE}\rho_0(1-gP)P$$

Dividing the extraction and the remainder by exploiter and producer numbers, respectively, we obtain the per capita resources for exploiters and producers:

$$\rho_P = \frac{\rho_0[1+(1-\epsilon)aE](1-gP)}{1+aE}$$

$$\rho_E = \frac{a\rho_0\epsilon(1-gP)P}{1+aE}$$

Substituting this expression for ρ_P into (A.10), we have the producer equation:

$$\dot{P} = \frac{\beta_1\rho_0[1+(1-\epsilon)aE](1-gP)P}{1+aE} - \delta_1 P \tag{A.11}$$

The population dynamics of the exploiters are derived analogously:

$$\dot{E} = (\beta_2\rho_E - \delta_2)E = \frac{\beta_2\rho_0\epsilon aE(1-gP)P}{1+aE} - \delta_2 E \tag{A.12}$$

These equation looks a bit complicated, but note that if we assume $\epsilon = 1$ then the model simplifies somewhat to

$$\dot{P} = \frac{\beta_1\rho_0(1-gP)P}{1+aE} - \delta_1 P$$

$$\dot{E} = \frac{\beta_2\rho_0 aE(1-gP)P}{1+aE} - \delta_2 E \tag{A.13}$$

These equations describe the situation of ruthless elites who are prepared to extract the maximum possible product from peasants, without regard to the effect on peasant population dynamics.

Demographic-Fiscal Model with Class Structure

Now that we have equations connecting P and E, we can use them to modify the basic demographic-fiscal model. To describe the dynamics of P and E I use the simplified model, equation (A.13). I assume that the parameter g that sets the carrying capacity of producer population in the absence of elites is a function of S in exactly the same way as is assumed in the basic demographic-fiscal model.

We now need an equation for the state resources, S. On the revenue side, a certain fraction of extracted resources should be transmitted by the exploiters to the state as taxes. I assume that when the resources extracted from producers are sufficient to maintain the consumption levels expected by elites, they will share the surplus with the state. However, when the exploiters do not obtain enough resource to maintain themselves and their dependents, they collectively resist the state's demands for increased taxes. This resistance can take the form of either collective action against the state demands, or action by individual officials who will divert the increasing proportion of taxes to their needs. In either case, the end result is that, when elites become impoverished, the state receives a decreasing fraction of the product extracted from the producers.

Specifically, let us assume that each exploiter family keeps the resources they need to maintain themselves, δ_2/β_2, and of the surplus they transmit a fixed proportion to the state. This implies that the state's revenues will be proportional to $\dot{E}$, as long as $\dot{E} > 0$, and 0 otherwise.

Next, arguing by analogy with the derivation of the basic model, I assume that state expenditures grow linearly with exploiter numbers, because the state has to provide employment to them as officers, bureaucrats, and priests. This argument assumes that state expenses associated with increased producer numbers are negligible compared to the demands made on the state by elites. (It is certainly possible to add producer-related expenditures, but this complicates the model and does not change the main result.) Putting together the assumptions about revenues and expenditures we have the following S equation:

$$\dot{S} = \gamma\dot{E} - \alpha E \qquad (A.14)$$

where γ is the proportionality constant related to the fraction of surplus remitted to the state by the elites when $\dot{E} > 0$ (if $\dot{E} \leq 0$, then $\gamma = 0$). The parameter α is the proportionality constant relating elite numbers to state expenditures. The complete model is

$$\dot{P} = \frac{\beta_1\rho_0[1 - g(S)P]P}{1 + aE} - \delta_1 P$$

$$\dot{E} = \frac{\beta_2\rho_0 aE[1 - g(S)P]P}{1 + aE} - \delta_2 E$$

$$\dot{S} = \gamma\dot{E} - \alpha E$$

$$g(S) = g_0 \frac{h + S}{h + (1 + c)S} \qquad (A.15)$$

The Selfish Elite Model

The model (A.16) assumes that political stability affects the productive capacity of the society. An alternative assumption is that the feedback acts on demographic rates (Section 7.1). Here I explore this alternative, with the goal of determining how it affects the results.

I assume that the presence of a strong state imposes peace on the elites. In contrast, when the state is absent or weak, the intraelite competition will take violent forms, and will lead to increased elite extinction rate. In other words, I argue that the parameter δ_2 in equation (A.12) should be a declining function of S. I assume the hyperbolic form $\delta_2 = c_1/(1 + c_2 S)$. Here, c_1 is the maximum extinction rate, which occurs when $S = 0$, and c_2 is the parameter that measures how fast the extinction rate declines with increasing S. Another way of thinking about δ_2 is as the coefficient of intraelite competition. As the amount of state resources S declines, the size of the pie over which the elites are fighting diminishes. This leads to intensified intraelite competition, causing increased mortality and downward mobility. Note that, by making δ_2 a function of S rather than E, we have built a time lag into the feedback effect of elite numbers on themselves. It is not the increased elite numbers per se that elevate the intraelite competition. Rather, increased elite numbers affect elite dynamics indirectly, by reducing the fiscal health of the state. The equations are (again, for simplicity, I set $\epsilon = 0$)

$$\dot{P} = \frac{\beta_1 \rho_0 (1 - gP)P}{1 + aE} - \delta_1 P$$

$$\dot{E} = \frac{\beta_2 \rho_0 aE(1 - gP) + P}{1 + aE} - \frac{c_1 E}{1 + c_2 S}$$

$$\dot{S} = \gamma \dot{E} - \alpha E \qquad\qquad (A.16)$$

I refer to this model as the *selfish elite* model, because the elites oppress the commoners without any regard for their well-being, and will transmit some taxes to the state if they have enough to live on. (Of course, elites in the demographic-fiscal model with class structure behave in exactly the same way; still, I need some handy labels to refer to the models, and this one is as good as any.)

In the analysis of the model, it helps to scale it. To do that, I define new variables: $P' = gP$, $E' = aE$, and $S' = c_2 S$. The scaled equations are

$$\dot{P} = \frac{\beta_1 P(1 - P)}{1 + E} - \delta_1 P$$

$$\dot{E} = \frac{\beta_2 E(1 - P)P}{1 + E} - \frac{\delta_2}{1 + S}E$$

$$\dot{S} = \gamma \dot{E} - \alpha E$$

where as usual, I suppressed the primes for better readability.

A.4 MODELS FOR ELITE CYCLES

The Ibn Khaldun Model

Let R be the amount of resources extracted from commoners, a constant. The per capita elite income, μ, is determined according to the following algorithm:

$$\mu = \begin{cases} (1-\gamma)R/E & \text{if } R/E \geq \mu_{\min}/(1-\gamma) \\ \mu_{\min} & \text{if } \mu_{\min}/(1-\gamma) > R/E \geq \mu_{\min} \\ R/E & \text{if } R/E < \mu_{\min} \end{cases}$$

The per capita rate of elite population change is

$$r = \begin{cases} \chi(\mu - \mu_0) & \text{if } \chi(\mu - \mu_0) < r_{\max} \\ r_{\max} & \text{otherwise} \end{cases}$$

The dynamic equations for E, S, and $\mu_{\min}$ are, assuming that $S \geq 0$

$$\dot{E} = rE$$

$$\dot{S} = (R - \mu E) - \alpha E$$

$$\dot{\mu}_{\min} = \delta_\mu$$

If $S < 0$, then we set $E = E_0$, $S = 0$, and $\mu_{\min} = \mu_0$ and repeat the cycle.

The Ibn Khaldun Cycle with Class Structure

The per capita income of commoners is

$$\nu = \frac{1 + (1 - \epsilon_0)aE}{1 + aE} \rho_0 (1 - gP)$$

The amount of resources extracted from commoners is

$$R = \epsilon_0 \frac{aE}{1 + aE} \rho_0 (1 - gP)P$$

The per capita elite income, μ, is calculated in exactly the same way as in the simple Ibn Khaldun model:

$$\mu = \begin{cases} (1-\gamma)R/E & \text{if } R/E \geq \mu_{\min}/(1-\gamma) \\ \mu_{\min} & \text{if } \mu_{\min}/(1-\gamma) > R/E \geq \mu_{\min} \\ R/E & \text{if } R/E < \mu_{\min} \end{cases}$$

The same applies to the per capita rate of elite population change:

$$r = \begin{cases} \chi(\mu - \mu_0) & \text{if } \chi(\mu - \mu_0) < r_{\max} \\ r_{\max} & \text{otherwise} \end{cases}$$

Finally, the dynamic equations are

$$\dot{P} = \chi_1(\nu - \nu_0)$$
$$\dot{E} = rE$$
$$\dot{S} = (R - \mu E) - \alpha E$$
$$\dot{\mu}_{min} = \delta_\mu$$

If $S < 0$, then we set $E = E_0$, $S = 0$, and $\mu_{min} = \mu_0$, and repeat the cycle.

The Parasitic Nomads Model

The amount of resources extracted from the agrarian state is

$$R = S \frac{E^2}{h^2 + E^2} R_{max}$$

Per elite capita income is

$$\mu = \frac{R}{E}$$

The per capita rate of elite population change is the same as in the Ibn Khaldun model:

$$r = \begin{cases} \chi(\mu - \mu_0) & \text{if } \chi(\mu - \mu_0) < r_{max} \\ r_{max} & \text{otherwise} \end{cases}$$

The dynamic equations are (assuming $S \geq 0$)

$$\dot{E} = rE$$

$$\dot{S} = \begin{cases} 0 \text{ if } \mu > \mu_0 \\ -\alpha & \text{otherwise} \end{cases}$$

If $S < 0$, then we set $E = E_0$ and $S = S_0$, and repeat the cycle.

Appendix B

Data Summaries for the Test of the Metaethnic
Frontier Theory

B.1 BRIEF DESCRIPTIONS OF "CULTURAL REGIONS"

ALB   Albania and Kosovo
AND   Andalusia
ANT   Anatolia from Ankara east (Roman Galatia and Cappadocia)
AQU   Aquitaine (including Gascony, Guyenne, Poitou, Limousain, Perigord)
       (Roman Aquitania)
ARG   Aragon (including Catalonia and Valencia)
AUS   Austria (without Tyrol) (Roman Noricum)
AZV   Steppe region north of Azov Sea between Don and Dnieper (includes
       Crimea)
BAL   Pomerania, Prussia, Lithuania
BEL   Belarus (Kievan Principalities of Polotsk and Turov–Pinsk)
BOH   Bohemia and Moravia
BUL   Bulgaria and Macedonia (Roman Thracia, eastern Macedonia)
BYZ   Western Anatolia and European Turkey (Roman Asia and Bythinia)
CAS   Castile, Leon (without Galicia), and Navarre
CRU   Central Russia (Vladimir–Suzdal Rus')
DAL   Croatia, Bosnia, and Slovenia (northern part of Roman Dalmatia,
       Illyricum)
DEN   Denmark, including Schleswig and Holstein
EFR   Champaigne, Lorraine, Alsace, Burgundy, and French Switzerland
       (roughly Roman Germania Superior plus eastern Lugdunensis)
EGE   Former East Germany (Brandenburg, Saxony)
EPL   Eastern Poland with center in Warsaw (Mazovia, Little Poland)
FIN   Finland
GAL   Western Ukraine (Galicia and Volhynia)
GRE   Greece
HUN   Hungary, Slovakia, and Vojvodina (Roman Pannonia plus land between
       Danube and Tisza)
IRL   Ireland (the whole island)
KAZ   Kazan (Great Bulgar, Kazan Khanate)
MOL   Moldova (Bessarabia) and Romanian province of Moldavia
NBL   Latvia, Estonia
NBR   Scotland

NED   Netherlands, Belgium, Luxemburg, and Rhineland (Roman northern
       Belgica and Germania Inferior)
NFR   Ile-de-France, Picardy, Normandy, Brittany, Anjou, Touraine, Orléannais
       (Roman western Lugdunensis and southern Belgica)
NIT   Italy north of Rome
NOR   Norway
NOV   Novgorodian land, Pskov, and Ingria
NRU   Northern Russia (Vologda, Vyatka and lands north)
POR   Portugal and Galicia
SBR   England and Wales
SER   Serbia (without Vojvodina) and Montenegro (Roman Moesia Superior, a
       piece of southern Dalmatia)
SFR   Toulousain, Provence, Auvergne, Savoy (Roman Narbonensis)
SGE   Swabia, Bavaria, German Switzerland, Tyrol (Roman Rhaetia and
       Germanic lands north)
SIT   Italy south of Rome (includes Lazio)
SRU   Soutern Russia (the "black-earth region")
SWE   Sweden
TRA   Transylvania (Roman Dacia)
UKR   Central Ukraine (Kiev, Chernigov, Novgorod–Seversk, Pereyaslavl)
VLG   Lower Volga region, south of KAZ (from Saratov to Astrakhan)
VLH   Wallachia: modern Romania without provinces of Transylvania and
       Moldavia; includes Dobrudja (Roman Moesia Inferior plus lands north
       of Danube)
WGE   West Germany north of Frankfurt (inclusive)
WPL   Western Poland with the center in Cracow (Great Poland) and Silesia
WRU   Western Russia (Principality of Smolensk)
ZAP   Zaporozhie (Southern Ukraine)

B.2 QUANTIFICATION OF FRONTIERS

Here, capital letters indicate cultural region codes and Roman numerals are centuries (for example, "during III" means "during the third century").

Typical score of a frontier of the Roman Empire (before Christianity):
religion = 1 (nonexclusive pagan religions), language = 2 (Latin versus Celtic,
Germanic, Illyrian, etc. languages), economy = 1 (urban settled agriculturalists versus backwoods agriculturalists), pressure = 1 (raiding, no frontier
depopulation); for a total of 5.

Typical score of a frontier of the Roman Empire (after Christianization):
religion = 3 (exclusive world religion versus pagan religions), language = 2
(Latin versus Celtic, Germanic, Illyrian, etc. languages), economy = 1 (urban
settled agriculturalists versus backwoods agriculturalists), pressure = 1 (raiding,
no frontier depopulation); for a total of 7. During III it goes to 8 in areas affected
by severe military pressure leading to depopulation.

ALB   Roman province of Epirus: score = 0 in I–V. Most probably subjected to increased raiding by Slavs and Turkic nomads from the second half of VI, although protected, to some degree by the mountainous terrain. Score = $(3+2+1+1)/2 = 4$ in VI. Slavic and Avar invasions, depopulation: score = $3+2+1+2 = 8$ in VII. A Byzantine-Slavic-Bulgar frontier (situation very confused): score = $3+2+1+1 = 7$ in VIII–X. From XI on, part of the Byzantine, Latin, Serbian, and Ottoman empires: score = 0.

AND   Roman province: score = 0 in I–V. Visigothic, score = 0 in VI–VII Muslim, score = 0 in VIII–XII. On the Castilian-Moorish frontier: score = $3+2+0+1 = 6$ in XIII–XV. Closure of the frontier, score = 0 from XVI on.

ANT   Deep in the Roman Empire, no frontier (except for raiding during the state collapse episodes of III and VI): score = 0 in I–VI. The Byzantine-Caliphate frontier: score = $3+2+1+2 = 8$ in VII–XI. After the battle of Manzikert is conquered by the Turks: score = $3+2+2+2 = 9$ in XII–XIV. From XV on, at the center of the Ottoman empire: score = 0.

AQU   Roman province: score = 0 in I–VI. 418 C.E.: Visigoths establish the Kingdom of Toulouse (until 507) (Wolfram 1997:xvii). 507: Frankish conquest. 587: the first record of raiding by the Vascones into plains of south Aquitaine; human captives taken (Collins 1990:84). Basque settlements spread into the plains of southern Aquitaine in VII (Collins 1990:96): score = $3+2+1+1 = 7$ in VII. The Basques were pagan through the whole of VII (Collins 1990:104). Basques living north of the Pyrenees were fundamentally Christianized by the middle of VIII (Collins 1990:152): score = $1+2+1+1 = 5$ in VIII. No significant frontier from IX on.

ARG   Roman province: score = 0 in I–V. The Basques become a problem for the Visigothic rulers during the VI; Basques raid urban population in the Ebro valley in VI and VII. Score = $3+1+1+1 = 6$ (it is uncertain whether mountaineers and lowlanders spoke a different language) (Collins 1990:82–98). The Basques were pagan through the whole of VII (Collins 1990:104). On the Iberian Christian/Muslim frontier: score = $3+2+1+2 = 8$ in VIII–XII. The closure of the frontier: score = 0 from XIII on.

AUS   Roman province: score = 0 in I–II. During troubled III Roman frontier shifts south; Germanic incursions; score = 5 in III. Score = 7 in IV (Christianization). Score = 8 in V (depopulation). On the Frankish-Avar frontier: score = $1+2+2+1 = 6$ in VI–VII. Score = $3+2+2+2 = 9$ in VIII. Score = $3+2+1+1 = 7$ in IX. Magyar invasions: score = $3+2+2+2 = 9$ in X. With Magyar Christianization, score = $2+2+1+1 = 4$ in XI and $0+2+0+0 = 2$ in XII–XV. On the Ottoman frontier: score = $3+2+1+2 = 8$ in XVI–XVIII.

AZV   Frontier between Bosporan Kingdom and the steppe: score = $1+2+2+1 = 6$ in I–II c. 375 C.E.: the Huns cross the Don River (Wolfram

1997:123). Stateless hinterland: score $= 0$ in III–VI. The steppe part incorporated into the Khazar Empire (Farrington 2002:83–85), a frontier with the Byzantine Crimea: score $= 3 + 2 + 2 + 0 = 7$ in VII–X. The Byzantine-steppe frontier with Pechenegs, Cumans, and Mongols: score $= 3 + 2 + 2 + 1 = 8$ in XI–XIV. Center of the Crimean Tatars: score $= 0$ in XV–XVI. Frontier with Russia: score $= 3 + 2 + 2 + 1 = 8$ in XVII and most of XVIII. Annexed by Russia in 1783.

BAL   Stateless hinterland: score $= 0$ in I–X. Pressure (raids, tribute) from christianized Kievan Rus (Gudz-Markov 1997:413): score $= 3 + 2 + 1 + 1 = 7$ in XI–XII. German *Drang nach Osten* into Pomerania, Prussia, and Lithuania: score $= 3 + 2 + 1 + 2 = 8$ in XIII–XIV. 1386–1417: Lithuanian conversion to Christianity (Palmer 1957:53) and the closure of the Baltic frontier: score $= 0$ from XV on.

BEL   Stateless hinterland: score $= 0$ in I–X. Incorporation into the Kievan state during the X (Gudz-Markov 1997:407). Again, no significant frontier: score $= 0$ in XI–XII. Mongolian conquest in XIII, then Lithuanian conquest in XIV, and finally Russian annexation in 1793: score $= 0$ from XI on.

BOH   Roman frontier north of Noricum and Pannonia. Score $= 5$ during I–III. Frontier moves south, score $= 0$ in IV–V. 454–560: spread of the Prague culture into the central Europe (Gudz-Markov 1997:28). Stateless hinterland: score $= 0$ in VI–VII. Pressure from the Frankish, then Ottonian Empires: Czechs made a tributary state; score $= 3 + 2 + 1 + 1 = 7$ in VIII–X. Czechs convert to Christianity in 880–1039 (Palmer 1957:53). Closure of the frontier in XI: score $= 0 + 2 + 0 + 0 = 2$ from XI on.

BUL   Roman province until III (score $= 0$). From 238 C.E.: more than a generation of disastrous Gothic assaults on the Balkans and Asia Minor (Wolfram 1997:44): score $= 6$ in III. Score $= 7$ in IV (Christianization). Score $= 8$ in V (depopulation). Frontier between Byzantium and Bulgar Khanate from VI: score $= 8$ in VI–IX. Bulgar conversion to Christianity occurrs in 863–900 (Palmer 1957:53): score $= 0 + 2 + 1 + 0 = 3$ in X. Part of the Byzantine Empire in XI–XII (Reed 1996), score $= 0$. An independent state surrounded by other Orthodox Christian states until the Ottoman conquest of late XIV: score $= 0$. Province within the Ottoman Empire "deep behind the lines" until XIX. Score $= 0$ in XI–XIX.

BYZ   Deep within the Roman Empire until III: score $= 0$ in I–II. 238: More than a generation of disastrous Gothic assaults on the Balkans and Asia Minor (Wolfram 1997:44). 252–3, 256, 258 C.E.: Gothic attacks in Greece and Asia (Le Glay et al. 1997:393). 378: Disaster at Adrianople (Le Glay et al. 1997:504), Goths at the gates of Constantinople (Wolfram 1997:307). 394–395: Hunnic attacks the Balkan provinces and Asia Minor (Wolfram 1997:124). Belisarius chases Kutriguri from the suburbs of Constantinople (Wolfram 1997:307). 626: Joint Avar/Persian siege of Constantinople fails (Wolfram 1997:xix). Score: 6 in III, 7 in IV, 8 in VI–IX. After Bulgar conversion to Christianity in 863–900 (Palmer 1957:53), score $= 0 + 2 + 1 + 0 = 3$ in X. Deep within the Byzantine Empire in XI; score $= 0$. After Manzikert and loss of most of Anatolia, becomes the frontier with the Turks: score $= 3 + 2 + 2 + 2 = 9$ in XII–XV. At the center of the Ottoman empire: score $= 0$ in XVI–XIX.

CAS   Roman province in I–V, then Visigothic kingdom: score $= 0$ in I–VII. On the Iberian Christian/Muslim frontier: score $= 3 + 2 + 1 + 1 = 8$ in VIII–XII. Closure of the frontier: score $= 0$ from XIII on.

CRU   Stateless hinterland, score $= 0$ in I–VIII. On the Kievan frontier: the Slavs begin to settle Suzdal Opol'e in the IX; increasing immigration in X–XI (Gudz-Markov 1997:438): score $= 1 + 2 + 1 + 0 = 4$ in XI–X. After Christianization (also, presence of nearby Muslim state of the Great Bulgar): score $= 3 + 2 + 1 + 0 = 6$ in XI–XII. The Mongol conquest of 1238: score $= 3 + 2 + 2 + 2 = 9$ in XIII–XVI. With the conquest of Kazan in 1552, the frontier moved away: score $= 0$ from XVII on.

DAL   Roman province: score $= 0$ in I–V. On the Avar frontier, Slavic settlement from the second half of VI: score $= (3 + 2 + 1 + 2)/2 = 4$ in VI, $= 8$ in VII. Stateless hinterland, score $= 0$ in VIII–XI. Conquest by the Hungarians around 1100: score $= 0$ in XII–XV. Conquest of Bosnia and then parts of Croatia by the Ottomans in late XV – early XVI. Score $= 3 + 2 + 1 + 2 = 8$ in XVI–XIX.

DEN   Stateless hinterland: score $= 0$ in I–VI. Pressure from Slavic raids: score $= 1 + 2 + 1 + 1 = 5$ in VII–VIII. Pressure from Carolingians: score $= 3 + 1 + 1 + 1 = 6$ in VIII–X. 1035: Danes convert to Christianity (Palmer 1957:53). On the Christian-Pagan frontier (with Swedes, who convert by 1150 C.E.): score $= 3 + 0 + 1 + 1 = 5$ in XI. Closure of the frontier, score $= 0$ from XII on.

EFR   Roman province: score $= 0$ in I–II. During troubled III Roman frontier shifts south; Germanic incursions; score $= 6$. Score $= 7$ in IV (Christianization). Score $= 8$ in V (depopulation). After the fall of the western Roman Empire, the major meataethnic frontier disappears. Only a Romance/Germanic linguistic frontier remains. Score $= 2$ from VI to XIX.

EGE   Stateless hinterland: score $= 0$ in I–VI. Slavic migration into central Germany sometime during VI (Gimbutas 1971:124). The Slavic-Saxon frontier: score $= 1 + 2 + 0 + 0 = 3$ in VII–VIII. The Slavic states under the influence (tribute) of the Carolingian empire during the IX (Shepherd 1973:56). German pressure on the Slavic lands intensifies during X (under Henry I and Otto I) (Barraclough 1998:116). 983: great Slavic revolt against the Germans (Barraclough 1998:116). Wends convert to Christianity between 900 and 1100 (Palmer 1957:53). 1125: German colonization resumes (Barraclough 1998:140). Score $= 3 + 2 + 1 + 1 = 7$ in IX–XII. Sorbs convert to Christianity during the 1200s (Palmer 1957:53). Baltic crusades: score $= 3 + 2 + 1 + 1 = 7$ in XIII–XIV. Frontier closure: score $= 0$ from XV on.

EPL   Stateless hinterland: score $= 0$ in I–X. Successively part of Poland, Poland–Lithuania, and Russia; no significant frontier: score $= 0$ from XI on.

FIN   Stateless hinterland: score $= 0$ in I–XI. On the Christian frontier with Novgorod: score $= 3+2+1+0 = 6$ in XII. 1100–1200: Finns convert to Christianity (Palmer 1957:53). No significant frontier after that. Score $= 0$ from XIII on.

GAL   Stateless hinterland, score $= 0$ in I–IX. Part of Kievan Rus, independent principality, then in Lithuania-Poland: score $= 0$ in X–XVI. On the Ottoman frontier (Podolia briefly conquered by the Ottomans): score $= 3+2+1+1 = 7$ in XVII. Frontier moves back south: score $= 0$ in XVIII. Taken over by Austria at the end of the XVIII.

GRE   Province deep within the Roman Empire until III: score $= 0$ in I–II. Gothic raiding, score $= 1+2+2+1 = 6$ in III: score $= 0$ in IV–V. From 540 on Bulgars and Sclavini continuously raid Trace, Illyria, and Thessaly (Gimbutas 1971:100). 558: Great invasion of Kutrigurs aided by Sclavini in Macedonia, Greece, Thrace (Gimbutas 1971:100). 610–626: Greece is attacked by Avars and Slavs (Gimbutas 1971:103). Slavic invasions ended before the end of VII (Gimbutas 1971:105). Score $= 3+2+1+2 = 8$ in VI–VII. A province deep in the succession of empires (Byzantine, Latin, Ottoman) from VIII until the war of liberation against the Ottomans in XIX. Score $= 0$ in VIII–XVII.

HUN   Roman frontier between the province of Moesia and a centralized polity of Dacia in I. Conquest of Dacia in 101–107 c.e. (Le Glay et al. 1997:271). Barbarian invasions in III (Wolfram 1997:35). Score $= 5$ in I–III. Christianization: score $= 7$ in IV–V. 547: Langobards are given parts of Pannonia and Noricum in a treaty with Constantinople (Wolfram 1997:xv). First Slavic groups make verifiable contact with Gepids and Langobards (Wolfram 1997:xx). Score $= 1+2+0+1 = 4$ in VI. 558–796: Avar khaganate (Wolfram 1997:305): score $= 1+2+2+1 = 6$ in VI–VIII. 788–796: Avar kingdom destroyed in war against the Franks (Wolfram 1997:xix). Slavic polities tributary to the Carolingian Empire (Shepherd 1973:56): score $= 1+2+1+1 = 5$ in IX. Magyars (Barraclough 1998:111): score $= 3+2+2+1 = 8$ in X. 950–1050: Magyars convert to Christianity (Palmer 1957:53): score $= 0+2+1+0 = 3$ in XI. Deep within the Hungarian state: score $= 0$ in XII–XV. Conquest by the Ottomans: score $= 3+2+1+2 = 8$ in XVI–XVII.

IRL   Conversion to Christianity in 440–493 c.e. (Palmer 1957:53). Stateless hinterland: score $= 0$ in I–VIII. Viking raids of IX. Viking settlement, Dublin founded in 841 (Cunliffe et al. 2001:62): score $= 3+2+0+1 = 6$ in IX. Viking adoption of Christianity in X (Cunliffe et al. 2001:65): score $= 1+2+0+1 = 4$ in X. Score $= 2$ (linguistic frontier) in XI. Linguistic assimilation of Vikings to the native Gaels complete during XII (Cunliffe et al. 2001:64), closure of the frontier: score $= 0$ from XII on.

KAZ   Stateless hinterland: score $= 0$ in I–VI. 650: After losing a battle with the Khazars, some of the Bulgars escape north up the Volga to KAZ (Artamonov 2001:243). Score $= 1+2+2+0 = 5$ in VII–IX. Volga Bulgars convert to Islam in early X (Artamonov 2001:635): score $= 3+2+2+0 = 7$ in X–XII. Mongolian conquest in 1236 (Channon and Hudson 1995:35): score $= 0$ in XIII–XIV. Kazan Khanate (early XV – late XVI): score $= 3+2+0+1 = 6$ in XV–XVI. Incorporated into Russian empire: score $= 0$ from XVII on.

MOL   Roman frontier north of Moesia Inferior from I: score $= 5$ in I–III. In IV Roman frontier shifted southwards to VLH. Hun invasion in 375 C.E. Avars at the lower Danube in 562 C.E. (Wolfram 1997:xix). Stateless hinterland, score $= 0$ in IV–XIV. On the Lithuanian-Ottoman frontier (XV on the Lithuanian side, after that on the Ottoman side): score $= 3+2+0+1 = 6$ in XV–XVIII.

NBL   Stateless hinterland: score $= 0$ in I–XII. 1186: Beginning of the German expeditions to conquer the Baltic; 1201: Riga established (Barraclough 1998:140): score $= 3+2+1+2 = 8$ in XIII. 1200s: Estonians convert to Christianity (Palmer 1957:53). 1309: Courland, Semgallen, and Livonia occupied; 1346: Estonia occupied (Barraclough 1998:140). Closure of the frontier: score $= 0$ from XIV on.

NBR   Stateless hinterland: score $= 0$ in I. Brief intrusion of the Roman frontier: in 81 C.E. Agricola pushes to the Forth–Clyde line. In 141 Antoninus builds his wall there; from 159 C.E. on Antoninus' wall is gradually abandoned: score $= 1+2+1+1 = 5$ in II. Stateless hinterland: score $= 0$ in III–V. Kingdom of Dalriada is founded in the second half of V, a dependency of Ulster (Musset 1975:111): score $= 1+1+0+1 = 3$ in VI. Conversion to Christianity (563–597) (Palmer 1957:53). Stateless hinterland: score $= 0$ in VII–VIII. On the Viking frontier: score $= 3+2+1+1 = 7$ in IX–X. Picts yield to the Scottish king macAlpin, a united kingdom is created, Alba, then renamed Scotland (Musset 1975:111). Closure of the frontier: score $= 0$ from XI on.

NED   Roman frontier established after the conquest of Gaul: score $= 5$ during I–II; increases to 6 in III (depopulation); 7 in IV (Christianization); 8 in V (depopulation). On the Saxon frontier: score $= 3+0+1+1 = 5$ in VI–VIII. Frontier closure, score $= 0$ from IX on.

NFR   Roman province: score $= 0$ in I–II. During troubled III Roman frontier shifts south; Germanic incursions: score $= 1+2+2+1 = 6$; score $= 7$ in IV (Christianization); score $= 8$ in V (depopulation). British migration to Armorica began about 450 C.E., reached a peak in 550–600, ended in early VII (Musset 1975:112): score $= 1+2+1+1 = 5$ in VI–VII. Viking intrusion; score $= 3+2+1+2 = 8$ in XI–X. Frontier closure: score $= 0$ from XI on.

NIT   Roman province: score $= 0$ in I–IV. Barbarian invasions, 405: Radagaisus (Ostrogoths) invades Italy (Wolfram 1997:xvi); 452: Huns invade Italy through Pannonia, take Aquilea, Pavia, Milan (Wolfram 1997:138); 493: Theodoric with Ostrogoths captures Ravenna; 497: imperial recognition of Ostrogothic kingdom (Wolfram 1997:xvii): score $= 3 + 2 + 1 + 2 = 8$ in V. No significant frontier: score $= 0$ from VI on.

NOR   Stateless hinterland: score $= 0$ in I–VIII. On the outer fringe of the Carolingian frontier: score $= 3 + 1 + 1 + 1 = 6$ in IX–X. Christianization by 1000 C.E. (Palmer 1957:53). With Christianization, the frontier closed down: score $= 0$ from XI on.

NOV   Stateless hinterland: score $= 0$ in I–VII. Slavic settlement by the beginning of the VIII (Gudz-Markov 1997:453). Linguistic frontier: score $= 2$ in VIII–XI. Conversion to Christianity by 1100 (later than the Kiev area): score $= 3 + 2 + 1 + 0 = 6$ in XII. Finns convert to Christianity in 1100s (Palmer 1957:53). Attacks of Teutonic knights and Swedes from 1223 (Channon and Hudson 1995:25): score $= 2 + 2 + 0 + 1 = 5$ in XIII–XIV. Increased intensity of conflict: score $= 2 + 2 + 0 + 2 = 6$ in XV–XVI. Lower intensity conflict: score $= 2 + 2 + 0 + 0 = 4$ in XVII. 1721: Russia gains the east Baltic, frontier closure: score $= 0$ from XVIII on.

NRU   Stateless hinterland: score $= 0$ in I–X. Part of Novgorodian then Russian lands: score $= 0$ from XI on.

POR   Roman province in I–V, then Visigothic kingdom: score $= 0$ in I–VII. On the Iberian Christian-Muslim frontier: score $= 3 + 2 + 1 + 2 = 8$ in VIII–XII. Closure of the frontier: score $= 0$ from XIII on.

SBR   Roman frontier following conquest in I (Le Glay et al. 1997:216): score $= 5$ in I. Frontier moved to NBR during II: score $= 0$ in II. Returned to northern SBR (the Hadrian wall, built in 122 C.E.) after the Antonine wall was gradually abandonded toward the end of II: score $= 5$ in III. Score increases to 6 in IV (Christianization). First incursions of Picts and Saxons in 429 C.E. (Wolfram 1997:xx), regular influx of Germanic immigrants into Britain begins in 430–440 C.E. (Musset 1975:101): score $= 3 + 2 + 1 + 2 = 8$ in V–VI. Conversion of Anglo-Saxons to Christianity by 670 (Palmer 1957:53): score $= 2 + 2 + 1 + 1 = 6$ in VII; $0 + 2 + 1 + 0$ in VIII. Viking invasions: score $= 3 + 1 + 1 + 1 = 6$ in IX–X. Closure of the frontier: score $= 0$ from XI on.

SER   Roman province: score $= 0$ in I–IV. Frontier of the Eastern Roman Empire shifts south to SER in late IV: score $= 3 + 2 + 1 + 2 = 8$ in V and VI. South Slavs on the steppe frontier with Avars, Bulgars, and Magyars: score $= 1 + 2 + 2 + 1 = 6$ in VII–IX. 900s: Serbs convert to Christianity (Palmer 1957:53): score $= 7$ in X. After Hungarians convert to Christianity (950–1050) (Palmer 1957:53), the score goes down to $0 + 2 + 0 + 0 = 2$ in XI–XIV. Conquest by the Ottomans in late XIV – early XV; SER is on the Ottoman frontier: score $= 3 + 2 + 2 + 2 = 9$ in XV. Frontier moves north: score $= 0$ in XVI–XVII. Frontier moves south: score $= 3 + 2 + 1 + 1 = 7$ in XVIII–XIX.

SFR   Roman province: score = 0 in I–V. No significant frontier: score = 0 from VI on.

SGE   Roman frontier established after the conquest of Gaul: score = 5 during I–II; 7 in IV (Christianization); 8 in V (depopulation). On the Frankish march: score = $3 + 2 + 1 + 1 = 7$ in VI–VIII. Closure of the frontier: score = 0 from IX on.

SIT   Roman center: score = 0 in I–V. Occupied by Ostrogoths, Langobards, Franks, Byzantines: score = 0 in VI–VIII. Persistent raiding by the Saracens: score = $3 + 2 + 1 + 1 = 7$ in IX. Norman conquest, then Spanish, then independent (Kingdom of Naples): score = 0 from X on. An interesting problem is presented by the Muslim occupation of Sicily in IX–X. However, the preexisting Muslim population was removed from Sicily after the Norman conquest, and Sicily was resettled from Liguria, Tuscany, and Provence (Abulafia 1990).

SRU   Stateless hinterland: score = 0 in I–VI. Slavic settlement (Vyatichi) in the north from VIII, resulting in a gradual assimilation of the Ugric population over the next five centuries. On the steppe frontier with the Khazars and the Volga Bulgars: score = $1 + 2 + 2 + 1 = 6$ in VII–X. Christinianization: score = $3 + 2 + 2 + 1 = 8$ in X–XII. Depopulation after the Mongol conquest and Tatar raiding: score = $3 + 2 + 2 + 2 = 9$ in XIII–XVI. Frontier moves south: score = 0 from XVII on.

SWE   Stateless hinterland: score = 0 in I–VII. On the outer fringe of the Carolingian frontier from 800 C.E. Swedes were subjected to an unusually prolonged pressure to convert to Christianity, from 829 to 1150 (Palmer 1957:53), which triggered development of a strong reaction from Nordic paganism: score = $3 + 1 + 1 + 1 = 6$ in IX–XII. With Christianization, the frontier closed down: score = 0 from XIII on.

TRA   Roman frontier between the province of Moesia and a centralized polity of Dacia in I. Conquest of Dacia in 101–107 C.E. (Le Glay et al. 1997:271). Barbarian invasions in III (Wolfram 1997:35). Score = 5 in I–III. Hinterland of the Hunnic, Gepid, Avar, Bulgar, and Magyar Empires. Protected by the Carpathian Mountains against direct influence of the steppe: score = 0 in IV–XV. Ottomanian conquest: score = $3 + 2 + 1 + 1 = 7$ in XVI–XVII. On the Austro-Hungarian side of the frontier in XVIII: score = $3 + 2 + 0 + 1 = 6$.

UKR   Stateless hinterland: score = 0 in I–VI. On the Khazar frontier: score = $1 + 2 + 2 + 1 = 6$ in VII–VIII; $3 + 2 + 2 + 1 = 8$ in IX–X (the Khazars converted to Judaism between 740 and 861 [Farrington 2002:82]). Conversion to Christianity in 988–1015 (Palmer 1957:53). On the Kievan Rus'-steppe frontier: score = $3 + 2 + 2 + 1 = 8$ in XI–XII. Depopulation: score = $3 + 2 + 2 + 2 = 9$ in XIII–XVI. Frontier moves south: score = 0 from XVII on.

VLG   Stateless hinterland: score = 0 in I–VI. On the steppe frontier of the Khazar Empire: score = $0 + 0 + 1 + 0 = 1$ in VII. Interior of the Khazar

Empire: score $= 0$ in VIII–X. Stateless hinterland: score $= 0$ in XI–XII. Center of the Golden Horde, then the Astrakhan Khanate: score $= 0$ in XIII–XV. On the Russian frontier: score $= 3 + 2 + 2 + 1 = 8$ in XVI. Conquest by Russia in 1556: score $= 0$ from XVII on.

VLH   On the Dacian frontier: score $= 1 + 2 + 1 + 0 = 4$ in I. Frontier shifts north: score $= 0$ in II. During troubled III Roman frontier shifts south; barbarian incursions; score $= 1 + 2 + 1 + 2 = 6$ in III. Score $= 3 + 2 + 1 + 1 = 7$ in IV–V (Christianization). On the Avar-Byzantium frontier: score $= 3 + 2 + 2 + 2 = 9$ in VI–VII (depopulation). 679: Bulgars cross the Danube; 681: Byzantium recognizes the Bulgar state (Hupchik and Cox 1996:8). On the Byzantium-Bulgar frontier: score $= 3 + 2 + 2 + 1 = 8$ in VIII. 802: Bulgaria expands in all directions, removing the frontiers from VLH (Hupchik and Cox 1996:10): score $= 0$ in IX–X. 972: Dobrudja is annexed by the Byzantines (Hupchik and Cox 1996:12). The Byzantine-Steppe (Pechenegs, Cumans) frontier: score $= 3 + 2 + 2 + 1 = 8$ in XI–XII. The Bulgarian-Steppe (Cumans, Mongols) frontier: score $= 3 + 2 + 2 + 1 = 8$ in XIII. Wallachia surrounded by Christian states (Hungary, Moldavia, Bulgaria) in XIV: score $= 0 + 2 + 0 + 0 = 2$. 1393: Wallachia becomes a vassal state of the Ottoman empire (Hupchik and Cox 1996:22). On the Ottoman frontier with Hungary: score $= 3 + 2 + 1 + 1 = 7$ in XV. The frontier moves north with the conquest of most of Hungary after Mohacs (1526): score $= 0$ in XVI–XVII. Back on the Austro-Hungarian/Ottoman frontier in XVIII: score $= 3 + 2 + 0 + 1 = 6$.

WGE   Roman frontier established after the conquest of Gaul: score $= 5$ in I–III. Frontier moves south: score $= 0$ in IV–V. On the Frankish frontier: score $= 3 + 1 + 1 + 1 = 6$ in VI–VIII. On the Slav frontier: score $= 3 + 2 + 1 + 1 = 7$ in IX–XII. As EGE was colonized during the XII and last Slavs converted (Sorbs, during the 1200s), frontier closed down: score $= 0$ from XIII on.

WPL   Stateless hinterland: score $= 0$ in I–V. Slavic migration into western Poland sometime during VI (Gimbutas 1971:124). Surrounded by other Slavic lands: score $= 0$ in VI–VIII. On the external fringe of the Carolingian frontier: score $= 3 + 2 + 1 + 0 = 6$ in IX–X. Poles convert to Christianity from 966 to 1034 (Palmer 1957:53): score $= 1 + 2 + 1 + 0 = 4$ in XI. German-Slavic linguistic frontier: score $= 2$ from XII on.

WRU   Stateless hinterland: score $= 0$ in I–VI. Massive immigration by the Slavs in VII–VIII (Krivichi) (Gudz-Markov 1997:422). WRU was situated in the middle of east Slavic settlement zone: score $= 0$. Conversion to Christianity around 1000. Conquest by the Mongols, then Lithuanians, and finally Russians. No significant frontier: score $= 0$ from VIII on.

ZAP   Frontier between Bosporan Kingdom and the steppe in I; addition of the Roman frontier in II–III: score $= 1 + 2 + 2 + 1 = 6$ in I–III. Visigoth hinterland: score $= 0$ in IV. 375 C.E.: Hun invasion (Wolfram 1997:123). Steppe (Huns, Bulgars, Magyars, Pechenegs, Cumans, Mongols) hinterland: score $= 0$ in V–XIV. Annexed by Lithuania in late XIV (Reed 1996). On the (1) Poland-Lithuanian and (2) Russian frontier with the Crimean Khanate and Ottomans: score $= 3 + 2 + 2 + 2 = 9$ in XV–XVIII.

B.3 QUANTIFICATION OF POLITY SIZES:
THE FIRST MILLENNIUM C.E.

My main source for polity sizes in Europe of 500–1000 C.E. was the Periodical Historical Atlas of Europe on CD-ROM (Nüssli 2002). The Atlas lists hundreds of polities, but we are interested in only a subset of them. First, we ignore all polities whose maximal size was less than 0.1 Mm², for reasons explained in Section 5.1.2.

Second, a number of polities have formed as a result of territorial disintegration of large empires. I refer to such polities as *relicts*. The defining feature of a relict is that its territory never grows: it secedes as a chunk of territory from a fragmenting empire and may either decline further or stay constant in area until it is conquered by some other polity. Polities that I classified as relicts are Austrasia and Neustria (Merovingian relicts); Asturia (a Visigothic relict); West Frankish and East Frankish Empires, Italy, and Burgundy (Carolingian relicts). Additionally, the Eastern Roman Empire of V is a relict (but not the Byzantine Empire of IX–X). I debated whether to treat Aquitaine as a relict of the Merovingian empire, but this polity actually grew in size during VII, so, to err on the conservative side, I classified it as an independent polity.

Third, we need to distinguish polities that developed in situ from those established by ethnies moving from elsewhere (such occurrences were particularly frequent during the period of 500–1000 C.E.). Here I distinguished three classes. The most clearcut cases are the Avars, the Caliphate, and the Magyars. Because these ethnies formed outside the boundaries of Europe, I classified them as *intruders* and omitted the polities they established from the analysis. The second class consists of the Visigoths and Ostrogoths. These two Gothic groups went through ethnogenesis in the area north of the Black Sea, but established their polities within the Iberian and Appenine peninsulas, respectively. The final class consists of polities forming in situ, such as the Frankish (Merovingians and Carolingians) and Byzantine Empires. I also classified the Bulgar Empire and Wessex-England as polities forming in situ, because in both cases diverse ethnic elements moved into the VLH and SBR areas, respectively, where they underwent ethnic fusion over a period of several centuries, eventually leading to the formation of new ethnies. Other in situ polities were the Burgundians (EFR), Alamans and Bavarians (SGE), Saxons (WGE), and Moravians (BOH). These polities probably were not true states, but ranged from complex chiefdoms to protostates. Very little is known about some of them, such as the Great Moravia.

Finally, one polity, Khazaria, was omitted because its center was located in the North Caucasus, which is outside the covered geographic area. And there were several polities who started developing toward the end of the first Millennium, and whose territorial peaks were achieved after 1000 C.E.: Holy Roman Empire,

Denmark, Kievan Rus', Hungary, Bohemia, and Poland. These polities, therefore, were analyzed as part of the 1000–1900 C.E. period.

B.4 QUANTIFICATION OF POLITY SIZES:
THE SECOND MILLENNIUM C.E.

This analysis proceeded in exactly the same manner as for the first millennium. My source for polity sizes was the electronic atlas CENTENNIA (Reed 1996). A number of familiar polities did not make the size cut, such as medieval Scotland (0.09 Mm^2 in 1140 C.E.) and Croatia (0.05 Mm^2 in 1080 C.E.); the early modern Bavaria, Saxony, and a host of lesser imperial states; and the modern Netherlands (0.04 Mm^2), Switzerland (0.04 Mm^2), as well as the modern microstates from Luxemburg down.

There were two intruders: Cumans (0.60 Mm^2 in 1200 C.E.) coming from outside Europe and the Teutonic order (0.18 Mm^2 in 1400 C.E.), which originated in EGE. One polity was classified as a relict: the Astrakhan Khanate (0.50 Mm^2 in 1550 C.E.), formed after the collapse of the Golden Horde and speedily conquered by Russia.

Finally, a number of polities formed after 1800 C.E. as a result of fragmentation of the Ottoman, Swedish, Romanov, Habsburg, British, Soviet, and Yugoslavian empires. These polities are Greece, Bulgaria, Romania, Serbia–Yugoslavia, Albania, Norway, Finland, Poland, Ireland, Czechoslovakia (later the Czech and Slovak Republics), Lithuania, Latvia, Estonia, Ukraine, Belarus, Moldova, Croatia, Slovenia, and Macedonia. Many of these polities may be relicts (as progressive fragmentation of at least some of them would seem to indicate). Others may turn out to be the incipient empires of the third millennium. In any case, the safest way is to omit all these polities from the analysis, as I omitted polities forming toward the end of the first millennium from the analysis of the 500–1000 period.

Bibliography

Abel, W. 1966. *Agrarkrisen und Agrarkonjunktur*, 2nd ed. Verlag Paul Parey, Hamburg, Germany.

Abulafia, D. 1990. The end of Muslim Sicily. In J. M. Powell, editor, *Muslims under Latin rule, 1100–1300*. Princeton University Press, Princeton, NJ.

Abulafia, D., and N. Berend, editors. 2002. *Medieval frontiers: Concepts and practices*. Ashgate, Aldershot, England.

A'Hearn, B. 2000. Could Southern Italians cooperate? Banche popolari in the Mezzogiorno. *Journal of Economic History* 60:67–92.

Alekseev, V. P. 1986. *Etnogenez*. Vysshaya Shkola, Moscow (in Russian).

Alekseeva, T. I. 1973. *Etnogenez vostochnyh slavian po dannym antropologii*. Moscow University Press, Moscow, (in Russian).

Alexander, R. D., and Borgia, G. 1978. Group selection, altruism, and the levels of organization of life. *Annual Review of Ecology and Systematics* 9: 449–474.

Ammerman, A., and L. L. Cavalli-Sforza. 1973. A population model for the diffusion of early farming in Europe. Pages 343–357 in C. Renfrew, editor, *Institute of Archeology Research Seminar*. Duckworth, London.

Armstrong, J. A. 1982. *Nations before nationalism*. University of North Carolina Press, Chapel Hill.

Artamonov, M. I. 2001. *Istoriya Khazar (The history of the Khazars)*. 2nd ed. Lan, St. Petersburg, Russia, (in Russian).

Artzrouni, M., and J. Komlos. 1996. The formation of the European state system: a spatial "predatory" model. *Historical Methods* 29:126–134.

Arutyunov, S. A. 1989. *Peoples and cultures: Development and interaction (in Russian)*. Nauka, Moscow.

Aston, T. H., and C. H. E. Philpin, editors. 1985. *The Brenner debate: Agrarian class structure and economic development in pre-industrial Europe*. Cambridge University Press, Cambridge.

Axelrod, R. 1997. *The complexity of cooperation: Agent-based models of competition and collaboration*. Princeton University Press, Princeton, NJ.

Axelrod, R., and W. D. Hamilton. 1981. The evolution of cooperation. *Science* 211:1390–1396.

Bagehot, W. 1895. *Physics and politics; or, thoughts on the application of the principles of "natural selection" and "inheritance" to political science.* D. Appleton, New York.

Banfield, E. C. 1967. *The moral basis of a backward society.* Free Press, New York.

Barfield, T. J. 1989. *The perilous frontier: Nomadic empires and China.* Blackwell, Oxford, England.

Barfield, T. J. 1990. Tribe and state relations: The Inner Asian perspective. Pages 153–182 in P. S. Khoury and J. Kostiner, editors, *Tribes and state formation in the Middle East.* University of California Press, Berkeley.

Barraclough, G. 1998. *Harper Collins atlas of world history.* Border, Ann Arbor, MI.

Barth, F. 1969. *Ethnic groups and boundaries: The social organization of culture difference.* Little and Brown, Boston.

Bartlett, R. 1993. *The making of Europe: Conquest, colonization and cultural change.* Princeton University Press, Princeton, NJ.

Bartlett, R., and A. Mackay, editors. 1989. *Medieval frontier societies.* Clarendon Press, Oxford, England.

Bates, D. 1995. Western Francia: The northern principalities. In T. Reuter, editor, *The new Cambridge medieval history.* Vol. III, Pages 398–419, c.900–c.1024. Cambridge University Press, Cambridge.

Benedict, P. 1985. Civil war and natural disaster in Northern France. Pages 84–105 in P. Clark, editor, *The European crisis of the 1590s.* George Allen and Unwin, London.

Biraben, J.-N. 1975. *Les hommes et la peste en France et dans les pays européens et méditerranéens.* Tome I. Mouton, Paris.

Black, D. 1998. *The social structure of right and wrong,* revised ed. Academic, San Diego, CA.

Blaut, J. M. 1993. *The colonizer's model of the world.* Guilford, New York.

Blaut, J. M. 2000. *Eight Eurocentric historians.* Guilford, New York.

Boehm, C. 1997. Impact of human egalitarian syndrom on Darwinian selection mechanics. *American Naturalist* 150:S100–S121.

Bois, G. 1984. *The crisis of feudalism.* Cambridge University Press, Cambridge.

Bois, G. 1985. Against the neo-Malthusian orthodoxy. Pages 107–118 in T. H. Aston and C. H. E. Philpin, editors, *The Brenner debate: Agrarian class structure and economic development in pre-industrial Europe.* Cambridge University Press, Cambridge.

Borsch, S. 2001. *The Black Death in Egypt and England: A comparative economic analysis,* Ph.D. Dissertation, Columbia University, New York.

Boserup, E. 1966. *The conditions of agricultural growth: The economics of agrarian change under population pressure*. Aldine, Chicago.

Boserup, E. 1981. *Population and technological change: A study of long-term trends*. University of Chicago Press, Chicago.

Boulding, K. E. 1962. *Conflict and defense: A general theory*. Harper and Brothers, New York.

Bourdieu, P. 1980. Le capital social: notes provisoires. *Actes de la Recherches en Sciences Sociales* 3:2–3.

Bowles, S., Choi, J. K. and Hopfensitz, A. 2002. *The co-evolution of individual behaviors and social institution*. Santa Fe Institute working paper.

Box, G. E. P., and N. R. Draper. 1987. *Empirical model-building and response surfaces*. John Wiley and Sons, New York.

Boyd, R., and P. J. Richerson. 1985. *Culture and the evolutionary process*. University of Chicago Press, Chicago.

Boyd, R., and P. J. Richerson. 1988. The evolution of reciprocity in sizable groups. *Journal of Theoretical Biology* 132:337–356.

Boyd, R., and P. J. Richerson. 1992. Punishment allows the evolution of cooperation (or anything else) in sizable groups. *Ethology and Sociobiology* 13: 171–195.

Boyd, R., and P. J. Richerson. 2002. Group beneficial norms spread rapidly in a structural population. *Journal of Theoretical Biology* 215:287–296.

Brass, P. R. 1991. *Ethnicity and nationalism: Theory and comparison*. Sage, New Delhi.

Braudel, F. 1972. *The Mediterranean and the Mediterranean World in the Age of Philip II*. Harper & Row, New York.

Braudel, F. 1988. *The identity of France*. Harper & Row, New York.

Brenner, R. 1985. The agrarian roots of European capitalism. Pages 213–327 in T. H. Aston and C. H. E. Philpin, editors, *The Brenner debate: Agrarian class structure and economic development in pre-industrial Europe*. Cambridge University Press, Cambridge.

Briggs, R. 1998. *Early modern France: 1560–1715*. 2nd ed. Oxford University Press, Oxford, England.

Bromley, J., and V. Kozlov. 1989. The theory of ethnos and ethnic processes in Soviet social sciences. *Comparative studies of society and history*, 31: 425–438.

Bromley, J. V. 1987. *Ethnosocial processes: Theory, history, modernity*. Nauka, Moscow (in Russian).

Brunt, P. A. 1971. *Italian manpower: 225 B.C. – A.D. 14*. Clarendon Press, Oxford, England.

Bulliet, R. W. 1979. *Conversion to Islam in the medieval period: An essay in quantitative history*. Harvard University Press, Cambridge.

Burns, T. 1984. *A History of Ostrogoths*. Indiana University Press, Bloomington.

Burt, R. S. 1992. *Structural holes: The social structure of competition*. Harvard University Press, Cambridge.

Cameron, R. 1989. *A concise economic history of the world: From paleolithic times to the present*. Oxford University Press, New York.

Cederman, L. E. 1997. *Emergent actors in world politics: How states and nations develop and dissolve*. Princeton University Press, Princeton, NJ.

Channon, J., and R. Hudson. 1995. *The Penguin historical atlas of Russia*. Penguin Books, London.

Chao, W.-L., and S.-C. Hsieh. 1988. *History of Chinese population*. People's Publisher, Peking (in Chinese).

Chapell, D. A. 1993a. Ethnogenesis and frontiers. *Journal of World History* 4:267–275.

Chapell, D. A. 1993b. Frontier Ethnogenesis: the case of New Caledonia. *Journal of World History* 4:307–324.

Chase-Dunn, C. K., and T. D. Hall. 1997. *Rise and demise: Comparing world-systems*. Westview, Boulder, CO.

Chase-Dunn, C. K., and T. D. Hall. 2000. Comparing world-systems to explain social evolution. In R. A. Denemark, J. Friedman, B. Gills, and G. Modelski, editors, *World system history: The social science of long-term change*. Rutledge, London.

Chatfield, C. 1989. *The analysis of time series: An introduction*, 4th ed. Chapman and Hall, London.

Chu, C. Y. C., and R. D. Lee. 1994. Famine, revolt, and dynastic cycle: population dynamics in historic China. *Journal of Population Economics* 7:351–378.

Coleman, J. S. 1990. *Foundations of social theory*. Belknap, Cambridge, MA.

Collins, R. 1978. Long-term social change and the territoral power of states. *Research in Social Movements, Conflicts, and Change* 1:1–34.

Collins, R. 1986. *Weberian sociological theory*. Cambridge University Press, New York.

Collins, R. 1990. *The Basques*, 2nd ed. Blackwell, Cambridge, MA.

Collins, R. 1992. *Sociological insight*. Oxford University Press, New York.

Collins, R. 1995. Prediction in macrosociology: The case of the Soviet collapse. *American Journal of Sociology* 100:1552–1593.

Coser, L. A. 1956. *The functions of social conflict*. Free Press, Glencoe, IL.

Culbert, T. P., and D. S. Rice, editors. 1990. *Precolumbian population history in the Maya lowlands*. University of New Mexico Press, Albuquerque.

Cunliffe, B., R. Bartlett, J. Morril, A. Briggs, and J. Bourke. 2001. *The Penguin atlas of British and Irish History*. Penguin Books, London.

Curet, L. A. 1998. New formulae for estimating perhistoric populations for lowland South America and the Caribbean. *Antiquity* 72:359–375.

Denemark, R. A., J. Friedman, B. Gills, and G. Modelski, editors. 2000. *World system history: The social science of long-term change*. Routledge, London.

de Vries, J. 1998. Review of The Great Wave: Price revolutions and the rythm of history. *Journal of Economic History* 58:92–94.

Dewar, R. E. 1991. Incorporating variation in occupation span into settlement-pattern analysis. *American Antiquity* 56:604–620.

Donnan, H., and T. M. Wilson. 1999. *Borders: Frontiers of identity, nation and state*. Berg, Oxford, England.

Dower, J. W. 1986. *War without mercy: Race and power in the Pacific War*. Pantheon Books, New York.

Duby, G. 1974. *The early growth of the European economy: Warriors and peasants from the seventh to the twelfth century*. Cornell University Press, Ithaca, NY.

Dunbabin, J. 1985. *France in the making: 843–1180*. Oxford University Press, Oxford.

Dunning, C. 1998. The preconditions of modern Russia's first civil war. *Russian History* 25:119–131.

Dupâquier, J., J.-N. Biraben, R. Ètenne, C. Pietri, P. Luce, H. Bautier, H. Dubois, A. Higounet-Nadal, C. Klapisch-Zuber, A. Sauvy, and E. Le Roy Ladurie. 1988a. *Histoire de la population française. I: Des origines à la Renaissance*. Presses Universitaires de France, Paris.

Dupâquier, J., J.-N. Biraben, R. Ètenne, C. Pietri, P. Luce, H. Bautier, H. Dubois, A. Higounet-Nadal, C. Klapisch-Zuber, A. Sauvy, and E. Le Roy Ladurie. 1988b. *Histoire de la population française*. Vol. II. Presses Universitaires de France, Paris.

Durand, J. D. 1960. The population statistics of China, A.D. 2–1953. *Population Studies* 13:209–256.

Durkheim, E. 1915. *The elementary forms of the religious life: A study in religious sociology*, translated from the French by J. W. Swain. Macmillan, New York.

Durkheim, E. 1933. *The division of labour in society*. Free Press, Glencoe, IL.

Dyson, S. L. 1985. *The creation of the Roman frontier*. Princeton University Press, Princeton, NJ.

Earle, T. 1997. *How chiefs came to power: The political economy of prehistory*. Stanford University Press, Stanford, CA.

Easterlin, R. 1980. *Birth and fortune*. Basic Books, New York.

Emberling, G. 1995. *Ethnicity and the state in early third millenium Mesopotamia*. Ph.D. thesis, University of Michigan, Ann Arbor.

Epstein, J. M., and R. Axtell. 1996. *Growing artificial societies: Social science from the bottom up*. Brookings Institution Press, Washington D.C.

Everitt, A. 1967. Farm labourers. Pages 396–465 in J. Thirsk, editor, *The agrarian history of England and Wales*. Vol. 4: 1500–1640. Cambridge University Press, Cambridge.

Fararo, T. J. 1989. *The meaning of general theoretical sociology: Tradition and formalization*. Cambridge University Press, Cambridge, England.

Farrington, K. 2002. *Historical atlas of empires*. Checkmark Books, New York.

Fehr, E., and S. Gächter. 2002. Altruistic punishment in humans. *Nature* 415: 137–140.

Fennell, J. 1983. *The crisis of Medieval Russia: 1200–1304*. Longman, London.

Ferguson, B. R., and N. L. Whitehead, editors. 1992. *War in the tribal zone*. School of American Research Press, Santa Fe, NM.

Fischer, D. H. 1996. *The great wave: Price revolutions and the rhythm of history*. Oxford University Press, New York.

Fisher, R. A. 1937. The wave of advance of advantageous genes. *Annals of Eugenics* 7:355–369.

Frank, A. G. 1998. *ReOrient: Global economy in the Asian Age*. University of California Press, Berkeley.

Frauental, J., and K. Swick. 1983. Limit cycle oscillations of the human population. *Demography* 20:285–298.

Fukuyama, F. 1995. *Trust: The social virtures and creation of prosperity*. Free Press, New York.

Galliou, P., and M. Jones. 1991. *The Bretons*. Blackwell, Oxford, England.

Galloway, P. R. 1986. Long-term fluctuations in climate and population in the preindustrial era. *Population and Development Review* 12:1–24.

Gambetta, D. 1988. *Trust: Making and breaking cooperative relations*. Basil Blackwell, Oxford, England.

Gambetta, D. 1993. *The Sicilian Mafia: The business of private protection*. Harvard University Press, Cambridge, MA.

Geary, P. J. 1988. *Before France and Germany: The creation and transformation of the Merovingian world*. Oxford University Press, New York.

Gellner, E. 1969. *Saints of the Atlas*. University of Chicago Press, Chicago.

Gellner, E. 1981. *Muslim society*. Cambridge University Press, Cambridge.

Gimbutas, M. A. 1971. *The Slavs*. Praeger, New York.

Godfray, H. C. J., and M. P. Hassell. 1989. Discrete and continuous populations in tropical environments. *Journal of Animal Ecology* 58:153–174.

Goldstein, J. 1988. *Long cycles*. Yale University Press, New Haven, CT.

Goldstone, J. A. 1986. The demographic revolution in England: A reexamination. *Population Studies* 40:5–33.

Goldstone, J. A. 1991a. The causes of long-waves in early modern economic history. in J. Mokyr, editor, Research in economic history. Supplement 6. *The vital one: Essays in honor of Jonathan R. Hughes*. JAI, Greenwich, CT.

Goldstone, J. A. 1991b. *Revolution and rebellion in the early modern world*. University of California Press, Berkeley.

Goldstone, J. A. 1994. Is revolution individually rational? Groups and individuals in revolutionary collective action. *Rationality and Society* 6:139–166.

Goldstone, J. A. 2002. Population and security: How demographic change can lead to violent conflict. *Journal of International Affairs* 56:3–21.

Goodnight, C. J., and L. Stevens. 1997. Experimental studies of group selection: What do they tell us about group selection in nature? *American Naturalist* 150:S59–S79.

Granovetter, M. 1978. Threshold models of collective behaviors. *American Journal of Sociology* 83:1420–1443.

Greengrass, M. 1985. The later wars of religion in the French Midi. Pages 106–134 in P. Clark, editor. *The European crisis of the 1590s*. George Allen and Unwin, London.

Grousset, R. 1970. *The empire of the steppes: A history of Central Asia*. Rutgers University Press, New Brunswick, NJ.

Gudz-Markov, A. V. 1997. *History of the Slavs*. VINITI, Moscow (in Russian).

Gumilev, L. N. 1971. *Ethnogenesis and Biosphere*, Gidrometeoizdat, Leningrad (in Russian).

Hall, T. D. 1998. The effect of incorporation into world-systems on ethnic processes: Lessons from the ancient world for the contemporary world. *International Political Science Review* 19:251–267.

Hall, T. D. 2000. Frontiers, and ethnogenesis, and world-systems: Rethinking the theories. Pages 237–270 in T. D. Hall, editor, *A world-systems reader*. Rowman and Littlefield, Lanham, MD.

Hall, T. D. 2001. Using comparative frontiers to explore world-systems analysis in international relations. *International Studies Perspectives* 2:252–268.

Hally, D. J. 1996. Platform-mound construction and the instability of Mississippian Chiefdoms. Pages 92–127 in J. F. Scarry, editor, *Political structure and change in the prehistoric southeastern United States*. University Press of Florida, Gainesville.

Hanneman, R. 1988. *Computer-assisted theory building: Modeling dynamic social systems*. Sage, Newbury Park, CA.

Hanneman, R. A., R. Collins, and G. Mordt. 1995. Discovering theory dynamics by computer simulation: Experiments on state legitimacy and imperialistic capitalism. *Sociological Methodology* 25:1–46.

Hatcher, J. 1996. Plague, population and the English economy, 1348–1530. In M. Anderson, editor, *British population history*. Cambridge University Press, Cambridge, England.

Heather, P. J. 1996. *The Goths*. Oxford University Press, Oxford.

Hechter, M. 1987. *Principles of group solidarity*. University of California Press, Berkeley.

Hedström, P. 1998. Rational imitation. Pages 306–327 in P. Hedström and R. Swedberg, editors, *Social mechanisms: An analytical approach to social theory*. Cambridge University Press, Cambridge.

Hellie, R. 1992. Editor's introduction: The frontier in Russian history. *Russian History* 19:1–8.

Ho, P. T. 1959. *Studies on the population of China: 1368–1953*. Harvard University Press, Cambridge.

Hopkins, R. F. 1973. Mathematical modelling of mobilization and assimilation processes. In H. R. Alker, K. W. Deutsch, and A. H. Stoetzel, editors, *Mathematical approaches to politics*. Jossey-Bass, San Francisco, CA.

Hosking, G. 2001. *Russia and the Russians: A history*. Belknap, Cambridge, MA.

Hudson, M. J. 1999. *Ruins of identity: Ethnogenesis in the Japanese Islands*. University of Hawaii Press, Honolulu.

Hummer, H. J. 1998. Franks and Alamanni: A discontinuous ethnogenesis. Pages 9–32 in I. Wood, editor, *Franks and Alamanni in the Merovingian period: An ethnographic perspective*. Boydell, San Marino, Republic of San Marino.

Huntington, S. P. 1996. *The clash of civilizations and the remaking of world order*. Simon and Schuster, New York.

Hupchik, D. P., and H. E. Cox. 1996. *A concise historical atlas of eastern Europe*. St. Martin's Press, New York.

Ibn Khaldun. 1958. *The Muqaddimah: An introduction to history*, translated from the Arabic by Franz Rosenthal. Pantheon Books, New York.

Johnson, A. W., and T. Earle. 2000. *The evolution of human societies: From foraging group to agrarian state*, 2nd ed. Stanford University Press, Stanford, CA.

Jones, D. 2000. Group nepotism and human kinship (with discussion). *Current Anthropology* 41:779–809.

Jones, E. L. 1981. *The European miracle: Environments, economies, and geopolitics in the history of Europe and Asia*. Cambridge University Press, Cambridge.

Kargalov, V. V. 1974. *On the steppe frontier* (in Russian). Nauka, Moscow.

Keely, L. H. 1997. *War before civilization: The myth of the peaceful savage.* Oxford University Press, New York.

Kennedy, P. 1987. *The rise and fall of the great powers: Economic change and military conflict from 1500 to 2000.* Random House, New York.

Keyfitz, N. 1972. Population waves. Pages 1–38 in T. N. E. Grenville, editor, *Population dynamics.* Academic, New York.

Khodarkovsky, M. 2002. *Russia's steppe frontier.* Indiana University Press, Bloomington.

Kidd, C. 1999. *British identities before nationalism: Ethnicity and nationhood in the atlantic world, 1600–1800.* Cambridge University Press, Cambridge.

Kliuchevskii, V. O. 1911. *A history of Russia.* J. M. Dent and Sons, London.

Kohler, T. A., and G. J. Gumerman, editors. 2000. *Dynamics in human and primate societies.* Oxford University Press, New York.

Kolmogoroff, A., I. Petrovsky, and N. Piscounoff. 1937. Étude de l'équation de la diffusion avec croisance de la quantité de matière et son application à une problème biologique. *Moscow University Mathematical Bulletin* 1:1–25.

Komlos, J., and S. Nefedov. 2002. A compact macromodel for pre-industrial population growth. *Historical methods* 35:92–94.

Kradin, N. N. 2000. Nomads, world-empires, and social evolution. Pages 314–336 in N. N. Kradin, A. V. Korotayev, D. M. Bondarenko, and V. A. Lynshi, editors, *Alternative routes to civilization.* Logos, Moscow (in Russian).

Kradin, N. N. 2002. *The Hunnu Empire.* Logos, Moscow (in Russian).

Kraus, J. S. 1993. *The limits of Hobbesian contractarianism.* Cambridge University Press, Cambridge.

Krugman, P. 1997. Seeking the rule of the waves. *Foreign Affairs* 76:136–141.

Laitin, D. D. 1998. *Identity in formation: The Russian-speaking populations in the near abroad.* Cornell University Press, Ithaca, NY.

Landes, D. S. 1998. *The wealth and poverty of nations: Why some are so rich and some so poor.* W.W. Norton, New York.

Lapidus, I. M. 1990. Tribes and state formation in Islamic history. Pages 25–47 in P. S. Khoury and J. Kostiner, editors, *Tribes and state formation in the Middle East.* University of California Press, Berkeley.

Lattimore, O. 1967. *Studies in frontier history: Collected papers 1928–1958.* Mouton, Paris.

LeDonne, J. P. 1997. *The Russian Empire and the world, 1700–1917.* Oxford University Press, New York.

Lee, J. S. 1931. The periodic recurrence of intrnecine wars in China. *The China Journal* March-April:111–163.

Lee, R. D. 1974. The formal dynamics of controlled populations and the echo, the boom, and the bust. *Demography* 11:563–585.

Le Glay, M., J.-L. Voisin, Y. Le Bohec, and D. Cherry. 1997. *A history of Rome*. Blackwell, Oxford, England.

Le Roy Ladurie, E. 1974. *The peasants of Languedoc*. University of Illinois Press, Urbana.

Levi, M. 1988. *Of rule and revenue*. University of California Press, Berkeley.

Levin, S. A. 1976. Population dynamic models in heterogeneous environments. *Annual Review of Ecology and Systematics* 7:287–310.

Lewis, M., and P. Kareiva. 1993. Allee dynamics and the spread of invading organisms. *Theoretical Population Biology* 43:141–158.

Lewit, T. 1991. Agricultural productivity in the Roman economy a.d. 200–400. *Tempus Reparaturm*, Oxford, England.

Lin, N. 1982. Social resources and instrumental action. Pages 131–145 in P. V. Marsden and N. Lin, editors, *Social structure and network analysis*. Sage, Beverly Hills, CA.

Lin, N. 2001. Building a network theory of social capital. Pages 3–29 in N. Lin, K. Cook, and R. S. Burt, editor, *Social capital: Theory and research*. Aldine de Gruyter, New York.

Lind, J. H. 2001. Consequences of the Baltic crusades in target areas: the case of Karelia. Pages 133–150 in A. V. Murray, editor, *Crusade and conversion on the Baltic frontier*. Ashgate, Aldershot, England.

Lurie, S. V. 1998. *Historical ethnology* (in Russian). Aspent Press, Moscow.

Malkov, S. Y., V. I. Kovalev, and A. S. Malkov. 2000. History of mankind and stability. *Strategicheskaya Stabil'nost'* 3:52–66 (in Russian).

Malkov, S. Y., and A. V. Sergeev. 2002. *Mathematical simulation of economical and geographical processes in agrarian society*. Unpublished manuscript (in Russian).

Malthus, T. R. 1798. *An essay on the principle of population*. J. Johnson, London.

Mann, M. 1986. *The sources of social power. I. A history of power from the beginning to* A.D. *1760*. Cambridge University Press, Cambridge.

Masters, R. D. 1998. On the evolution of political communities: the paradox of Eastern and Western Europe in the 1980s. In I. Eibl-Eibesfeldt and F. K. Salter, editors, *Ethnic conflict and Indoctrination*. Berghahn, Oxford.

McEvedy, C., and R. Jones. 1978. *Atlas of world population history*. Facts on File, New York.

McNeill, W. H. 1963. *The rise of the West*. New American Library, New York.

McNeill, W. H. 1964. *Europe's steppe frontier*. University of Chicago Press, Chicago.

McNeill, W. H. 1982. *The pursuit of power*. University of Chicago Press, Chicago.

McNeill, W. H. 1986. *Polyethnicity and national unity in world history*. University of Toronto Press, Toronto.

Melotti, U. 1987. In-group/out-group relations and the issue of group selection. In V. Reynolds, V. Falger, and I. Vine, editors, *The sociobiology of ethnocentrism : Evolutionary dimensions of zenophobia, discrimination, racism and nationalism*. University of Georgia Press, Athens.

Meskill, J., editor. 1965. *The pattern of Chinese history: Cycles, development, or stagnation?* D. C. Heath, Lexington, MA.

Miller, D. H. 1993. Ethnogenesis and religious revitalization beyond the Roman frontier: the case of Frankish origins. *Journal of World History* 4:277–285.

Mironov, B. N. 2000. *A social history of Imperial Russia, 1700–1917*. Westview, Boulder, CO.

Modelski, G., and W. R. Thompson. 1996. *Leading sectors and world powers: The coevolution of global politics and economics*. University of South Carolina Press, Columbia.

Mollison, D., editor. 1995. *Epidemic models: Their structure and relation to data*. Cambridge University Press, Cambridge.

Moore, J. H. 2001. Ethnogenetic patterns in native North America. Pages 31–56 in J. E. Terrell, editor, *Archaeology, language, and history: Essays on culture and ethnicity*. Bergin and Garvey, Westport, CT.

Morgan, K. 1999. Review of The Great Wave: Price revolutions and the rhythm of history. *American Historical Review* 104:866–867.

Moynihan, D. P. 1993. *Pandaemonium: Ethnicity in international politics*. Oxford University Press, Oxford.

Mulroy, K. 1994. Ethnogenesis and ethnohistory of the Seminole maroons. *Journal of World History* 4:287–305.

Munro, J. H. 1999. Review of David Hackett Fischer, *The Great Wave: Price Revolutions and the Rhythm of History*. EH.Net, H-Net Reviews, URL:http://www2.h-net.msu.edu.

Murdoch, W. W., B. E. Kendall, R. M. Nisbet, C. J. Briggs, E. McCauley, and R. Bolser. 2002. Single-species models for many-species food webs. *Science* 417:541–543.

Murray, A. V., editor. 2001. *Crusade and conversion on the Baltic frontier, 1150–1500*. Ashgate, Aldershot, England.

Murray, J. D. 1993. *Mathematical biology*. 2nd ed. Springer-Verlag, Berlin.

Musset, L. 1975. *The germanic invasions: The making of Europe A.D. 400–600*. Pennsylvania State University Press, University Park.

Neeley, J. A., and H. T. Wright. 1994. Early settlement and irrigation on the Deh Luraw plain. *University of Michigan Museum of Anthropology Technical Report 26*, Ann Arbor.

Nefedov, S. 1999. *The method of demographic cycles in a study of socioeconomic history of preindustrial society*. Ph.D. dissertation, Ekaterinburg University, Ekaterinburg, Russia (in Russian).

Nefedov, S. 2002a. On the theory of demographic cycles. *Ekonomicheskaya Istoriya* 8:116–121 (in Russian).

Nefedov, S. A. 2002b. On the demographic cycles in the history of medieval Russia, *Klio* 3:193–203 (in Russian).

Nettle, D. 1999. *Linguistic diversity*. Oxford University Press, New York.

North, D. C. 1985. The growth of government in the United States. *Journal of Public Economics* 28:383–399.

Novoseltsev, A. P. 2001. The Khazar state and its role in the history of western Eurasia. Pages 59–72 in B. N. Florya, editor, Slavs and their neighbors Issue 10, *Slavs and the nomadic world*. Nauka, Moscow (in Russian).

Nüssli, C. 2002. *Periodical historical atlas of Europe*, Version 1. Euratlas.com (http://www.euratlas.com), Yverdon, Switzerland.

Olson, M. 1965. *The logic of collective action: Public goods and the theory of groups*. Harvard University Press, Cambridge, MA.

Otterbein, K. F. 1985. *The evolution of war: A cross-cultural study*. HRAF, New Haven, CT.

Palmer, R. R. 1957. *Rand McNally atlas of world history*. Rand McNally, New York.

Paszkievicz, H. 1983. *The rise of Moscow's power*. Columbia University Press, New York.

Phelps-Brown, E. H., and S. Hopkins. 1956. Seven centuries of the prices of consumables, compared with builders' wage-rates. *Economica* 23:297–314.

Pomeranz, K. 2000. *The great divergence: China, Europe, and the making of the modern world economy*. Princeton University Press, Princeton, NJ.

Postan, M. M. 1973. *Essays on medieval agriculture and general problems of the medieval economy*. Cambridge University Press, Cambridge.

Power, D., and N. Standen, editors. 1999. *Frontiers in question: Eurasian borderlands, 700–1700*. St. Martin's, New York.

Presniakov, A. E. 1918. *Moskovskoe tsarstvo*. Ogni, Petrograd.

Putnam, R. D. 2000. *Bowling alone: The collapse and revival of American community*. Simon and Schuster, New York.

Putnam, R. D., R. Leonardi, and R. Y. Nanetti. 1993. *Making democracy work: Civic traditions in modern Italy*. Princeton University Press, Princeton, NJ.

Quigley, C. 1961. *The evolution of civilizations: An introduction to historical analysis*. Macmillan, New York.

Rashevsky, N. 1968. *Looking at history through mathematics*. MIT Press, Cambridge, MA.

Reed, F. E. 1996. CENTENNIA *for Windows*. Clockwork Software, Chicago.

Reinhard, M. R., A. Armengaud, and J. Dupaquier. 1968. *Histoire générale de la population mondiale*. Editions Montchrestien, Paris.

Reynolds, S. 1997. *Kingdoms and communities in Western Europe, 900–1300*, 2nd ed. Clarendon Press, Oxford.

Riazanovsky, N. V. 2000. *A history of Russia*, 6th ed. Oxford University Press, New York.

Richerson, P. J., and R. Boyd. 1998. The evolution of human ultrasociality. In I. Eibl-Eibesfeldt and F. K. Salter, editors, *Ethnic conflict and indoctrination*. Berghahn, Oxford.

Richerson, P. J., and R. Boyd. 2001. The evolution of subjective commitment to groups: A tribal instincts hypothesis. Pages 186–220 in R. M. Nesse, editor, *Evolution and the capacity for commitment*. Russel Sage Foundation, New York.

Rogers, E. M. 1995. *Diffusion of innovations*, 4th ed. Free Press, New York.

Rokkan, S. 1975. Dimension of state formation and nation building: a possible paradigm for research on variations within Europe. Pages 562–600 in C. Tilly, editor, *The formation of national states in Western Europe*. Princeton University Press, Princeton, NJ.

Rokkan, S., and D. W. Urwin. 1982. Introduction: Centres and peripheries in Western Europe. Pages 1–17 in S. Rokkan and D. W. Urwin, editors, *The politics of territorial identity: Studies in European regionalism*. Sage, London.

Roosens, E. E. 1989. *Creating ethnicity: The process of ethnogenesis*. Sage, Newbury Park, CA.

Rozov, N. S. 1997. An apologia for theoretical history. *History and Theory* 36:336–352.

Rozov, N. S. 2000. *Approaches to a rational philosophy of history: The research program, models, and hypotheses*. Vol. 5. Novosibirsk State University, Novosibirsk, Russia (in Russian).

Ruelle, D. 1989. *Chaotic evolution and strange attractors*. Cambridge University Press, Cambridge.

Ruse, M. 1999. *The Darwinian revolution: Science red in tooth and claw*, 2nd ed. University of Chicago Press, Chicago.

Russell, J. C. 1985. The control of late ancient and medieval population. *American Philosophical Society*, Philadelphia.

Sahlins, P. 1989. *Boundaries: The making of France and Spain in the Pyrenees*. University of California Press, Berkeley, CA.

Salmon, J. H. M. 1976. *Society in crisis: France in the sixteenth century*. St. Martin's Press, New York.

Sanders, S. K. 1999. *Social transformations: A general theory for historical development*. Rowman and Littlefield, Lanham, MD.

Savage, W. W., and S. I. Thompson, editors. 1979. *The frontier: Comparative studies*. University of Oklahoma Press, Norman.

Schaffer, W. M., and M. Kot. 1985. Nearly one-dimensional dynamics in an epidemic. *Journal of Theoretical Biology* 112:403–427.

Scheidel, W., editor. 2001. *Debating Roman demography*. Brill, Leiden, Netherlands.

Schelling, T. C. 1978. *Micromotives and macrobehavior*. Norton, New York.

Scherman, K. 1987. *The birth of France: Warriors, bishops and long-haired kings*. Random House, New York.

Searle, E. 1988. *Predatory kinship and the creation of Norman power, 840–1066*. University of California Press, Berkeley.

Service, E. R. 1975. *Origins of the state and civilization: The process of cultural evolution*. Norton, New York.

Shaskolsky, I. P. 1978. *The struggle of Russia against the crusader aggression on the Baltic shores in the twelfth–thirteenth centuries*. Nauka, Leningrad, (in Russian).

Shaw, R. P., and Y. Wong. 1989. *Genetic seeds of warfare*. Unwin and Hyman, Boston.

Shepherd, W. R. 1973. *Shepherd's historical atlas*, 9th ed. Barnes and Noble, New York.

Simiand, F. 1932. *Les fluctuations économiques à longue période et la crise mondiale*. Félix Alcan, Paris.

Simmel, G. 1955. *Conflict. The web of group-affiliations*. Free Press, Glencoe, IL.

Slicher van Bath, B. H. 1964. *The agrarian history of Western Europe, A.D. 500–1850*. St. Martin's Press, New York,.

Smith, A. D. 1986. *The ethnic origins of nations*. Blackwell, Oxford, England.

Smith, A. D. 2000. *The nation in history: Historiographic debates about ethnicity and nationalism*. University Press of New England, Hanover, NH.

Sober, E. and Wilson, D. S. 1991. *Unto others: The evolution and psychology of unselfish behavior*. Harvard University Press, Cambridge.

Sokal, R. R., and F. J. Rohlf. 1981. *Biometry: The principles and practice of statistics in biological research*. 2nd ed. W. H. Freeman and Company, New York.

Song, J., C. H. Tuan, and J. Y. Yu. 1985. *Population control in China: Theory and applications*. Praeger Scientific, New York.

Sorokin, P. A. 1927. *Social mobility*. Harper, New York.

Stark, R. 1984. The rise of a new world faith. *Review of Religious Research* 26:18–27.

Stark, R. 1996. *The rise of Christianity: A sociologist reconsiders history*. Princeton University Press, Princeton, NJ.

Stark, R., and W. S. Bainbridge. 1996. *A theory of religion*. Rutgers University Press, New Brunswick, NJ.

Stone, L. 1972. *The causes of the English revolution*. Harper and Row, New York.

Stone, L. 1974. The size and composition of the Oxford student body, 1580–1909. Pages 3–110 in L. Stone, editor, *The university in society*. Cambridge University Press, Cambridge.

Taagepera, R. 1978a. Size and duration of empires: Systematics of size. *Social Science Research* 7:108–127.

Taagepera, R. 1978b. Size and duration of empires: Growth-decline curves, 3000 to 600 B.C. *Social Science Research* 7:180–196.

Taagepera, R. 1997. Expansion and contraction patterns of large politices: Context for Russia. *International Studies Quarterly* 41:475–504.

Tainter, J. A. 1988. *The collapse of complex societies*. Cambridge University Press, Cambridge.

TeBrake, W. H. 1985. *Medieval frontier: Culture and ecology in Rijnland*. Texas A&M University, College Station.

Tilly, C. 1975. Reflection on the history of European state-making. Pages 3–83 in C. Tilly, editor. *The formation of national states in Western Europe*. Princeton University Press, Princeton, NJ.

Tilly, C. 1990. *Coercion, capital, and European states, A. D. 990–1990*. Blackwell, Cambridge, MA.

Tocqueville, A. de. 1984. *Democracy in America*. Anchor Books, Garden City, NJ.

Treadgold, W. 1997. *A history of the Byzantine state and society*. Stanford University Press, Stanford, CA.

Triandis, H. C. 1995. *Individualism and collectivism*. Westview, Boulder, CO.

Trivers, R. L. 1971. The evolution of reciprocal altruism. *Quarterly Review of Biology* 46:35–57.

Turchin, P. 1998. *Quantitative analysis of movement: Measuring and modeling population redistribution in animals and plants*. Sinauer Associates, Sunderland, MA.

Turchin, P. 2003. *Complex population dynamics: A theoretical/empirical synthesis*. Princeton University Press, Princeton, NJ.

Turchin, P., and T. D. Hall. 2003. Spatial synchrony among and within world-systems: Insights from theoretical ecology. *Journal of World Systems Research* 9:37–64.

Turchin, P., and A. Korotayev. 2003. *Relationship between population density and internal warfare in prestate societies*. Unpublished manuscript.

Turchin, V. F. 1977. *The phenomenon of science*. Columbia University Press, New York.

Turner, F. J. 1921. *The frontier in American history*. H. Holt and Company, New York.

Turner, J. H. 1995. *Macrodynamics: Towards a theory on the organization of human populations*. Rutgers University Press, New Brunswick, NJ.

Usher, D. 1989. The dynastic cycle and the stationary state. *American Economic Review* 79:1031–1044.

Varien, M. D. 1999. *Sedentism and mobility in a social landscape*. University of Arizona Press, Tucson, AZ.

Vermeulen, H., and C. Govers. 1994. *The Anthropology of Ethnicity: Beyond 'Ethnic Groups and Boundaries'*. Spnihuis, Amsterdam.

Wachter, K. W., and R. D. Lee. 1989. US births and limit cycle models. *Demography* 26:99–115.

Wallerstein, I. M. 1974. *The modern world-system*. Academic, San Diego, CA.

Wallerstein, I. M. 1980. *The modern world-system II: Mercantilism and the consolidation of the European world-economy, 1600–1750*. Academic, New York.

Wallerstein, I. M. 1989. *The modern world-system III: The second era of great expansion of the capitalist world-economy, 1730–1840s*. Academic, San Diego, CA.

Weber, E. J. 1976. *Peasants into Frenchmen: The modernization of rural France, 1870–1914*. Stanford University Press, Stanford, CA.

Whitmore, T. M., B. L. Turner, D. L. Johnson, R. W. Kates, and T. R. Gottschang. 1993. Long-term population change. Pages 25–39 in B. L. Turner, W. C. Clark, and R. W. Kates, editors, *Earth as transformed by human action*. Cambridge University Press, Cambridge.

Whittaker, C. R. 1994. *Frontiers of the Roman Empire*. Johns Hopkins University Press, Baltimore, MD.

Whittow, M. 1996. *The making of Byzantium, 600–1025*. University of California Press, Berkeley.

Wickham, C. 1981. *Early medieval Italy: Central power and local society, 400–1000*. Macmillan, London.

Wieszynnski, J. L. 1976. *The Russian frontier: The impact of borderlands upon the course of early Russian history*. University of Virginia Press, Charlottesville.

Williams, D. 1997. *The reach of Rome: A history of the Roman imperial frontier 1st–5th centuries A. D.* St. Martin's Press, New York.

Williamson, S. H. 1991. The history of cliometrics. *Research in Economic History*, Supplement 6:15–31.

Wolfram, H. 1997. *The Roman empire and its Germanic peoples*. University of California Press, Berkeley.

Wolfram, H., and W. Pohl, editors. 1990. *Typen der Ethnogenese unter Besonderer Berücksichtigung der Bayern*. Denkschriften der Österreichischen Akademie der Wissenschaften, Vienna.

Wood, J. B. 1980. *The nobility of the élection of Bayeux, 1463–1666*. Princeton University Press, Princeton, NJ.

Wood, J. W. 1990. Fertility in anthropological populations. *Annual Review of Anthropology* 19:211–242.

Wood, J. W. 1998. A theory of preindustrial population dynamics (with discussion). *Current Anthropology* 39:99–135.

Wright, N. 1998. *Knights and peasants: The Hundred Years war in the French countryside*. Boydell, Rochester, NY.

Wrigley, E. A. 1969. *Population and history*. McGraw-Hill, New York.

Wrigley, E. A., Davis, R. S., Oeppen, J. E., and Schofield, R. S. 1997. *England population history from family reconstruction: 1580–1837*. Cambridge University Press, Cambridge.

Wrigley, E. A., and R. S. Schofield. 1981. *The population history of England: 1541–1871: A reconstruction*. Harvard University Press, Cambridge, MA.

Yorke, J. A., and W. P. London. 1973. Recurrent outbreaks of measles, chickenpox and mumps. II. Systematic differences in contact rates and stochastic effects. *American Journal of Epidemiology* 98:469–482.

Zimmerman. 1995. Western Francia: the southern principalities. Pages 420–455 in T. Reuter, editor, *The new Cambridge medieval history*. Vol. III. c.900–c.1024. Cambridge University Press, Cambridge.

Index